DATE DUE			

SCHOOL FOR SOLDIERS

SCHOOL FOR SOLDIERS

★★★★★★★★★★★★★★★★★★★

West Point and

the Profession of Arms

★★★★★★★★★★★★★★★★★★★

JOSEPH ELLIS
AND
ROBERT MOORE

New York
Oxford University Press
1974

Library of Congress Catalogue Card Number: 74-79638

Printed in the United States of America

For Toni, Diana, Randall,
and Robin

Preface

THE purpose of this book is to describe and analyze the operation of the United States Military Academy at West Point. Since the Academy is a national institution sustained by federal funds, we believe that Americans should know more about the school's day-to-day operation. The book, then, is an extended answer to a simple question: how does West Point train the nation's future military leaders? Our intention is to provide an account of institutional life which will contribute to an informed dialogue about West Point's role in America during the last quarter of the twentieth century.

Throughout its history the Academy has served as a Rorschach test for the divergent values and sensibilities of its various interpreters; its susceptibility to diverse interpretations is itself a problem requiring explication. Our research thus began as a concerted effort to withhold judgment until we felt that we understood how West Point viewed itself. To this end, we focused on both the rhetoric and the actions of West Point officers and cadets. In the process we have discovered that the issues are more complex and far-reaching than we initially suspected, that they involve different definitions of education, different views of tradition, different attitudes toward soldiers, and, most important, different expectations for America.

Since a balanced account of West Point life required something more than reliance on our personal reminiscences as former faculty members and our unofficial sources, we asked the Academy superintendent, Lieutenant General William A. Knowlton, for access to officers, cadets, and institutional documents. We wrote: "While much of the material for our book is readily available from libraries, government agencies, USMA graduates and other sources as well as from our own experiences at West Point from 1968 to 1972, the accuracy and completeness of our account can be further assured with the . . . assistance of your office. We are especially interested in . . . how West Point has dealt with its problems and challenges of recent years, and we are also committed to giving individuals at West Point the fullest opportunity to express in their own words their understanding of their roles in the life of the Academy."

In early 1973 General Knowlton granted our request. His cooperation set the tone for our dealings with the dean of the Academic Board, Brigadier General John R. Jannarone, his successor, Colonel John Somers Buist Dick, and the heads of the academic departments, as well as with Brigadier General Philip R. Feir, the commandant of cadets, and the agencies under his command. We also profited from the professional help and assistance of officers assigned to West Point's Public Affairs Office, especially Lieutenant Colonel Thomas P. Garigan, and the director of the Office of Institutional Research, Colonel Gerald W. Medsger. Our greatest debt is to those West Pointers, officers and cadets, who consented to hours of official and unofficial taped interviews; they contributed immeasurably to our understanding. The idiosyncrasies of their remarks are preserved throughout the text as well as in the notes, where West Pointers' comments frequently serve to amplify matters discussed in the text.

Since most West Pointers are highly partisan supporters of their alma mater, they may find portions of our account disagreeable. But readers of differing persuasions would do well to remember that, in a time when it has been commonplace for America's public officials to be evasive and deceptive, most of those we consulted were responsive and candid.

In the early months of this project Dan T. Carter, Marcia Higgins, Joyce Johnson, and Ann Ray Martin encouraged us to develop a tentative prospectus into a book-length study. Other friends and colleagues who read one or more chapters in various manuscript stages include Richard Duncan, Michael Getler, Linda Greenhouse, John A. Knubel, James H. Lesher, Colonel James L. Morrison (ret.), Mancur Olson, Robert E. Pechacek, John D. Russell, and Sam C. Sarkesian. We benefited from critiques of the completed manuscript draft by our former West Point colleague Daniel A. Carrell as well as John P. Lovell, a West Point graduate and director of graduate studies in political science at Indiana University, William F. McFeely and Charles H. Trout of the Mount Holyoke College History Department, and Richard J. Schoeck of the University of Maryland English Department. Morris Janowitz and Adam Yarmolinsky read and commented on a late draft of the manuscript.

We are grateful to Sharon Landolt for typing scores of interview transcripts, to Catherine La Rose for clerical assistance, and to our respective departments for their support. Sheldon Meyer and Vivian Marsalisi of Oxford University Press and Theresa Silio were most helpful as the manuscript was prepared for publication. Although the book has been strengthened by the labors of these people, the final responsibility for what follows is ours alone. We shared equally the initial research and the writing of the preliminary drafts and subsequent revisions, and we agreed jointly on every particular of the final text.

South Hadley, Massachusetts J.J.E.
College Park, Maryland R.H.M.
June 1974

Contents

★★★★★★★★★★★★★★★★

SCHOOL FOR SOLDIERS

Chapter One

★★★★★★★★★★★★★★★★★

OUTSIDERS AND INSIDERS

. . . If any boy wanted to go to the Point, the General said, it was a pretty good thing for him to start as a pretty simple kid with just a few essential loyalties. . . . You could not possibly, the General said, explain the place satisfactorily to an outsider, any more than you could explain what went on inside yourself. West Point's primary function was to turn out leaders who could win wars for their country. It was not intended to turn out philosophers or artists. West Point was neither a boys' school nor a university. It was a professional institution for professionals. Its product was a soldier who could fight, who could submerge his individuality in prompt implicit obedience and still be an individual.

General Goodwin in John P. Marquand's Melville Goodwin, USA (*1951*)

The perception of mission is the biggest constraint we have. . . . We exist here just for one purpose—to prepare a man to become an officer in the Regular Army. And this is the only institution in the world that has that sole specific mission.

Brigadier General John R. Jannarone, Dean (*1973*)

★ ★ ★ IN 1808, West Point's first superintendent, Jonathan Williams, issued a warning: unless the institution was moved to Washington, D.C., the fledgling school for Army engineers would remain "a foundling, barely existing among the mountains and nurtured at a distance out of sight, almost unknown to its legitimate parents." [1] Since then the heirs to the superintendency have come to regard West Point's isolation as a fortunate accident of history, a natural asset that must be preserved. Even the proliferation of gray, gothic buildings, many of which were constructed from 1965 to 1974, have been designed to preserve the atmosphere from which Williams hoped to escape. As a result, Americans who tour the military monuments and buildings on the 16,000 acre reservation in the picturesque highlands above the Hudson River often feel that they have been transported back in time to the nineteenth century and to a world insulated from the ravages of progress.

The surrounding countryside reinforces this impression. Although West Point is only fifty miles north of New York City, it is part of the Hudson River valley, which also appears to be a refuge from modernity. This is the area immortalized in the work of Washington Irving, the province of the seventeenth-century Dutch patroons which later became home for American aristocrats in the eighteenth and nineteenth centuries, the majestic landscape that inspired and gave its name to an entire school of American painting.[2] And yet the fortress effect of West Point's mammoth stone buildings is an inspired architectural metaphor for the Military Academy's relationship to the Hudson River valley. The valley is natural and peaceful, with the nostalgic quality of an old charm bracelet that contains mementos representing different centuries of an early America. West Point is a man-made fort that recalls a more distant, medieval past. A feudal fief in the midst of an early American paradise, West Point is an anachronism within an anachronism.

Anyone traveling up the Palisades Parkway toward West Point in one of the fogs that regularly settles on the region might justifiably conclude that he has entered a fantasy land. The area recalls the mysterious scenes depicted in the short stories of Edgar Allan Poe (who was a cadet at West Point for a short time). And West Point, like its locale, is rich in local legends and susceptible to imaginative distortions of mythical proportions. The Military Academy's capacity to generate preposterous and often inconsistent impressions makes any inquiry into its operation doubly difficult, for it requires that one cast out the ghosts which haunt the castle before exploring the interior.

VISITORS

Most of the thousands of tourists and other outsiders who visit West Point every year already possess a highly developed mental picture of the Academy even before they arrive. Films such as *The Long Gray Line* have contributed to the national lore about West Point, a lore which provides most visitors with dramatic expectations. And perhaps more than any other American monument, West Point looks the way it is supposed to look, the way most visitors knew it looked before they set foot on the grounds. The Cadet Chapel, Battle Monument on Trophy Point, the Plain, the cadets on parade—all convey the sense of solidity and permanence most visitors expect to find. Even graduates of West Point, who realize that the physical appearance of the Academy reinforces a public craving for tradition, often seek inspiration from trips back to alma mater. The Protestant chaplain, the Reverend James Ford, recounts the story of a graduate who "had an important decision ahead that had all sorts of ethical implications, a difficult decision, and he took the day off and drove up to West Point. He walked out on to the Plain. He looked up at the Chapel. And he knew what he had to do." Chaplain Ford is aware that this "sounds a little syrupy," but, he adds, "it *was* a *true* story." [3]

The Cadet Chapel has dominated the Academy landscape since its construction in 1910. It is an imposing structure of native granite built into the hillside overlooking the Plain, and it set the architectural style for a major renovation of the Academy which began at the turn of the century. In its own literature West Point notes that the chapel "architecture combines the techniques and shapes of Gothic with the massiveness of medieval fortresses" and this "architectural theme" has subsequently shaped the construction of Academy buildings into the 1970's. Although the exterior of the chapel does not bear distinctive West Point markings, the interior is characterized by the "great Sanctuary Window, inscribed with the words of the motto of the Academy, 'Duty, Honor, Country,' " and by class memorial windows. At the "first pew are silver plates, engraved with the signatures of previous superintendents. Among them are the names of Generals MacArthur, Taylor, and Westmoreland." [4]

The immediate effect of entering the chapel is described by Colonel George S. Pappas, an Academy graduate:

> Stepping through the center doors into the Nave, the visitor immediately finds his attention focused on the altar, its reredos, and the Sanctuary Window by the unbroken expanse of the center aisle and the battle flags which hang above the arcade arches. Nowhere else does the Chapel so vividly reflect the military character of its worshippers as here where flags carried in battle in many wars hang in serene stillness broken only by the voices of the Corps at Sunday worship.
>
> These battle flags hanging from the triforium have caused the Chapel to be compared often to St. George's Chapel, Windsor, England, and to the Church of St. Louis at Les Invalides in Paris. Old National and regimental colors are alternated. The regimental flags include artillery standards and infantry colors carried in the Civil War, the Spanish American War, and the Philippine Insurrection. Famed old regiments are honored here—the 3rd, 4th, and 5th Ar-

> tillery Regiments; the 6th, 14th, 17th, 18th, and 19th Infantry Regiments, to name but a few. The American flags displayed include that of the 4th United States Artillery carried in the Civil War and four carried by the Corps of Cadets—two during the Civil War period, one from 1890 to 1897, and one about 1912.[5]

Military memorabilia are everywhere. On the sides of Battle Monument at Trophy Point are inscribed the names of 2230 members of the Regular Army killed in the Civil War. Links from "The Great Chain" that stretched across the Hudson during the American Revolution are displayed on the west side of the Trophy Point flag pole; the top of the pole reportedly comes from the battleship *Maine*, which was sunk in Havana harbor in 1898. Dozens of cannon, most of them captured during the Mexican War, flank the shaft of Battle Monument, which the Academy describes as "the largest piece of granite turned in the Western Hemisphere." A similar claim is made for the organ in the chapel; it has 14,297 pipes and is described as "the largest church organ in the Western Hemisphere." The view up the Hudson from Trophy Point has also inspired superlatives. Nathaniel Parker Willis, a nineteenth-century naturalist and writer, exclaimed that "of the river scenery of America, the Hudson, at West Point, is doubtless the boldest and most beautiful." [6]

Although hundreds of thousands of tourists visit the Cadet Chapel and Trophy Point each year, the central attraction at West Point is the lush green lawn known as the Plain, especially when it is filled with cadets on parade. On specified days in the fall and spring, two of the four cadet regiments march out from the MacArthur and Eisenhower wings of the barracks. Visitors sit in specially constructed grandstands and, on crowded football weekends, the overflow crowd stands three abreast on the walkways adjacent to the Plain in order to watch the immaculately turned-out cadets execute their impressive turning movements at precise points marked by small wooden markers, which are driven into the ground so that they cannot be seen from the grandstands.

Many visitors admire the orderliness of a cadet parade. To them, the behavior of the cadets in their dining hall would be awe-inspiring. But few visitors ever see the inside of Washington Hall, which faces the Plain and into which the Corps of Cadets enters and sits down in unison for its meals. The dining hall is a cavernous area, its original three wings emanating from the main entrance and its high ceiling supported by deep cross beams. The interior is decorated by paintings, murals, stained-glass windows, state flags, and statutes set in the stone walls. A brightly colored mural by T. Loftin Johnson covers the entire south wall and depicts twenty great battles and generals in world history. The west wall is decorated with a huge stained glass window which portrays the life of George Washington.[7]

Each of the six spoke-like wings of the building has its own artistic or architectural attraction, but the most fascinating attraction of all is the Corps of Cadets at the noon or evening meal. Each of the approximately four hundred ten-man tables is identical. On each table the water pitcher, ketchup, peanut butter, A-1 sauce, salt and pepper shakers, and sugar bowl are neatly aligned in rows. At each meal the entire Corps marches to assigned chairs at assigned tables. A battery of more than fifty waiters serves the food. At each table there are two or three plebes (freshmen), who perform the duties of "gunner," the man responsible for ensuring that the food and dishware are in order; "cold beverage corporal," entrusted with the milk, juice, and water; "hot beverage corporal," in charge of coffee and tea; and "dessert cutter," who ensures the equal distribution of cake and pie. Cadet regulations specify that plebes "will know the beverage preferences of the upperclassmen sitting at their table." These are the same regulations that require plebes to sit erect on their chairs, to "gaze only at their plates in the dining hall unless otherwise directed," to place eating utensils on their plates before beginning to chew their food, and to "speak only prescribed phrases when performing their duties." [8]

At a time when much of the American landscape is cluttered

with neon signs, dilapidated billboards, soot-covered skyscrapers, and various other forms of architectural blight, when virtues associated with a bygone agrarian era appear to have disappeared beneath asphalt highways and suburban sprawl, West Point's environment remains remarkably intact. Whether the casual tourists or the VIP visitors see the Cadet Chapel and the Corps on parade or whether they get a rare outsider's glimpse of the dining hall, the effect is a rejuvenated faith in the continuity between past and future. Despite the enormous costs, increased by the need to import stonemasons from Italy, new buildings like Mahan Hall have been constructed so that they blend in with the older granite structures and preserve the traditional atmosphere.[9]

During the last ten years the Corps of Cadets has increased by about 70 per cent in size, but the parades are as precise as ever. And plebes today, like their predecessors, are still able to tell an upperclassman on demand that there are 340 lights in Cullum Hall or that Lusk Reservoir contains "78 million gallons, sir, when the water is flowing over the spillway." [10] One former cadet recalled the evening a visiting general returned to his father's old cadet room, reached through the loose board in the wall and pulled out the crystal set he had hidden there when he was a cadet. The general gleefully enforced an old regulation by reporting the residents of the room for "concealing unauthorized equipment." [11] Samuel Huntington summed up the opinion of many visitors and West Pointers alike when he noticed that the village of Highland Falls, just beyond West Point's Thayer Gate, was a town of the sort "familiar to everyone: the First National Bank with venetian blinds, real estate and insurance offices, yellow homes with frilly victorian porticos, . . . a motley, disconnected collection of frames coincidentally adjoining each other, lacking common unity or purpose." By contrast, West Point was "a different world. There is ordered serenity. . . . Beauty and utility are merged in gray stone. . . . a gray island in a many colored sea, a bit of Sparta in the midst of Babylon." [12]

ALUMNI

The American scholar Philip Rieff recently wrote that much of contemporary American education is characterized by "that critical openness to possibility in which nothing remains true" and in which "all oppositions are welcomed as if life could be an endless experience of political, technological or interpretive breakthroughs, against orders recognized only for purposes of disestablishment." [13] Few other undergraduate institutions in the country would seem less susceptible to such remarks than West Point. The visible solidity of West Point's buildings and monuments and the precision of the public rituals such as cadet parades convey a sense of stability, a sense of roots that reach far back into the past. In 1968, Bob Hope accepted the Sylvanus Thayer Award from the Academy and articulated the dominant reaction of most outsiders when they visit West Point. Hope lashed out at "the character of those demonstrators who are trying to make patriotism a dirty word." He extolled "all those cadets moving in perfect unison," noting that the cadet parade "restores my faith in life." And then Hope added, "it is nice to know there are still teen-agers who can agree on something." [14] For those countless Americans who, like Bob Hope, regard the turbulence and instability of modern life as unsettling, West Point is a source of reassurance. West Point is the place where their version of America lives on.

Visitors to West Point are inevitably dependent on the most obvious symbols of Academy culture. But the graduates of West Point, men who have spent four years at the Academy and who, presumably, have an understanding of the West Point world that goes beyond the impressionistic, tend to express similar opinions. They also regard the Academy as a haven for the old-fashioned virtues. Most college alumni tend to be nostalgic about their alma mater, but when West Pointers gather for Founders Day banquets at Army posts throughout the world each spring, or when they exchange opinions in *Assembly*, the alumni quarterly, they reinforce for themselves a deep-felt conviction that West Point represents older values that are on the verge of extinction elsewhere. Like the visitors who gather to watch cadets parade on the Plain, West Point graduates who assemble for alumni banquets engage in a ritualistic affirmation of "the tried and true."

An example of such affirmation appears in a letter from Superintendent William H. Knowlton, published in *Assembly.* Lieutenant General Knowlton told his fellow West Pointers that he was concerned about "the cynicism of modern generations." He then quoted at length from what he identified as "a letter . . . published . . . in a small-town newspaper" written by a cadet who had recently arrived at West Point but who had already begun to adopt the language and express the sentiments of countless Academy alumni. General Knowlton cited the cadet's words:

> I know now what makes this place what it is. West Point is like the rock; it is built on ever-lasting. I have only been here two months. I am not yet a member of the Corps, but the feeling of Duty, Honor, and Country has already begun to build in me. I know now why Patton, MacArthur, and other men like them have given so much to their Country. It is because West Point has instilled in them a faith in God and in our Country that overrules all other feelings. . . .
>
> What I have written may be hard for you to understand. It is just a feeling that comes from being part of this place. . . .
>
> This sums up what I am trying to say: ". . . With eyes up, thanking our God that we of the Corps are treading where they of the Corps have trod. . . ." [15]

The more exuberant and extravagant statements of graduates frequently do not stand up under scrutiny. Nonetheless, these statements are commonplace. Alumni comments in Academy publications tend to take on the form and language of prayers, and the various activities of West Point's Association of Graduates create the effect of a congregation of the faithful with a litany best understood by "the elect"—the graduates themselves. And what

William James said about a religious experience, many alumni say about West Point: if you have not had the experience, no one can explain it to you. "You could not possibly . . . explain the place satisfactorily to an outsider," explained General Goodwin in John P. Marquand's novel *Melville Goodwin, USA*, "any more than you could explain what went on inside yourself." [16] In fact, one alumnus, perhaps frustrated with the emphasis on the mysterious character of the West Point way, decided to do a book-length study of the Academy's impact on the values of cadets. He used sociological models, as well as the methods of political science, checked the data with a computer, and discovered that he was unable to definitively verify the hypotheses he had postulated. His work had unwittingly confirmed the convictions of the staunchest alumni. West Point seemed impervious to logical analysis.[17]

Most alumni refer to their West Point years as the formative period of their lives and credit the Academy with providing the direction that guided their subsequent careers. There are exceptions, notably Ulysses S. Grant, who was seldom given to nostalgic appraisals of anything. In 1871 Grant wrote a friend that he looked forward to the day he would retire from public life. "That day is at hand," he wrote, "and I hail it as the happiest of my life, except possibly the day I left West Point[,] a place I felt I had been at always and that my stay at had no end." [18] Even Dwight D. Eisenhower had reservations about the value of his experience as a cadet. He once confessed that "if any time had been provided to sit down and think for a moment, most of the 285 of us would have taken the next train out." [19] But toward the end of his life, Eisenhower too made clear his sense of indebtedness to the Academy. "West Point and all it means is so deep inside you," he said, "that you are not so articulate about it. West Point did more for me than any other institution." [20]

George S. Patton, Jr., went even further. He claimed that West Point had "a power that no other place would have had in my case." Patton said that it was "a holy place and I can never think of it without reverence and affection." [21] Patton's use of religious language reflects an imagery that pervades the reminiscences of prominent alumni. Maxwell D. Taylor, for example, described the ideal of service inculcated at the Academy as "something like the Church; it is not for everyone, only for those with a true vocation." [22] Similarly, Lucius D. Clay said that he regarded each trip back to West Point as "a pilgrimage to seek inspiration which renews faith." [23]

The more recent comments of Academy graduates express a more specific version of this religious imagery. West Point is described not just as a conversion experience, a holy land, a church, or a training ground for missionaries, but as a sanctuary. The overriding impression conveyed by many Academy alumni is that West Point is the single safe repository for national values which are under constant attack in the civilian world. In 1970 General Knowlton sounded this theme when he told the alumni that the social ferment of the present era made it necessary "to reaffirm the unique role of West Point" as a place where men "understand that man struggles upward more successfully within society than under moral anarchy." [24] The following year *Assembly* noted that Founders Day speakers had emphasized a particular theme: "References to 'Duty, Honor, Country' took on special meaning at a time when our Nation seems to be convulsing from the strains of dissent. . . ." [25]

In short, it appears that many Academy graduates have come to believe that the Academy has the cure for many of the social ills currently afflicting America. Samuel Huntington, an alumnus not of West Point but of Yale and Harvard, said it most succinctly in 1957: "Today America can learn more from West Point than West Point from America." [26] During a visit to the Academy in 1964, General Westmoreland put it more forcefully when he told the cadets that "all mankind feel themselves weak, beset with infirmities, and surrounded with danger. . . . They want above all things a leader with the boldness, decision, and energy that, with shame, they do not find in themselves." [27] An elderly graduate, Abbott Boone, spelled out an alumnus' vision in even greater detail at a West Point Founders Dinner in the late 1960's:

> The United States is today drifting slowly but unmistakably into a subtle form of anarchy. The military virtues of governmental authority and self-discipline in its people are gradually being eroded. The time has come when subtle influences are invading the military forces of the country, and only the military virtues hold the key to national and governmental authority and obedience to law. We do not know when the great fountain of honor, duty, and love of country as stored in the hearts and minds of the some twenty-five thousand graduates of West Point . . . will be the granite strength which will preserve this country from the evil forces now seeking to undermine it. . . . [A]uthority in the government and self-discipline in the citizenry are the urgent needs of the day.[28]

CRITICS

Impressions of West Point based primarily on a reading of several of the more popular anti-military books are the antitheses of impressions conveyed by alumni. Critics tend to invert the "West Pointer as Jack Armstrong" stereotype into the "West Pointer as Machiavelli" or to contend that West Point is the cause of, rather than the cure for, the ills afflicting contemporary America. Some of the critics even cite *Assembly* as an invaluable source of information, finding abhorrent the very accomplishments the alumni discuss with pride. Like the impressions generated by alumni, impressions of West Point obtained from critics such as Anthony Herbert, Edward King, Bruce Galloway, and Robert Johnson are more fully developed than the impressions of casual visitors. Taken together, however, West Point's journalistic critics and alumni defenders are both so preoccupied with their idiosyncratic versions of "the truth" that the limitations of their commentaries are evident on a close reading.

Lieutenant Colonel Anthony Herbert became a national celebrity in 1971 after his appearance on the *Dick Cavett Show;* this was followed by a series of television and magazine interviews, his controversial retirement from the Army in February 1972, and the subsequent publication of his book *Soldier* in 1973.[29] During this period, Herbert argued that the United States Army had been victimized by a group of self-serving West Pointers who destroyed Army morale in Vietnam: "Vietnam was no accident of fate, but rather the goal toward which our Army had been doggedly headed for years. And now the line is drawn; the professional officer corps, the 'clique,' must accept responsibility for the major role it played."[30] In Herbert's view, by far the most powerful clique within the clique of the officer corps is the West Point Protective Association, an old-boy network of Academy graduates that allegedly perpetuates an elitist attitude in the officer corps for the primary benefit of West Point graduates. In *Soldier* Herbert traced his experience with West Pointers back to his days as a second lieutenant and instructor in Ranger School and gave an account of "a certain class of Ranger students made up entirely of West Point graduates. It was the only class in Ranger history that ever quit en masse." According to Herbert,

> They were on a survival exercise in the swamps, without food or water, without anything except their native intelligence and their weapons. They just threw down their rifles and walked out on the theory that, if they all did it together, nobody could do anything about it. . . .
>
> The Army covered up the West Pointers' failure and the class was allowed to continue, but when I heard about it, I drew my first distinction between West Point officers and the others. It was, perhaps, an unfair judgment based on only a smattering of evidence. But I made it and followed it for the rest of my life. West Pointers were different, I decided. You had to watch them.[31]

Herbert's Army career, by his own account, was ruined after he filed charges against two West Pointers for allegedly covering up war crimes he reported to them in Vietnam. And Herbert described these men, Colonel J. Ross Franklin and Major General John Barnes, as the products of "their type of training—the West Point-type training." It was a training, wrote Herbert, which taught that the "junior man had no rights; he never did. Everything was for the good of the commander's image, for the good of the brigade." In Herbert's view this too often meant "for the good of Barnes and Franklin. The key phrase used to justify any type of illegal action was always 'for the good of the brigade.' We can't let this get out and spoil our image. The civilians wouldn't understand. For the good of the brigade, you could cover up fraud and theft, rape and murder." [32]

While charges such as those cited above created considerable attention when they were first made, Herbert's veracity has been challenged by many civilians and soldiers alike, most tellingly by Mike Wallace on a CBS-TV *60 Minutes* program, "The Selling of Colonel Herbert." [33] Herbert also undermined his own critique by his inclination to generalize about the inevitable effect of West Point training and by his vociferous bias against graduates, whom he tended to lump together as "ring-knockers"—"West Point graduates wear these big class rings, and they're always tapping them on tabletops in case you forgot they're wearing one." [34] But the principal genesis of Herbert's charges—West Point's elitism and its main corollary, the West Point Protective Association—continues to be of serious concern to many observers of the Academy. One such observer, Lee Ewing, congressional reporter for the *Army Times* paper, reported that although the Army had ruled that Herbert's charges against Barnes and Franklin were unsubstantiated, it refused to release its investigations of the two officers. Unless this information is made public, Ewing warned, "the Herbert affair could drone on interminably and inconclusively" and Herbert "will be an albatross around the neck of the Army." [35]

Edward L. King is another widely celebrated critic of the Army who discovered that much which he disliked in the Army had its source at West Point. His *The Death of the Army: A Pre-Mortem* was extensively advertised with a prominent endorsement by Seymour M. Hersh which asserted that King "describes exactly what is wrong with the Army and what should be done about it. His facts and integrity are beyond reproach." [36] King, like Herbert a retired lieutenant colonel, shares Herbert's concern about West Point's impact on the Army. He charged that the "Army's top managers" were guilty of "indoctrinating all members of the officer corps from the time of their commissioning to accept the myth of superiority of an elitist group from West Point." Like Herbert, King tends to deal in absolutes: all means *all.* He also charged that "At each level the West Point managers weed out increasing numbers of those officers who are no longer useful. Only the most cooperative and best indoctrinated non-West Pointers are permitted to progress to the general officer ranks." King invoked another critique of the Army and West Point, Ward Just's *Military Men,* which calls the Academy "the place where the professional Army begins . . . , the Army alma mater." King noted: "Just . . . says, 'There is no doubt that a sort of West Point Protective Association exists in the Army.' " And King added, "The WPPA does exist and it is constantly at work to protect and promote classmates from West Point at the expense of the rest of the officer corps." [37] "By the time a non-West Pointer reaches major," King argued, "he has begun to prepare himself unconsciously to accept the fact that he will probably be fortunate to [ever] make colonel." Continuing the extravagant generalizing that characterizes Academy critics and partisans alike, King wrote: "While the West Point officer automatically gets his ticket punched with good assignments, the rest of the officer corps must scurry around desperately trying to avoid the dead-end jobs that so often fall to their lot." Similar charges were also echoed by a West Point faculty member, Major Josiah Bunting, in his Vietnam novel, *The Lionheads.* The national attention Bunting attracted annoyed Academy officials, not only because he was a Virginia Military Institute graduate but because he was resigning from the Army as he launched his attack.[38] And so, while Academy graduates have pointed to the fact that over half of the division commanders in World War II and the majority of the Army's current three- and four-star generals are West Pointers as an indication of the superiority of West Point training, critics have cited these career patterns as proof of discrimination. And throughout their books the critics implied that many of the Army's problems, and much of the horror of Vietnam, were the result of a nefarious military camaraderie originating during cadet years at the Academy.

The books by Herbert, King, and Bunting did not focus on the actual operation of the Academy and cadet life; their conclusions were based on observations of Academy graduates in the Army. In *West Point: America's Power Fraternity*, K. Bruce Galloway and Robert Bowie Johnson, a 1965 West Point graduate, did focus on the training received at West Point. Moreover, they insisted that Academy graduates have infiltrated the upper echelons of American industry and government as well as the Army. Like other critics of West Point, the authors seemed most comfortable with impassioned rhetoric. In the third paragraph of their first chapter, they announced:

> West Pointers have played a major role in the reduction of this country to a democracy without a people, and they are fearful of any effort to change this condition. The power and influence to prevent any move from the status quo is theirs—the Army and the Air Force are under their control, they boss the foreign and domestic intelligence community, they act as the lubricants in the military-industrial-educational machine, and, above all, they hold top policy positions in government both here and abroad. This is a dangerous situation because these are dangerous men—men whose personal code is identical to the one that appears again and again in the ideology of totalitarianism: "Duty, Honor, Country." This code leaves little room in the life of a West Pointer for a more familiar one, the one that says "Liberty and justice for all." [39]

Some three hundred and sixty-six pages later, Galloway and Johnson concluded their *West Point* on this note: "The West Pointers seek to apply the 'techniques' of Vietnam to the 'solution' of America's problems. Morality is their possession, order is their cry, and stability is their goal—a uniformed America marching on a West Point Plain that extends from coast to coast." [40]

Another one of the many curious ironies associated with West Point emerges upon examination of Galloway and Johnson's primary sources. Although their book recalls the scathing attacks on West Point published during the nineteenth century, it relies to a remarkable extent on evidence, carefully selected and ingeniously edited, from back issues of the Academy's own *Assembly* and a companion volume, the *Register of Graduates*. This material enabled them to develop their long lists of West Pointers who are serving on the National Security Council, the Rand Corporation, the Federal Aviation Administration, the Atomic Energy Commission, the White House staff, and in certain Latin American regimes as well as various governmental agencies and assorted defense contractors.[41] These lists buttressed their contention that West Pointers have increasingly come "to dominate the military and assume an inordinately powerful role in civilian affairs"; they also sought to prove how "a 'school' that professes to train 'defenders of freedom' . . . instead hammers out an elitist group of automatons who are prisoners of their education and afraid of the very concept they are supposed to defend." In short, they argued that West Point is intricately arranged to prevent critical thinking, to promote socialization rather than education, to indoctrinate rather than teach, to transform "idealistic youths" into like-thinking men "whose self-imposed mission is to determine our country's destiny." [42]

Responses by Johnson's fellow West Pointers to the book's account of Academy life and its graduates are frequently a mixture of indignation about its antagonism toward the Academy and puzzlement over its thesis of West Point's uniquely powerful role in military and civilian life. Johnson and Galloway singled out the institution's Social Sciences Department as crucially instrumental in selecting and training West Pointers for what they call "the capture of [American] foreign policy." [43] This contention elicited an initially bemused response of "Well, I think it's all very flattering" from the current head of the department, Colonel Lee D. Olvey. Then he elaborated:

> The idea that the Military Academy, much less the Department of Social Sciences, has that range of influence on the affairs of the nation is really very flattering. I think they have overstated the case a bit. I think there is an element of elitism here. That's simply nothing more than an effort to get the very best people here and a reasonable amount of success in doing it. It really isn't surprising that they turn out to be successful Army officers. Indeed, successful in almost any walk of life in which they enter upon. Quite a few of them are retired, out of the service, and have assumed other vocations and are successful. The place where I part company with them [Galloway and Johnson] is with the conspiracy idea. The idea that there's a great plot to do something particular in the affairs of the country is utter nonsense.[44]

Unlike Colonel Olvey, many West Point officers are not disposed to make temperate responses to the public attacks of the 1970's. The speeches of Superintendent William Knowlton to the staff and faculty at West Point and to Academy alumni groups throughout the country were filled with calls to "band together with the other Service Academies in withstanding the onslaught of a hostile outside world" and with ominous references to "the influences which have been loose in the environment from which come our cadets . . . to our rock-bound highland home." But General Knowlton reserved his most scathing denunciations for that "erratic fraction of one percent" of West Pointers "who have not performed to the standards we expect, or who have been embarrassments to the institution. About 5 to 10 of these receive constant national publicity," although "they amount to $^{1}/_{20}$th of 1%" of living Academy graduates. While "there have always been a few such individuals," General Knowlton noted, "there is something new about this latest wave":

> In former times, those who went out of our institution and failed the test disappeared quietly into the undergrowth. Now, they have press conferences and write books. Has one's checkered career included relief from the rigors of the battlefield in Vietnam and a rather pathetic performance even in safe jobs? Then, write a book explaining that the fault cannot be within one's self—the fault must be in the institution from which one graduated. Did one refuse command of an Infantry unit on the battlefield? Then one should write a novel denouncing those who accepted command as being "ticket punchers." Did one get reported in the national newspapers for running up hundreds of dollars of telephone calls to a phony credit card? Then, one should offer the publishing houses an exposé of the horrors of the high standards demanded by the Honor Code and the Code of Ethics. While CBS may have uncovered a whole series of lies by Colonel Herbert in that large segment of its "60 Minutes" program, his book still remains among the best sellers. And so it goes.[45]

Just as the alleluia quality of alumni praises of West Point tends to make even Academy defenders uneasy, the ideological intensity of contemporary critics tends to make even those skeptical of West Point sympathetic. After a strong dose of *Assembly,* followed by a few of Galloway and Johnson's chapters, one gets the impression that what is being explored is not the complexities of the Military Academy, but the outer perimeters of an ideological controversy. "Read those guys [Galloway and Johnson] and then go listen to some grad on Founders Day," said one West Pointer, "and then go get a T-square and figure out the point that lies equidistant from each. That's the *real* West Point." [46] But this transparently sensible advice confuses the problem with its implication that "the truth" always lies between ideological extremes. It is useful to know that West Point has the capacity to generate antithetical impressions, that the different factions argue their cases with a religious-like zeal, that West Point has come to symbolize some of the most basic credal beliefs of Americans. But the first order of business is not to calibrate one's ideological instruments in order to locate "the point that lies equidistant" from two imaginary West Points. For West Point is not a Land of Oz with a separate existence in everyone's imagination. It is a highly complex institution shrouded from the public, and frequently itself, by an intricate array of myths. Most visitors, alumni, and critics of West Point deal in mythology rather than fact, or at least bend the facts to satisfy their particular need for gods and devils. Beneath the myths, far removed from the polarized rhetoric, inside the gothic buildings so easily appropriated as symbols, lies a more pedestrian West Point. This is the West Point inhabited by cadets.

CADETS

The bedrock of the West Point world is the Corps of Cadets. Everything in the West Point environment is intended to do something for or to cadets, and everyone seems to have an impression about the kind of person who inhabits that individually tailored gray uniform. But the officers who teach cadets, the girls who date them, and, most especially, the cadets themselves are quick to post warnings. "You don't get to know them very quickly," said one Mount Holyoke student, "and if you expect to get beyond their veneer quickly, you are going to be disappointed." [47] Cadets seem particularly eager to assert that there is no such thing as a "cadet personality," that each cadet is a distinctive person who should be understood on his own terms. They are also eager to make it clear that the impression most Americans have of cadets is excessively romantic, although they admit that cadets themselves consciously encourage such an impression. "The Military Academy is a national shrine," said one first classman (senior), "and the people come here to watch us go through the military rituals. So we oblige them." [48] Another cadet added, "If the visitors knew that guys in the middle of a formation during a parade were straining to get a shot [look] at some honey who's wearing a see-through blouse and who's sitting in the bleachers as we march by, well, if they knew that, then they wouldn't think of us as 'cadets.' "[49] Dubious reasoning, but a clear indication that many cadets feel the need to play the roles they believe the public has assigned to them. And this need, according to one highly successful first classman, has its basis in a calculated self-interest: "Performing all the time takes its toll, but I'm willing to pay the price in order to keep the West Point image what it is. . . . Other cadets in earlier classes have done it and now I'm going to benefit. . . . You don't destroy the place in which you have so much invested."[50]

Yet, after all these warnings, it must be acknowledged that perhaps more is known about the Corps of Cadets than about any other undergraduate student body in the country. The Office of Institutional Research is an Academy agency devoted to the assemblage of data on cadets and graduates of West Point. Each year it turns out studies of the Corps of Cadets which are used by other West Point departments and agencies to compile charts, slides, multi-colored transparent overlays, information booklets for parents, and lectures for visiting educators.[51]

From these studies one learns that the typical cadet in the class of 1976 has a mean height of 70.28 inches and weight of 161.58 pounds. He is from a family whose range of income is between $12,500 and $20,000. He graduated from a public high school in the top fifth of his class. He had a B+ average in high school and scored 554 on the verbal scholastic aptitude test and 624 on the mathematical test. Over 80 per cent of the class of 1976 earned a varsity letter in high school, 33.8 per cent were team captains, and 13.4 per cent of their fathers are military careerists. Just over 3 per cent of the class is black.[52]

The attitudes of entering cadets differ from the attitudes of entering freshmen at other colleges in several ways. More cadets are interested in pursuing their education after West Point: 48.5 per cent aspire to an M.A. degree and 22.1 per cent intend to seek a Ph.D. Fewer cadets describe themselves as liberals; fewer believe marijuana should be legalized; fewer think grades should be abolished. More cadets than their civilian college peers think that the chief benefit of college is monetary, that student publications should be regulated, that a college has a right to ban speakers, that student protestors have been treated too gently, that recognition from one's peers is important, that they will marry within the next five years.[53]

At West Point each cadet will take between 152 and 158 credit hours (compared to a normal load of 120 to 128 credits at most civilian colleges). He will be paid $12,700 in salary during his four years. His West Point education will cost the American taxpayer at least $65,000. During his four years at West Point his motivation for a military career will decrease each year until he becomes a first classman, when it will stabilize. His idealism will also wane at about the same rate, so that as a first classman he will exhibit greater cynicism than he did in his earlier years. Over 60 per cent of the entering cadets will graduate, about 70 per cent of the graduates will serve beyond the minimum five-year obligation, and 75 per cent of those that make the Army a career will go on to graduate school.[54] Most cadets have unrealistic expectations about their ultimate rank. (As one major put it: "When I graduated the commencement speaker said that only 20 of the 600 of us would be generals. So I looked around to see who the other 19 were.")[55] Retired West Pointers from the classes of 1920 to 1949 should offer long-range encouragement to the young cadet, for on average they earn between $22,000 and $30,000 annually.[56]

Some West Point faculty members endorse the notion that there are three degrees of untruth, each worse than the other: "lies, damned lies, and statistics."[57] Many cadets agree and seem to regard the enormous bank of statistical information maintained on them by the Academy as fundamentally misleading. One first classman insisted that cadets fill in the blank spots on the surveys without thinking: "You look over to the guy next to you and put down the answers he had. A lot of times the right answer is not listed on the questionnaire. . . . You tell them what they want to hear." [58] Philip Linder, West Point's fifty-second Rhodes scholar, agreed: "You're talking to a guy who's in the position to answer those questions about cadets, and who's given a lot of thought to them, but I can't answer them. . . . Don't trust the answers I put down." [59]

No one likes to believe that his personality can be reflected in a computer print-out, but cadets often claim that they are not capable of being understood by any means. "The Academy is so different from anything else you ever encountered that it's really hard to make a person understand what being a cadet is all about," said one recent graduate. "People tried to make me understand before I came, but I just couldn't get close to it. I just couldn't hear what they were saying." Another cadet expressed the same idea: "Until you have given as much of your time, your energy, and yourself to this place as I did, you'll have to be satisfied in the knowledge that cadets are incomprehensible." [60] Such views hark back to the alumni version of "West Point as mystery" and help explain why so many cadets are content to act out stereotypical roles for visitors. In the end, they suggest, most visitors prefer a stereotype to an enigma.

But the comments of cadets challenged their claim that beneath the breastcoat lies the unfathomable. Consider the following comments by cadets about cadets. First, a recent graduate on cadet motivation:

> A typical night at West Point could consist of writing a half-assed paper aimed at an adequate B−, studying for a test so as not to flunk, cleaning one's rifle so as not to lose weekend privileges, writing a half-assed letter so as not to lose one's girl, and reading an assignment while standing in line to use the phone to call another girl. Throughout, the goal is adequacy.[61]

Or a first classman's critical account of the Academy's insistence on responsibility:

> It seems to me a fearful thing to take a boy of seventeen and rob him of his freedom to be irresponsible, frivolous, absent-minded and silly. West Point always makes you think of the cost involved; it attaches extrinsic costs to things with inherent costs. . . . It seems to me that adolescence is something to be outgrown, not something to be scoffed at as childish and abruptly confiscated without a minute's notice.[62]

Or the views of a former cadet, who resigned in his final year, on what he called the "cadet neurosis":

> West Point makes you up-tight. It's designed to make you up-tight. What else can you be after listening for footsteps in the hall to hear whether the shoes have taps [a sign that a tactical officer is approaching]? . . . Cadets are aware they are up-tight, that something is dying in them. But they hold out the hope that the free education will compensate and they'll be able to get out of the Army in five years, have a Jaguar, a good job at Bell and Howell and a girl on each arm. They want to believe they are Horatio Algers and West Point is their lucky break.[63]

Or a black cadet's judgment of the reasons for the harassment and deprivation:

> All cadets are niggers here, living in a ghetto. . . . But like one man [Chaplain Ford] said, it's a "beautiful ghetto and it has a purpose." It's all designed to give us a hard edge that will cut through shit . . . and do the job other people can't do. Most cadets bitch about the hassles, but deep down they know it's for a purpose . . . and worth the price.[64]

From the stereotypes of West Point as picture postcard, as seminary, as sanctuary, as conspiracy, even as enigma, there is much to be learned; and, there is also much that confuses and contradicts. It is as if a bird-watcher asked for his binoculars and were given a kaleidoscope. But the cadet statements quoted above constitute evidence that the quest for an understanding of West Point is not like the proverbial snipe hunt. Despite the Academy's various masks, it is possible to probe beneath the myths and stereotypes to find real people and the patterns of their culture. But the predominance of polarized stereotypes constitutes a warning: West Point is sufficiently complex and ambiguous to serve as a Rorschach test for the values of its different interpreters. In order to avoid transforming an effort at understanding into a reaffirmation of one's personal prejudices, outsiders should approach West Point with the critical but sympathetic attitude of an anthropologist studying a different culture.

Chapter Two

★★★★★★★★★★★★★★★★★★★★

FIRST PRINCIPLES

It is perhaps more than any other educational institution sui generis; *and in its adherence to an organic standard and a characteristic ideal it is more conservative and consistent than any but theological seminaries of the most orthodox type.*

Charles Larned, Professor of Drawing, West Point (1902)

The United States Military Academy provides a superior education. We are modern in concept and staff. During this decade we have made great advancement in our academic program, providing a more flexible curriculum and a growing diversity of electives. We offer some of the finest and most advanced educational and physical development facilities in the world.

Lieutenant General William A. Knowlton, Superintendent (1972)

I find in talking to cadets that most of them say that they would like to have more freedom and more options in taking academic courses. But, when you probe this a little more deeply, I think there are indications there that they're not saying that they think it's the best way to prepare them for a military career, but for some other things.

Brigadier General John R. Jannarone, Dean (1973)

★ ★ ★ WEST Point's susceptibility to a variety of different, even inconsistent impressions is not the result of a conspiracy among Academy officials. Public confusion is a natural consequence of two related developments: first, West Point has come to regard itself as both an undergraduate college with an academic purpose and as a professional school for Army officers with an essentially military mission; second, the pressure to combine these antithetical goals, to be both Athens and Sparta, has meant that the Academy has evolved in a way that makes it unlike any other educational or military institution in America. People who are unaware of the Academy's unique development invariably attempt to analogize, compare, or contrast West Point with other institutions with which they are familiar. Such analogies, comparisons, and contrasts are inevitably misleading because they fail to take into account West Point's unique set of goals and the idiosyncratic mode of operation necessary to pursue those goals.

As a hybrid, if not schizophrenic institution, West Point has always been wary of interference from outsiders who would upset its delicate institutional balance. Succeeding generations of West Point officials have attempted to insulate the Academy from "Army types who want to turn us into a Fort Benning" and civilian educators "who want to turn us into a Harvard or Berkeley." [1] Although West Point has been remarkably successful in deflecting outside influence, its insularity has also shielded the Academy from public scrutiny and its uniqueness has become a convenient excuse for in-breeding. Who else, the argument goes, but West Point graduates can comprehend the complexities and peculiarities of life at the Academy sufficiently well to serve as teachers and administrators? The graduates who have run the Academy over the years have self-consciously rejected most of the reforms that have reshaped American higher education in the twentieth century, arguing that West Point's unique goals render such reforms inappropriate. And change in the name of progress has never made sense to most Academy officials, because they are convinced that the pedagogic principles most likely to produce effective military leaders have not changed during the last few centuries. As a result, West Point is one of the most anomalous institutions in America, a willful anachronism more comprehensible to a nineteenth- than to a twentieth-century man.

Which is not to say that West Point has remained unchanged since the nineteenth century. Many of the older gothic buildings, reminiscent of the Middle Ages, were actually constructed between the Spanish American War and World War I. In the last fifty years the size of the Corps of Cadets has increased from a few hundred to over four thousand. When Dwight Eisenhower and Omar Bradley graduated in the famous "class the stars fell on" in 1915, they knew each other, and most of the other 162 graduates, on a first-name basis. When the 939 members of the class of 1973 graduated, less than half of them had any personal acquaintance with James Pelosi, despite the fact that Pelosi was a *cause célèbre* and a classmate they had agreed "to silence" for nineteen months.[2]

What General Knowlton refers to as the "facilities" have also changed radically since the days of Eisenhower and Bradley. The classrooms and hallways of the academic buildings offer a closed-circuit television network, equipment to make and show films and tapes, Xerox machines, a Honeywell-635 computer system, and one hundred and twenty computer terminals available for use by any cadet who wishes to tabulate his current grade and class standing in every subject.[3] Yet continuity rather than change governs the Academy's operation. For West Point culture is grounded in several nineteenth-century traditions that have become sacrosanct Academy fixtures. These traditions were established during the Academy's "golden age" between the War of 1812 and the Civil War. These same traditions were reaffirmed at the turn of the century, when American higher education moved away from wholly prescribed academic programs. It was not until the late 1960's that West Point implemented reforms that raised serious questions about the survival of traditional doctrines. But at West Point those eager to predict the future usually begin by studying the past. And at West Point this requires going back to the golden age, to the year 1817 and the patriarch of the Long Gray Line, Sylvanus Thayer.[4]

THE THAYER SYSTEM

Thayer was a cold, severe graduate of Dartmouth (1807) and West Point (1808) whose personal correspondence reads like a set of battle orders. During his tenure as superintendent (1817–33) he developed a formidable reputation as a disciplined but independent thinker whose main goal was to make West Point a prominent national institution. And he succeeded. When Thayer arrived, West Point was a floundering school for sons of the well-born. One of Thayer's first actions was a general examination of every cadet. The examination revealed that forty-three cadets, almost one-fifth of those enrolled, had serious academic deficiencies and over half of the deficient cadets had failed to move beyond the first year's course in more than three years of attendance. But the most bizarre circumstance involved two young South Americans who had been carried north by an American naval officer "on a cruise from Chile and dumped at the Academy" for schooling. Thayer found these men lacking "in the first rudiments of education, reading, writing and orthography. They manifest no desire to learn and accordingly make no progress. They are besides extremely troublesome as they cannot be made to observe any of the police regulations. They have been advised, admonished, and punished but entirely without effect. They are real nuisances." [5] Nuisances were short-lived under Thayer's reign. Within a few years West Point was the premier engineering school in the United States. By 1826 a member of the Board of Visitors reported that when the topic of Thayer's successor came up, officers were saying that "no man would be indiscreet enough to take the place after Thayer; it would be as bad as being President of the Royal Society after Newton." [6]

The educational reforms Thayer introduced at West Point were modeled on French technical institutes, especially the École Polytechnique. He insisted that all cadet classes remain small enough to allow for daily recitations by each cadet. The subjects cadets studied were wholly prescribed and were designed to produce technically trained graduates who were intellectually equipped to enter the Corps of Engineers. The daily recitations were intended not only to enforce rigorous study habits but also to provide practical experience in leadership and to foster competition among members of the class. The grades for the recitations were posted regularly and the classes were "re-sectioned" (educators now would say "re-tracked") on the basis of grades. Finally, there was a "general order of merit" in which all cadets of the same year were ranked according to grade. Along with these academic practices, Thayer regularized the entire cadet schedule, and insisted on a high standard of appearance, weekly attendance at chapel, and a strict enforcement of rules against lying, stealing, and other "irregular or immoral practices." Eventually this combination of rules, policies, and prohibitions became known as the Thayer System.[7]

Thayer's reforms gave the Military Academy a distinctive atmosphere. The rules and regulations seemed to blend into an organic whole. West Point was an institution that knew what it was about, a place where a young American was remade in the image of Thayer himself. One tended to surrender his individuality when he entered Thayer's West Point, because he had confidence in the wisdom, if not the clairvoyance, of Thayer and his colleagues. Thayer exuded a confidence and a certitude that proved infectious. West Point was a place where men knew what they were doing, a school that operated according to rules that possessed a sanctified character, as if Thayer had received his inspiration from divine sources. And over time the mythology fed on itself, so that graduates of

Thayer's West Point had a genuine sense that they were privy to archetypal insights denied to others and that the mental training and character traits ostensibly acquired as cadets separated them from other men.

When Horace Mann, the most prominent and progressive educator in America at the time, observed the Thayer System in operation, he remarked that he had "rarely if ever seen anything that equalled the excellence of the teaching or the proficiency of the taught." [8] That was in 1849. Now, a century and a quarter later, the Thayer System still dominates Academy pedagogy. In recent years the desire to portray West Point as a modern and progressive institution committed to educational reform has been forced to compete with the desire to maintain the Thayer traditions in pristine form. In some cases Academy supporters have simply asserted both views simultaneously and ignored their incompatibility. For example, in 1972 the Curriculum Review Board headed by Frederick R. Kappel, president of American Telephone and Telegraph, said, "We have been impressed with the progress made by the Academy during the past decade in keeping the curriculum in tune with recent social changes and the changing requirements of a modern Army." But the Kappel board also strongly endorsed the continued relevance of Academy policies dating back to Thayer. As for the faculty, "composed almost entirely of military officer personnel," the civilian board insisted: "We are convinced they are doing an excellent job." [9]

Much of the board's report is addressed to those at the Academy and on the outside who are not convinced that "keeping the curriculum in tune" means clothing Thayer's tenets in modern dress. "The man showed a lot of wisdom in places and a lot of wisdom for the time," one department head acknowledged. "Unfortunately there are vestiges of his ideas that still remain which shouldn't. Occasionally you see papers coming out of the Academic Board that look like the Yale Report—1828." [10] A young Army major who served very successfully as a faculty member in the early 1970's offered a melancholy view of West Point academics:

> A person who is going to serve in the Army for 20 or 30 years and who spends part of that time obtaining a graduate degree in order to teach at the Academy knows that he is not going to be a full-time academician and that accounts for much of the unhappiness at West Point. Because people don't really know what they are. They have been exposed to what it takes to be a first-rate scholar in graduate school. Most of them responded quite well to that, but they knew that even while they were at the Academy it would be almost impossible to be a first-rate scholar or even a first-rate teacher. The faculty member's job is to pass out the poop, not to continue his own academic development. And besides, the quality of the teacher is largely dependent on the quality and dedication of the students. Cadets rarely get involved in any kind of academic pursuit other than that directly covered in the class. It takes a cerebral relationship between a teacher and his students to allow one to become a really good teacher. And although there are potentially great students at the Academy, very few of them ever attain that status.
>
> This is because all of the other things at the Academy—pressures from the Corps, pressures athletically, pressures from the curriculum; things that people have to do at a certain time and in a certain phase of the year. They simply don't have the leisure to explore things intellectually because that takes a lot of skulking and rambling around. And they don't have time to do that.[11]

Most West Point professors are less critical of the Thayer System. In fact, most of the thirteen full professors who head the academic departments consider themselves the guardians of the Thayer tradition and equate substantive challenges to the Thayer System with heresy. They tend to discuss the weaknesses of the Thayer System in the manner Edmund Burke discussed flaws in the British Constitution, like "the wounds of a father" to be approached only "with pious awe and trembling solicitude." Along with the dean, the department heads constitute the only permanent members of the Academic Board, another legacy of the Thayer era, a legacy which has made possible the preservation of the other legacies. It is to West Point what the Curia Romana is to the Catholic Church, except that at West Point the superintendent, unlike the Pope, normally serves for only three years instead of for life.

Although the Military Academy has always been under the official control of Congress and the War Department (now the Secretary of the Army in the Defense Department), in practice the Academic Board has assumed on-the-scene control of policy-making. And since Thayer's day the permanent members of the Academic Board have usually been West Point graduates who have seen themselves as the heirs of Thayer, entrusted with the defense of West Point's unique mode of operation against encroachments from outsiders. Some professors can even trace the academic appointments they hold back through Thayer-trained predecessors all the way to Thayer himself. This academic version of apostolic succession provides continuity, but it also creates an atmosphere in which educational reform is sometimes perceived as a repudiation of semi-sacred procedures. And so while many civilian colleges are debating the reliability and value of any kind of grading system, a cadet's average can be recomputed to the third decimal point every day; or while civilian educators debate the advantages of an open classroom, cadet recitations in most mathematics classes are still governed by a modestly revised Thayer ritual which begins "Gentlemen, I was required to prove. . . ." [12]

Given the idiosyncracies of the Thayer System, it is easy to understand why visiting educators are frequently bewildered when they attend Academy classes or confer with West Point officials. The language which West Pointers use to discuss classroom procedures requires translation before it can be comprehensible to the uninitiated. For example, cadets "take boards" (go to the blackboard for written work), are "pro" (passing), or "tangent" (barely passing), or "D" (deficient or failing), or have been "found" (discharged from the Academy for deficiency in studies or conduct); good students are "hives" and poor students are "goats." And when Academy officials explain that these terms are vestiges of pedagogic practices instituted by Sylvanus Thayer, it is possible the visiting educator will think that name requires translation too, since Thayer is virtually unknown outside the Military Academy. Nor is it likely that those civilian educators who come to understand and admire the Thayer System will ever recommend its implementation elsewhere, because few civilian schools could afford to hire the number of faculty required to teach the multiple fifteen-man sections.[13]

A NEW RATIONALE

Although it too dates from the Thayer era, the core curriculum is not considered part of the Thayer System. In the nineteenth century virtually every American college, not just Thayer's West Point, offered students a standardized and prescribed curriculum centered on the classics. Latin and Greek were supplemented with courses in logic and moral philosophy, plus a smattering of mathematics and natural philosophy.[14] The Academy replaced the classics with courses in mathematics, the physical sciences, and technical subjects like mechanical drawing. French was required but only to permit the reading of textbooks imported from the École Polytechnique. The technical character of the Thayer curriculum made pedagogic sense because military tactics, especially the employment of artillery, depended heavily on engineering skills. The prescribed character of the West Point curriculum also made sense to educators of the time, because they believed that there was an essential group of subjects that an educated man must master. In the case of West Point, there were clearly defined disciplines and skills which all Army officers must master.

During the fifty years separating the Civil War and World War I, both American higher education and the American army underwent drastic reorganization. Much influenced by Charles Eliot of Harvard, American colleges abandoned the prescribed curriculum in favor of elective programs that allowed students to pursue individual academic interests in order to acquire specialized knowledge in one discipline.[15] At the turn of the century, Secretary of War Elihu Root initiated reforms which led to the establishment of advanced schools of the various arms and services, a development which also accelerated the tendency toward specialization in the Army.[16] Meanwhile, the Military Academy's organizational ties with the Corps of Engineers were greatly reduced and the majority of West Pointers were commissioned into non-technical branches of the service for the first time. During this era of academic and military ferment, the Military Academy remained committed to a prescribed engineering curriculum and to the stable world of Sylvanus Thayer.[17]

Ironically, Thayer himself recommended a complete overhaul of the West Point curriculum in 1865. But even Thayer could not compete with the mystique that had grown up around his name. Officials at West Point ignored his recommendations, despite Thayer's warning that "All human work and institutions are imperfect and subject to the laws of progress. To stand still and not advance is to retrograde." And as Thayer feared, West Point dropped from the ranks of the nation's leading schools of engineering after the Civil War. Developments in the sciences made possible by specialization were not incorporated into the Academy's program; it became increasingly clear that West Point graduates did not possess technical expertise comparable to that of graduates of first-rank civilian schools. West Point professors conducted their own surveys of prominent civilian institutions like MIT and Harvard and returned with the good news that West Point surpassed them all. For instance, in 1873 Professor Peter Smith Michie reported that MIT's extensive use of laboratory facilities was "of no value other than to educate the hand and eye in the use and application of apparatus." Michie dismissed Harvard's elective program as an academic fad that placed unwarranted responsibility "upon young men, who, in the nature of things can know less about what is fit for them than experienced instructors and professors." [18]

Surveys of civilian schools by Academy officials were primarily intended to amass evidence that the Academic Board could use to justify the status quo. "It is with pleasure," Michie concluded in his 1873 survey, "that I have to report that so far as the Military Academy is concerned, the character, scope and method of its instruction considering the end in view, is much superior to that of any institution either technical, special or general." But few civilian educators took West Point's claims of academic supremacy seriously. The inflated assertions of the Academic Board were generally regarded as symptoms of West Point's increasing defensiveness about its drop from academic prominence.[19]

The officials at West Point faced a choice: either reform the curriculum along the lines of civilian colleges in the hope of recapturing the Academy's former prestige as an engineering school or retain the old and wholly prescribed curriculum and devise a new rationale for the old practices. Gradually, the Academic Board adopted the latter option. The prescribed curriculum remained, because to abandon it would be to confess that there was no longer a formal body of knowledge or a special technique of instruction which West Point could claim as its particular province. The emphasis on mathematics and the applied sciences also remained, but between 1875 and 1900 these subjects were justified for an entirely new and different set of reasons. They were not justified as basic skills of practical utility in the Corps of Engineers or the Artillery. Mathematics and technical subjects were described as disciplines that developed mental rigor and character. West Point began to portray itself less as an engineering school that produced competent technicians armed with a particular expertise than as a character-building institution that produced moral and tough-minded men.[20]

For example, during the Thayer era cadets had been required to take massive doses of mathematics because mathematical skills were essential for engineers and artillery officers. In the early years of the twentieth century mathematics still dominated the curriculum, but now it was rationalized as a "mental toughener." In 1908, a committee charged with a study of the curriculum reported that the study of mathematics was the primary cause of the accomplishments of West Point graduates: "It is believed that mathematical training at the Military Academy has been the main factor in all the accomplishments of graduates; that it, more than any other factor, has generated that power of the graduate for profound and logical thinking; it has been a means for the installation of proper self-confidence, for understanding unhesitatingly the unfamiliar, and for going unerringly and indomitably after results whenever demanded by Duty of any nature." Or as Samuel Tillman, a West Point professor, put it: "It is not so much a knowledge of the subject that you wish to get into the boy; it is the mental training." [21]

The argument that officials at West Point began to make in the late nineteenth and early twentieth century—and some West Pointers still make in the 1970's—was really a modified version of a much older pedagogic theory. In most eighteenth-century American colleges the study of Latin and Greek was justified on the grounds that it "tempered the mind." Although Latin and Greek were "dead" languages of little practical utility, the student who mastered them, so the argument went, was intellectually disciplined.[22] By the turn of the century this pedagogic theory had been labeled "transferral of learning" or "transference," the notion that one could transfer the skills acquired in one area (e.g. Latin, Greek, mathematics) into a wholly unrelated area (e.g. troop leadership). The nub of this theory was the assumption that the human mind was like a muscle; education was a form of intellectual exercise that improved the strength and tone of one's mental muscles. Requiring the cadet to recite every day in mathematics class sharpened his powers of analysis, so that when confronted with a difficult combat decision, he would be able to think quickly and accurately, even if the decision had nothing to do with mathematical calculations. Like athletics and military drill, classroom learning was essentially a form of training in which constant repetition of prescribed exercises developed habits of mind that might prove useful in a wide variety of unrelated endeavors.

Most West Point officials refused to believe that the study of Latin or Greek provided such exercise. It was only mathematics courses, which West Point had in abundance, that gave an Army officer the requisite mental discipline. "We had a man come to West Point that graduated from Harvard that had never studied geometry," explained one nineteenth-century member of the Academic Board. "He couldn't do anything in the Army, although I expect he read Latin and Greek very well. He couldn't do anything else." [23] Although by the 1920's Edward L. Thorndike and other educational psychologists had discredited the notion that unrelated mental skills were transferable, many officials at West Point continue to find the theory compelling.[24]

The new emphasis on mental toughness, moral development, and character found expression in the "Duty, Honor, Country" motto that was engraved on the official crest, which was adopted in 1898. This was also the time when West Point professors began to emphasize their concern for "the Whole Man" and to express belief in the value of "general education" as opposed to intensive study of selected subjects.[25] No longer an engineering school, West Point also shunned comparisons with traditional liberal arts colleges and proclaimed itself a unique educational institution committed to producing a military version of the Renaissance man. According to Charles Larned, professor of drawing, the Thayer System was the most "perfectly arranged educational system ever devised by man." In 1902 Larned assured the guests at West Point's centennial celebration that the Academy was "more than any other educational institution *sui generis* . . . , a machine in which a heterogeneous mass of raw material is transformed in the short space of four years into a finished product, molded, tested, and stamped with the sterling mark which has come to be recognized the world over." [26]

Neither Larned nor his colleagues on the Academic Board had national academic reputations. In 1901, the librarian at West Point, himself an Academy graduate and a distinguished scholar, regretfully observed that "No member of the Academic Board is a member of the National Academy of Sciences. No member has received an honorary degree from any [other] college for work done. So far as I know, no publication on a scientific matter has been made in any scientific journal by anyone connected with the Academy as a professor or a cadet since about 1857." [27] Although several of the members of the Academic Board during the Thayer era were prominent scholars, by the twentieth century the West Point professors thought of themselves primarily as administrators entrusted with the conservation of the Thayer System. They simply had no time left for scholarly research. As watchdogs over the Thayer traditions, members of the Academic Board successfully opposed reform-minded superintendents, critical civilian educators, and activist congressmen. They could afford to lose some battles because their tenured status guaranteed them the longevity required to wait out critics of the Thayer System and eventually win the war. Unknown outside West Point, but indomitable and revered within the confines of the Military Academy, the members of the Academic Board maintained the Thayer System and the core curriculum remarkably intact, isolated from what Larned called the "contaminating impurities of the world," until the middle of the twentieth century.[28]

THE IMPULSE TO CONSERVE

In certain fundamental ways the Academy of the 1970's remains wedded to the Thayer System. Most of the members of the Academic Board still regard themselves as sentries whose primary duty is to protect the unique Thayer heritage from what Colonel Gilbert Kirby, head of the Department of Earth, Space, and Graphic Sciences, has called "these outside pressures." And the pressures are constant:

> Rather than allowing us to make institutional evaluations of the curriculum, as any good institution would, we get these outside pressures. Everytime we get a new Secretary of the Army, a new Chief of Staff, or a new DCSPER (Deputy Chief of Staff for Personnel Operations), we have to make a new curriculum study. And God Almighty, we have plowed this ground so many times. And all of these men have their particular little fetishes. Here's a guy who says, "Well, here I am. I am Chief of Staff of the Army and I like *area x;* therefore, cadets ought to have *area x.*" Here I am, as Froehlke would sit down there, as Secretary of the Army [1971–73], and say, "I never had a course in math. Why does anybody need math?" But because of the directive nature of the thing, we are forced to react. So in curriculum matters we have great difficulty here. We have a hard time trying to maintain our balance because we do have so much directed at us.[29]

Like Charles Larned and Samuel Tillman, contemporary West Point professors are administrators rather than scholars. They spend a great deal of their time explaining their nineteenth-century pedagogy to civilian and military officials who are skeptical about the relevance of the tried and true. Colonel Edward Saunders, head of the Department of Physics, points out that the supervision of "how the whole thing ties together" is a full-time job:

> The fact is that the people who sit in jobs like mine really don't devote much of their effort, their real effort, to the specific disciplinary aspects of their job. Most of us don't. . . . But the point is that many of us . . . devote the primary portion of our time to the operation of the institution as a whole, as opposed to our own disciplines. It's an extremely important factor in understanding and analyzing the institution because it's probably unique in educational institutions. The fact that I, with the responsibility for the curriculum content in physics, am also so intimately involved with the interrelationships with other disciplines, with the over-all mission of the Academy, and how the whole thing ties together.[30]

Academic Board members take their institutional responsibilities seriously, not because they have a perverse desire to keep West Point tied to hidebound traditions but because they are career officer administrators who believe that through the Thayer System West Point conserves and inculcates attitudes which are absolutely essential for military men. The combination of prescribed mathematical and applied science courses and the formalized classroom procedures, most Academic Board members argue, develop a respect for order, for duly constituted authority, and for rigorous attention to detail. Occasional public pretensions to the contrary, West Point puts a premium on these traits rather than on intellectual curiosity. And many of West Point's more forthright officers are wary of comparisons between West Point and prestigious civilian schools which expose the relative superficiality of the Academy's intellectual life. "I don't give a shit about academics here, really," said a third-generation West Pointer who was actively involved in enforcing new cadet regulations during the 1973–74 school year. "As long as they get a broad general education and a man can lead a rifle platoon and respects the dignity of man, then I don't give a shit what they teach him. . . . What we've got to teach these guys here is 'savvy.' That means that they've got to go out and teach a guy who's getting ready to throw a grenade into their tent and make him think of only one thing, 'What can I do to help that lieutenant get over the hill?' " [31]

This earthy expression of West Point objectives would embarrass Academic Board members, but it summarizes central principles of a 1970's view of the Thayer System—that West Point should provide what can be certified as "a broad general education" and that in the last quarter of the twentieth century it should continue to produce men who can lead even their most recalcitrant fellow Americans in ground combat. And these latter principles underlie the civilian and military defense of the Academy as the alma mater of men who have led the nation to victory in two world wars.[32]

These principles are also inherent in Colonel Gilbert Kirby's response to people who are overly inclined "to tinker with the curriculum" in the name of modernization. Kirby remarked: "I like to fall back on what Somers Dick, the head of the Department of

Mathematics says—'I hate to give up on a winner.' For better or for worse, the curriculum we have had in hand has worked and I hate to fiddle around with this too much on the odd chance that it might work better." Lieutenant Colonel James B. Hall, Assistant Dean for Plans and Programs, summed up the view that the conservatism of the Academic Board is the source of its strength:

> I think there is a tremendous strength in the system organizationally. There are certain weaknesses perhaps, depending on how you look at it, and just the Academic Board itself is a conservative, unwieldy type organization and a difficult organization to get any rapid progress out of. In the longer view, I think its strength is there. It is a conservative view. You look at Oxford and they haven't changed their curriculum very much over the years and nobody has faulted them for it. A larger university can afford to introduce new courses at the drop of a hat. It's all done with malice aforethought here.[33]

West Point's first civilian visiting professor of history (1972–73), Morten Jay Luvaas, also affirmed the value of "the strong sense of mission that pervades the Military Academy and shapes every program here." Professor Luvaas found it "refreshing to work with men who basically agree on what they are trying to accomplish and who do not feel compelled to insist that what they are teaching has nothing to do with character." He contrasted West Point's old but coherent program with civilian colleges where "courses and programs [tend] to proliferate without any particular sense of direction until the curriculum often resembles . . . 'a monster carrying with it all kinds of rudimentary organs and even sprouting new horns.' "[34] In Luvaas' mind, then, as well as in the minds of most West Point professors, it would be foolish for the Academy to pattern itself after civilian colleges. Douglas MacArthur, Dwight D. Eisenhower, Maxwell D. Taylor, Omar N. Bradley, and George S. Patton, Jr., are merely a few of the prominent "sons of Thayer" whose careers are invoked to confirm the effectiveness of mental training as opposed to a liberal education. The invocation is particularly effective if one's sense of history stops in the 1940's.

In 1973, a majority of the almost 23,000 living graduates of West Point concurred with the traditional orientation of the Academic Board. Over 97 per cent of the alumni belong to the Association of Graduates, perhaps the most powerful and best organized alumni association in the country. The Association of Graduates, founded under the leadership of Sylvanus Thayer in 1869, uses its enormous influence to "acquire and disseminate information on the history, activities, objectives, and methods of the United States Military Academy; to acquire and preserve historical materials relating to that institution; and to encourage and foster the study of military science there by worthy young men." [35] In addition to supporting a world-wide series of events and activities, the association works through the West Point Alumni Foundation Inc., to publish the Academy's alumni magazine, *Assembly*, and its extraordinary yearbook, *The Register of Graduates and Former Cadets.* [36] This volume appears annually in a revised edition and contains the name of every man admitted as a cadet "from the establishment of the institution in 1802 to the present time." [37] The 1973 edition contains in its 866 pages a biographical summary of association members with annual updates as well as the continued listing of ex-cadets such as "Poe, Edgar A. . . . . . x 1834" and "Leary, Timothy F. . . . . . x Jun 43." (The "x" indicates a "non-graduate" and the date identifies the class with which he first entered the Academy.) [38]

The most important development in the association's recent history has been the presentation since 1958 of the Sylvanus Thayer Award to an American "whose service and accomplishments in the national interest exemplify devotion to the ideals expressed in the Military Academy motto: 'Duty, Honor, Country.' " Many graduates view this award as an opportunity for West Point to identify itself with a distinguished American whose career symbolizes the commitment to national service and to values West Pointers associate with the Thayer System. Five of the first six winners of the award were men of great national prominence whose sympathies to the military could scarcely be questioned—John Foster Dulles, Henry Cabot Lodge, Dwight D. Eisenhower, Douglas MacArthur, and John J. McCloy. But in recent years the Vietnam conflict has eroded the prestige of the award and has required the reigning superintendent to preside over ceremonies for two public personalities, Bob Hope (1968) and Billy Graham (1972); two embattled diplomats, Dean Rusk (1969) and Ellsworth Bunker (1970); and one astronaut, Neil A. Armstrong (1971).[39]

The awards to Hope and Graham were a source of embarrassment for many graduates, who felt that neither a comedian nor a preacher should receive the honor. In 1973 the association seemed determined to redeem itself by returning to the generation of Eisenhower and MacArthur to honor "the soldiers' general"—Omar Bradley. General Bradley's appearance at West Point was a welcome change from that of his immediate predecessor, Billy Graham, who began his acceptance speech by declaring, "I feel a little bit like the man I heard about on Resurrection Day. He got up out of the grave and looked at his tombstone and read the epitaph and said, 'Either someone is a terrible liar or I'm in the wrong hole.' " General Bradley's style was much more self-effacing. "As leaders you will have to act and you will have to command," the General advised, "As leaders you will have to listen." Then, unexpectedly, he added, "There is an old Missouri proverb that says, 'If one man tells you you are a jackass it might not mean much. But, if five men tell you you are a jackass it is time to go out and buy a saddle.' " Whereas Billy Graham lauded West Point and self-consciously invoked the name of Thayer—"I believe it is of paramount importance that the moral and spiritual values that Sylvanus Thayer held be rekindled and revived, and that once again they become the beacon lights to guide our nation through this perilous period"—Bradley cautioned, "There is no question we [the Army] look to West Point for our leaders, but some of our finest leaders have received their commissions from other sources. I need only remind you of General George Marshall [a graduate of Virginia Military

Institute] to prove the truth of that." Whereas Graham concluded by exhorting the cadets to be inspired by Thayer's values, "Until a moral and spiritual glow can be seen throughout the world," Bradley said simply, "June will come soon for all of you. I know you will go out into the world of reality not as tourists but as active participants. Participate fully—participate well. Our nation's future depends on it." [40]

General Bradley's belief that the national well-being was inexorably linked to the quality of the West Point education underscored the sense of importance the Academic Board and the Association of Graduates attach to the retention of established traditions. They are convinced that, if West Point bends to accommodate its critics, if it abandons the Thayer System, eliminates the prescribed curriculum, endorses the tendency toward academic specialization and student freedom, if it does any or all of these things, the future of the republic will be less secure.

The organization of the Military Academy guarantees that the advocates of change will not easily gain the upper hand. Twelve of the department heads and the dean are tenured professors who have a vested interest in the maintenance of the status quo. The major threat to their control comes from the superintendent, a lieutenant general who officially has complete responsibility for the immediate government and military command of the Academy and the military post at West Point. A lesser threat is the commandant, a brigadier general who heads the Department of Tactics and has official responsibility for the administration and military training of the Corps of Cadets. But despite their rank and their official responsibilities, the superintendent and commandant have only one vote apiece in Academic Board deliberations and, most significantly, they are assigned to their posts for only one tour of duty, which rarely exceeds three years. Although the Office of Superintendent and the Office of Commandant are coveted positions which attract bright, ambitious, "on the way up" career officers who are often eager to leave their marks on West Point by initiating reforms, the dean and his Academic Board represent an institutionalized check to such ambitions.[41]

In addition to the direct restraint exercised by the permanent members of the Academic Board and the indirect restraint exercised by the Association of Graduates, the West Point superintendent is accountable to the deputy chief of staff for personnel operations in the Army. During much of General Knowlton's tour as superintendent this position was filled by Lieutenant General Bernard W. Rogers, who was commandant of cadets during the late 1960's. General Knowlton graduated seventh in his January 1943 class of 409 and General Rogers, a Rhodes scholar, thirteenth in his June 1943 class of 514.[42] According to some observers, their considerable talents, identical class years, and respective positions precipitated an on-again, off-again battle of wills. Among some Academy officials, General Rogers had the reputation of trying to run West Point from Washington.[43] But despite the conflicts between strong personalities like Knowlton and Rogers, the balance of power is still vested in the members of the Academic Board. In short, thc government of West Point operates according to an elaborate system of checks and balances which constrains ambitious superintendents and ensures that policies will be measured against first principles, which at West Point means the tenets of Thayer.

THE IMPULSE TO CHANGE

In the years immediately following World War II the Military Academy conducted an exhaustive review of its curriculum and operation. Many similar reviews had taken place at West Point before, usually in response to pressures from the War Department, Congress, or civilian educators. According to Brigadier General John R. Jannarone, who was academic dean from 1965 to 1974, "it was a time for everybody to look around and see what needed to be changed. We were no exception to this general trend. I particularly want to indicate that we weren't doing this because we felt that there was something wrong. But it seemed to be the logical thing to do. So the first thing that was done was to have a group get together to try to set forth the qualities and attributes that would be desirable in an Army officer of the future." In the dean's view "this was a logical way to start the study" of curriculum needs; this group then interviewed "prominent military and civilian leaders of World War II, prominent businessmen and educators." [44] It was quite natural for the Academy to turn to people whom it believed were instrumental in "winning the war" for guidance in planning for the future. Many of these men were West Point graduates who could be counted on to endorse the principles of the Thayer System. (Even when referring to actions that took place over two decades ago, General Jannarone was careful to repudiate the notion that the postwar survey of West Point was an indication that "something was wrong" with the old policies.) Equally reassuring were the criteria against which the West Point program was to be judged. These were essentially military as opposed to academic criteria, "the qualities and attributes that would be desirable in an Army officer of the future," the very qualities the disciples of Thayer regarded as their special province.

General Jannarone acknowledged that it was "pretty hard to translate" the study group's recommendations into tangible policies, but the Academy did find "several factors which we thought were quite significant . . . particularly in terms of our own kind of mission":

> [1.] The first one involved the increasingly complex technologies that were associated with military weapons systems, communication systems, etc. In many instances these involved words that were not even in the lexicon before World War II. Words like ionic propulsion, nuclear energy and so forth. And we found that the Army, Navy, and Air Force were developing for the future a lot of material which would require a more profound and intimate knowledge of the underlying sciences than had heretofore been the case. We felt that if these men were going to be the managers of these systems

they should have a pretty firm foundation in some of the basic principles which were involved in these systems.

[2.] The military in the foreseeable future would be cast in political-military responsibilities to a much greater extent than had been the case before. . . . And we realized that this meant that future military leaders had to know much more about the history, geography, the economics, the aspirations of a lot of people all over the world. This pointed to the need for more emphasis on the social sciences and humanities. So we were being pushed from both ends of the spectrum and this indicated that there were some things that we were going to have to change.

[3.] The Army in 1947 had embarked on a rather large scale of expanded graduate education for the officer corps. . . . And what this meant to us is that we had to prepare these young men to go off into any one of a different number of graduate level experiences even though we could not identify what that would be with respect to a particular cadet.

[4.] The fourth factor was the explosion of knowledge, a factor which everyone was contending with. And this required a hell of a lot of reorganization of courses.[45]

The Academic Board's response was predictable: committed to extend the nineteenth-century traditions of Sylvanus Thayer into the second half of the twentieth century, officials at West Point argued that the Thayer System was sufficient to meet the technological, political, educational, and scientific challenges of the future. In 1953 a board of officers appointed by Superintendent Frederick A. Irving to review Academy curriculum reported that "the mission of West Point is clear, distinct, and directly applicable to each individual cadet." The Thayer System, the board concluded, was not in need of modification. And this conviction held through the superintendency of Blackshear M. Bryan in the mid-1950's. But revolutionary views found expression when Major General Garrison H. Davidson came to power as superintendent. In his annual report of 1957 Davidson announced that "the time has come for a more searching and fundamental review of what our goals should be and how best to attain them." [46]

General Davidson initiated an unprecedented series of studies to reinterpret West Point's "mission." This reinterpretation was meant to be substantially influenced by the findings of a board of officers, the Ewell Board, which in January 1958 reported its conclusions as to "the qualities and attributes . . . most essential in the regular army officer in the period 1968–78." [47] The Ewell Board found "that the individual capable of fulfilling the leadership demands of the military profession in the future will require all the military virtues of his predecessors, many of them to a greater degree." And in addition:

> . . . He will require a wealth of knowledge and a capacity for applying that knowledge beyond any requirements of the past. Character, leadership qualities, intellectual capacity, and a fairly fixed body of knowledge are no longer enough. The inroads of physical science and political science into the military realm demand military leaders who are well based in these areas and who have the intellectual curiosity, the initiative, and the quality of creative thinking which will enable them to expand their base of knowledge in a flexible manner, and apply it to ever-changing situations. The unrelenting compression of time-space, the geometric progression of man-force relationships, and the ideological overtones that will continue to pervade the course of events make flexible, creative knowledge and wisdom ever more significant in the direction of military affairs. [48]

The tenets of Sylvanus Thayer, in other words, were no longer enough. The Ewell Board's endorsement of "intellectual curiosity," "creative thinking," and "creative knowledge and wisdom" represented a dramatic shift away from the qualities that had dominated the concern of the staff and faculty since the Civil War. Despite its ponderous tone and its deference to "the military virtues of . . . predecessors," the report was a manifesto for sweeping reforms which would move the Academy in the direction taken by American colleges and universities half a century earlier.

The *Superintendent's Curriculum Study* that appeared in the fall of

1958 reflected some of the sentiments of the Ewell Board, but only rhetorically. Although General Davidson seemed convinced that West Point could no longer insulate itself from the trends that had transformed American higher education since the nineteenth century, the permanent members of the Academic Board did not concur. Davidson favored the Academy's priority commitment to the production of military professionals; but he also insisted that West Point must become, once again, a first-rate academic institution. Professor Sumner Willard speculated that "one reason that General Davidson adopted the view that he did was that we were about to be accredited again in 1959 and he had children who went to places like Cornell, the University of North Carolina, maybe to Harvard, one son to Williams. And they all came home and told their father what was going on in liberal arts colleges and universities." [49]

Such outside influence from youthful civilians "was not to General Davidson's credit," as one senior faculty member put it. And a decisive majority of department heads declined to support General Davidson's convictions. However, the *Superintendent's Curriculum Study* reflected the concerns of the Ewell Board and even appeared to suggest that West Point academic life must undergo root and branch reform. The study observed that "the educational problems" associated with "the Sputnik-Explorer era" had stimulated "the sudden . . . realization that our national survival is more closely related to educational accomplishment than any but the most far-sighted had previously suspected." [50] But, despite the boldness of this rhetoric, the study proceeded to endorse the quite modest reforms proposed by a subcommittee chaired by Colonel John R. Jannarone, then head of the Physics and Chemistry Department. The conclusions of Colonel Jannarone's subcommittee exemplified the most important bureaucratic fact about the Academy; in most confrontations between the superintendent and the Academic Board, the superintendent was destined to lose:

> The Evaluation Committee concludes that the curriculum should continue to be an essentially standard one, but with increased oppor-

tunities for advanced and elective work for qualified cadets. The preponderance of weight should continue to be on the mathematics-science-engineering area, with a ratio of emphasis of that area to the social science-humanities field between 60/40 and 55/45. This distribution of emphasis is based on the fact that more graduates will be called on to do postgraduate work in the engineering and physical science field than in other fields and on the concept that a strong science-engineering base, if it is to be acquired at all, must be developed in formal courses, whereas, in the social science-humanities field, a good base is equally desirable but there are greater opportunities for individual development and growth after graduation.[51]

In the words of one former West Point professor, General Davidson was "faulted by the Academic Board for trying to move too far—too fast—too soon." [52] The report underscored the reluctance of Academy professors to endorse major departures from past practices. Cadets would be allowed to select a few courses on their own; the social sciences and humanities courses would be increased slightly. But that was as far as the Academic Board would go. Even the implementation of these modest changes was quite gradual. The opportunity for a cadet to select two elective courses was installed in the curriculum in 1961. Two more electives were added in 1964. By 1969 there were a total of eight.[53]

From his vantage point in 1973, General Jannarone offered a self-consciously judicious view of these changes. "We have a core curriculum now which consists of 40 courses of which 21 are in the social sciences and humanities area; and, 19 are in the math, science, and engineering area," but he added:

We've changed the unbalance from what it used to be to the present situation; and, some people argue that, if you look at the credit-hour ratings of some of the courses involved there, that the imbalance is still slightly in favor of the math, science and engineering area. The reason for this is that we have four credit-hour courses in most of the math, science, and engineering program and two and a half for the others. The imbalance is in favor of the social sciences and humanities in terms of the number of courses, and there is an

> imbalance in the other direction if you look at it in terms of credit hours. But, if you take the electives available to you, you can imbalance the program in a number of different ways.[54]

This opportunity for cadets to "imbalance" their programs was extremely disturbing to a number of West Point professors. There was no credible way to disguise the fact that this development constituted one of the most important dilutions that has ever occurred in the Thayer System. Despite the modest character of the reforms initiated in 1961, the implications of the curriculum changes were dramatic. The enormity of the change is reflected by a 1959 graduate who remembered "the daily grind in math," which, while still an integral part of the required curriculum, has been cut back by one course and is subject to advance placement and cadet validation. He approved of the electives development, but recalled, "If anyone thought very seriously about what he was doing in academics . . . he would probably say (I'm sure I would have said) that you did it because there really was no alternative. You either went to mathematics every day except Sunday or you left the Military Academy. Those were the alternatives; you either did it or you got out." Underscoring the paradoxical nature of his own response, he added, "that feeling of futility, I suppose, has been somewhat lessened by having electives. Yet, I suspect that the elective options encourage people to think more, to see that things can be changed and to think more about alternatives. . . . I suspect cadets now think more about that."[55]

In the minds of many disciples of Thayer, the varied and voluntaristic characteristics of the new curriculum challenged the basic assumptions of the old Thayer System. And from their perspective, they were correct. What was involved in the addition of electives and the erosion of the math-science-engineering dominance was fundamental. Cadets were allowed to make judgments about the direction of their education. The presumption that there was a basic course of study essential for all Army officers and that the officials at West Point knew what that course of study should be, these old and entrenched presumptions were brought into question. Electives opened up a Pandora's box that had been sealed shut at West Point for half a century, for they not only implied that individual choice was as reliable as institutional authority but they also suggested that the peculiarities of an individual's intellectual process were as important as the "transferable mental skills" acquired in the learning process. The freedom of choice accorded a cadet was still very limited and the math-science-engineering courses, the courses best suited for Thayer pedagogy, still occupied the bulk of a cadet's academic time. But long-standing articles of faith had come under question. The advocates of the Thayer System had always argued that a school for soldiers could not be like other schools, that it required a special curriculum, a conservative pedagogy, a uniform and regularized academic atmosphere. By the 1970's there was a faction at West Point which echoed the exhortations of the Ewell Board and which argued that soldiers should be educated in much the same way as civilians, that the Army needed West Pointers with undergraduate academic specialties, that the Academy should provide cadets with a rich intellectual diet and not worry about the potentially subversive consequences of the liberalized curriculum.

DISAGREEMENTS AND PUBLIC OPINION

Few faculty members of any rank will talk openly about their fear that electives, a majors program, and the increase in social sciences and humanities courses will subvert the discipline and respect for authority required of soldiers. It not only threatens the vested interests of the mathematics, science, and engineering departments but it is such a psychologically troublesome issue that serious reflection about it is as rare as conversations about how it feels to see men die in combat. And the public statements made by Academy spokesmen frequently conceal rather than reveal what is at issue. Superintendent Knowlton represented the Academy's public stance in a 1973 Founders Day speech on the West Coast:

> . . . For the past few years I have explained that the last decade has seen tremendous changes in the academics at West Point. Gar Davidson started stirring this pot in the late 1950's when he was the Superintendent. The changes which eventually came out of what he started are now widely hailed by almost everyone as very beneficial to West Point and to the Army. But having been stationed at West Point during that period, I can tell you that this acceptance was not terribly great when it all started.
>
> To put things very simply, having all cadets take the same courses regardless of prior college experience was wasteful of talent. We cannot afford it when we are faced with the explosion of knowledge which has occurred in the last quarter of a century. So a procedure was set up whereby a cadet who has taken a college course in one of the subjects in the core of our curriculum may validate that course by a combination of his college record and the passing of an exam taken at West Point. Successful combination of those make it unnecessary for a cadet to take that particular course.
>
> To fill the gap thus created, a series of electives has been introduced into the curriculum. There are now about 160 of these electives covering almost every field of intellectual endeavor at West Point. All cadets take at least 6, and those with quite a bit of prior college take many, many more. When a cadet groups his electives in a certain field of academic interest and completes certain minimums, he has what we have called an *area of elective interest.* Harvard has done away with the word *majors,* and calls them *areas of concentration.* While we have shied away from the word *majors* as well, the elective program makes it possible for a cadet to get a good minor and in some ways approach a major in a civilian college—but all the while retaining the balance of the West Point educational experience.[56]

Although these remarks may have been well received on the West Coast, they would not have been welcomed at the Academy by those Academic Board members whose "acceptance" of change was, as General Knowlton put it, "not terribly great." Since General Davidson "started stirring this pot" in 1957, the pressure has been building steadily over the years; during General Knowlton's tour the pressures were at times explosive. When the issue of West Point electives came up in meetings among department heads, one participant described the sessions as "very open, very candid discussions"; but, he added, "they are frequently very vitriolic. Many times people aren't even nice in what they say to each other. But I think it is a good thing and I think it is a healthy thing." [57] Terms such as "electives" and "specialization" have become code words in the West Point culture; like "law and order" and "busing" they are euphemistic symbols of deep-felt convictions which are seldom articulated in public.

At issue is how soldiers should be educated. Every department head at West Point recognizes that the Academy produces professional soldiers and concurs that the Academy's curriculum and pedagogy must be tailored to fit that goal. But no member of the Academic Board argues that West Point should offer only courses in military science or only courses that provide direct and practical training in the skills of troop leadership. All agree that West Point is interested in providing something called general education, but they disagree over what that term means. The dominant faction believes that a West Point education must develop characteristics historically associated with the Thayer System. These include discipline, dependability, what they call "mental toughness," and an orderly approach to work. West Point professors who advocate this view are critical of efforts to open up the curriculum, to expand electives, and to give cadets freedom of choice, because they regard the drift toward a more individualistic concept of education as fundamentally antithetical to the Academy's military mission. "I really think that you find here a crashing ignorance in the fundamental precepts of structuring curricula," said one professor. "The rationale that 'they do it at other places, so we ought to do it here' just doesn't work. I think what has been lost here is what we are trying to do. . . . other schools don't have our mission of, you know, trying to graduate Army officers." [58] Meanwhile, a minority faction believes that the old Thayer values are less relevant to the needs of a modern Army officer. They would like to see West Point become more like other colleges because they think that intellectual curiosity, specialized knowledge, and individual initiative are likely to make future officers more effective. In the end, then, the debate boils down to an argument about what a soldier should be. And the West Point curriculum of the mid-1970's features the contradictory commitment to the goals of both factions.

Colonel Somers Dick of the Math Department was perhaps more associated than any other faculty member with the faction of the Academic Board which warred against the development of the electives program. He is a 1935 graduate of the Academy; and, until he became interim dean in 1974, one of the three department heads without a Ph.D. "I'm not one that really supports the choosing of an area of concentration," Colonel Dick said; and, he offered three principal reasons for this view. First, "very few people . . . as Army officers have a field speciality such as physicist, historian, etc., and, if they are such a beast, they've got doggone few places where they can be sent. And I think their whole life is curtailed by this specialization." He also contended that "most undergraduates don't know what they want to do; and when they choose, they choose for any number of reasons that are perhaps not academic. It's either because their friends did; they've been exposed to someone influencing them by saying: 'This is a good idea.' It's really not a decision of their own you might say." And, finally, the most frequently cited justification for the prescribed curriculum, that "the areas of concentration . . . earmarks the boy, perhaps restricts the ability for him to *perform* in later life in the service." [59]

Colonel Elliott Cutler of the Electrical Engineering Department did not share Colonel Dick's acute apprehension about electives; however, he did reinforce the principle that the basic rationale for the Academy's required curriculum was "utilization in the service." Cutler agreed with Dick that the Academy's first priority is the production of officers for the Army, officers with the attitudes and skills that will meet what are called "the Army's needs." Like Dick, he did not believe the Academy is a place where young men should be allowed to pursue their intellectual interests without regard for military requirements.[60] Colonel Edward Saunders of the Physics Department saw the prescribed courses in their present form as essential in preserving what he referred to as "those fundamental threads." Saunders argued that "it would be a serious error to encroach upon those basic threads in order to allow the guy to be a specialist." The concept of allowing a young man to specialize in his education raised for Colonel Saunders an issue that "we sometimes lose sight of. We're an expensive place and the only way we can justify our existence is by doing what we're getting paid for doing. And that's to *produce* professional *Army* officers." [61]

The Academy's youngest department head, Colonel Lee D. Olvey of Social Sciences, was a particularly articulate advocate for a sophisticated electives program. He argued that "it is terribly important that the military leadership of the country be politically literate" and what the Social Sciences Department is "aspiring to do *at a minimum* is to make our graduates politically literate." He bristled at suggestions that traditional Thayer concepts such as the "transfer of training" assumption are applicable to the education of cadets in the 1970's. Olvey's emphasis was on education as opposed to training and he said, "I suppose training is involved with teaching a set of answers and education is involved with teaching the people how to ask the right questions." While his colleagues on the Academic Board shied away from such traditionally civilian concerns, Olvey argued:

> If the military is going to be able to perform its function effectively, then it needs to be literate in political, domestic, and other kinds of considerations. It simply won't do to argue that the military can make a purely military input and that at some higher level all the other considerations will be entered in and that we will come up with some magic calculus which balances it all out. All of the participants in the process need to have some appreciation of not only

> their own particular area of responsibility but for some of the other types of considerations as well. And it is very much in the best interest of the nation that its military leadership understands some of the political and non-military issues domestically and internationally which face the nation. And to that end we require all graduates to take a certain amount of course work in political science, international relations, and economics and we think that it is very useful that they do that.[62]

Despite Olvey's argument for a broader and more intellectually sophisticated curriculum, the general consensus of department heads remains strongly opposed to academic specialization and still wedded to the belief that mental discipline, not intellectual curiosity, is the proper goal of a West Point education. Underlying this belief in discipline is the conviction that the modern soldier, like his nineteenth-century predecessor, must have an ingrained respect for order and authority. The specialized knowledge required to formulate national and international policies is unnecessary, they argued, because policy-making is the province of civilians, not soldiers. General Jannarone expressed the majority opinion of his colleagues:

> I can understand why cadets might feel that they would like to be studying more social sciences or more mathematics or more English if they had in mind some other vocation when they graduate. But I don't think it would be fair to take the attitude that this institution ought to bend to accommodate them if they do not intend in fact to be an officer in the Regular Army.
>
> I find in talking to cadets that most of them say that they would like to have more freedom and more options in taking academic courses. But, when you probe this a little more deeply, I think there are indications there that they're not saying that they think it's the best way to prepare them for a military career, but for some other things.[63]

The Academy dean capped his argument with a comparison between West Point and the Air Force Academy:

> Our sister Academy, the Air Force Academy, moved in this direction [instituting electives] about ten years ago. They were almost using it as a public relations gimmick. They were sloganizing—"A Major For All," or something like that. And they have found from their experience that they went too far in that direction. I get this information from my counterpart out there, General Woodyard. He tells me that he's a little bit disturbed, that their cadets begin to feel like they are physicists or historians instead of "cadets." They are worried about it and they are beginning now to move back away from the direction they had been moving in and back to a position which is closer to ours.[64]

From Jannarone's perspective it would be hard to imagine a more satisfying reaffirmation of the conservative values associated with the Thayer System. This endorsement from the humbled Air Force Academy dean came at a time when the Air Force Academy was experiencing the most serious attrition problem in its history.[65] Much of the impetus for change at West Point in the 1950's and 1960's came from the fear that the Air Force Academy, with its more diverse curriculum and its public emphasis on academic as opposed to military concerns, would out-recruit West Point and eventually become a demonstrably superior institution. But the attrition rate at the Air Force Academy and the higher resignation rate among its graduates appear to have confirmed what the old guard at West Point has said all along: a military man cannot receive a liberal education and be counted on to remain in the military.

But unofficial jubilation by those who believe that West Point's academic policies have been vindicated seldom takes official form. In fact, General Knowlton, the Academy's senior spokesman in the early 1970's, delivered public statements which frequently suggested that West Point was a New York State version of Princeton with an unusually vigorous ROTC program. And in the catalog sent to over 25,000 young men who wrote the Academy seeking information about its programs in 1972–73, General Knowlton said:

"The United States Military Academy provides a superior education. We are modern in concept and staff. During this decade we have made great advancements in our academic program, providing a more flexible curriculum and a growing diversity of electives." General Knowlton's celebration of a West Point "modern in concept and staff' with its "flexible curriculum" is similar to the misrepresentations that pass for truth in most college catalogs. But the reasons behind West Point's need to associate itself with liberal arts colleges help explain why members of the Academic Board do not insist that Academy spokesmen emphasize the values of which they are genuinely most proud: they are afraid that the unvarnished truth is unpalatable to most young Americans.[66]

"We are interested in appealing to the sort of guy," said Colonel Manley Rogers, the director of admissions, "who has the potential to make it medically, physically and academically and *who has the desire to give a career of service to his country an honest try.*" Such candidates are scarce. As Kenneth Keniston has observed, the college-age population of the early 1970's is "discouraged, exhausted and depressed." A career of public service has little appeal. "Far from being won over," contended Keniston, "students have if anything become even more discouraged about the political process." [67] Colonel Rogers, a thoughtful, soft-spoken West Point graduate, acknowledged that "the guy who is really looking forward to service, like I was in World War II, is in short supply. It was a grand crusade for the country and I was young and I was thinking that the war was going to be over before I had a chance to get in it and prove myself. A lot of us felt that way, but I'm convinced that this picture of World War II is completely different from what it [attitude toward service] is today." [68]

West Point has often suffered recruitment problems. It has always represented a challenge to certain enduring American convictions, such as the belief in the superiority of the citizen-soldier, distrust of a professional army, antipathy toward a self-professed elite, unease about a school where men are trained in the increasingly sophisticated art of killing other men. But the pervasive disenchantment with public service that characterizes many students of the 1970's has further decreased the size of the pool from which the Academy might draw prospective candidates. According to a survey commissioned by the Department of Defense in 1971 and a related survey of college-age Americans by George Gallup, the number of men who are medically, physically, and academically qualified for the four service academies and who aspire to a career of national service is about 10,000.[69] As Colonel Rogers observed, "there are hundreds of colleges who are looking for that kind of guy. That also is a number which almost equals the total number of available cadetships at all [service] academies plus the four year ROTC scholarships awarded each year." In order to attract candidates from what was always a small and has now become an even smaller student population, the Academy cannot afford to publicize its devotion to the principles of Sylvanus Thayer. Colonel Rogers candidly acknowledged that the Academy "has resisted most of the trends throughout the country which allow students to develop on their own." [70] But at a time when service to country is out of favor, particularly if service requires allegiance to the tenets of a governmental agency, more particularly if that agency is military, most particularly if that military agency has very strong attachments to unpopular ideas about what constitutes education, it is easy to understand why West Point prefers to advertise itself as a college rather than a unique school for soldiers.

Chapter Three

★★★★★★★★★★★★★★★★

BEAST AND BEYOND

By electing to attend the United States Military Academy, your son has chosen to make sacrifices the nature of which may be unknown to him. On other campuses across our country the life-style of students is undergoing rapid change. Selecting West Point precludes participation in that phenomenon.

From The New Cadet: Information for the Parents of the Class of 1977 (*1973*)

I'd like to think that the types of stress West Point provides in Beast Barracks, and in other ways, do not relate to the types of stress a cadet has to face when he leaves here as an officer. It seems to me that it's phoney stress. Who gives a good goddamn whether you can change your clothes in thirty seconds or thirty minutes because it seems to me that stress . . .

[A second officer interrupting] Anybody who studies this business of operation under stress will argue that . . . you can create conditions of stress and force people to operate in them. OCS is built on this notion, basic training is built on this, and West Point is built on this. It isn't the [kind of] stress that is important; it is the immediate acceptance of the stress on the part of the individual concerned and his realizing that he has got to respond. . . . Good tactical officers here and in OCS spend a great deal of time trying to maximize these situations of stress. And if in Beast Barracks, in the first few encounters, you can get the individual to accept the fact that he can't do anything as well as you want him to but that he had better do something, once you get him that way, you can work with him.

Exchange Between West Point Officers (*1973*)

★ ★ ★ ALTHOUGH few West Point professors would claim that the Academy has the same academic goals or is comparable to Ivy League colleges in any significant ways, the analogies between West Point and institutions like Harvard linger on in casual conversations at the Academy as well as in the public imagination. Such analogies are a historic part of the Academy's conception of itself. When pressed to specify the particular similarities between Harvard and West Point, officials explicitly repudiate the comparison. But official repudiation does not force comparisons to the Ivy League, like old soldiers, to fade away. They endure in spite of, often because of, claims to the contrary. The very act of denying that West Point and Harvard are alike reinforces the widely held impression that the two institutions can be mentioned in the same breath. In point of fact, West Point is so unlike America's first-rate colleges and universities that any comparison invariably raises a question about West Point's stature as an academic institution.

For example, Professor Daniel P. Moynihan told the class of 1976 at Harvard that they would determine the shape of their school in the future. Moynihan based his remarks on Joseph A. Schumpeter's *Capitalism, Socialism, and Democracy* and Lionel Trilling's novel, *The Middle of the Journey*, two books the students had been asked to read prior to their arrival at Harvard.[1] "[Y]ou are living in the future about which they wrote," said Moynihan, a time in which institutions "have changed almost beyond recall . . . and none so drastically as institutions like Harvard." [2] Professor Moynihan's analysis of the staggering pace of change at Harvard suggested that the future was ominous:

> Attack from *within* is wholly new to its [Harvard's] experience and brings forth few of the brave and honorable qualities that so charac-

> terized the university's response to attack from *without* in the 1950's. One has the sense of a somewhat overbred community that had the instinct to bring in new blood, but did not understand that in doing so it would bring in also new conditions of argument, and resentment of its very existence. In the face of ideas that intend nothing less than the destruction of what Harvard has stood for, Harvard seems to have almost no defense save good manners. . . . The fact, as I see it, is that the ideological initiative at Harvard has been conceded to the extremists. . . . the institution remains trapped in its own decency, its moral authority gradually eroding, such that in the end all that will be left will be the good manners, and then it will not any longer matter.

The major point of Moynihan's address was not that Harvard's future was bleak, but that it was in the hands of his audience: "[A]n altogether new and quite uncertain development . . . takes place this week. A new class has arrived. You. It is now your university, also. It will impart some of its qualities to you, and partake of some of yours." Having passed part of the responsibility for institutional survival on to these newly arrived men and women, he concluded, "I would wish you to know that you are well spoken of and genuinely welcome." [3]

At West Point the members of the incoming plebe class are not asked to read scholarly books prior to their arrival; they are advised to get themselves in good physical shape. The emphasis is not on the uncertain and ominous future, but on the stability of the past and the reliability of tradition. The young men are not told that they are about to shape the future of the Military Academy; they are congratulated for giving themselves over to the character-building processes which are about to shape them. Like the students at Harvard, they are told that they are special, but their official welcome comes from a soldier rather than a scholar. And within a few minutes they find themselves stripped of all personal possessions, standing at attention in their shorts, staring at the back of the soon-to-be shorn head of another new cadet while waiting to be issued an athletic supporter. They have just entered what West Pointers call Beast Barracks. From the point of view of an entering plebe, Professor Moynihan could have been talking about events, people, and an institution in another cosmos.

THE FIRST DAY

As recently as the 1950's, some West Pointers tended to regard their weeks as new cadets in Beast Barracks and their subsequent activities in the Corps of Cadets as the principal characteristics which set them apart from their peers at elite eastern schools like Princeton, Dartmouth, Harvard, and Yale.[4] According to this view, West Point was an Ivy League college with a demanding set of military requirements added on to the normal academic routine. In the 1970's Colonel Frederick A. Smith, Jr., head of the Department of Mechanics, insisted that the rigors of Beast Barracks and the military requirements of cadet life do not inhibit but rather enrich the academic environment at West Point. Colonel Smith described the Academy as an ideal educational environment in which the student "can't take it easy; he can't go back to the library whenever he wants to or when he has free time; he's got to spend that time sort of maximizing all of his endeavors. And he can't go to sleep on any one." Colonel Smith prefers West Point's regimented academic atmosphere because it "teaches him a way of thinking that is probably better than the average student at a prestige university. Now I realize that there are gifted students on the campus at Harvard who could make students here stand up and take notice. There are probably more students at Harvard and Yale who could do this than at many places because you have a better cut of input there." But, Colonel Smith added, "what I am thinking is that maybe the gifted students at Harvard, given the pressures we have here, would probably be infinitely better. So I would say that basically we do develop a product which thinks better." In Colonel Smith's view, the genesis for the institutional pressures which would make Harvard students "infinitely better" is the military training program that begins with Beast Barracks and is called the Fourth Class System.[5]

Every West Pointer, Colonel Smith noted, "has the Fourth Class System to survive. He has to survive as a fourth classman learning the ropes here. No other institution puts their students under that kind of pressure." [6] The intent of the institutional pressure which greets incoming freshmen is spelled out in a booklet the Academy sends to parents after their son's appointment to West Point. In prefatory remarks the superintendent cautions, "For many, the transition from a permissive civilian environment to a strenuous, disciplined one will be difficult and trying. Your understanding and encouragement will be necessary to help your son overcome the many challenges and obstacles he will encounter along the way." [7] And the function of this "strenuous, disciplined" environment is then explained, not to the incoming cadets, but to their parents:

> The Fourth Class System is an essential element in the development process designed to change a young man from a civilian to a cadet and ultimately to an Army officer. There are three basic functions which the Fourth Class System performs. They are the conversion of a young man into a professional soldier, the identification of those cadets who cannot function under stress, and the provision of a vehicle by which upperclasses can improve their leadership techniques.
>
> When the first few letters arrive from your son, he may tell you how much he dislikes this or that; what he will be talking about is the System from which New Cadet Barracks draws its strength: the Fourth Class System. This System, this code, looms over him during NCB [New Cadet Barracks] and the entire Plebe Year. He really is not angry with his cadet superiors, nor his tactical officer, nor even the Academy—he is angry with the Fourth Class System. As parents, you can be of great value in helping your son through the rough times.
>
> Your son may tell you many things, some will be quite true—others inaccurate. You must listen sympathetically and carefully and

> supply the salve of moderation when appropriate. It is important to keep in mind that the System is operated by upperclass cadets under the supervision of Army officers in the Department of Tactics. Cadets thus learn by doing; but in such situations honest mistakes are sometimes made. Injustices may occur, but fair treatment and respect for regulations are the norm, and practices contrary to these concepts are few and far between.[8]

Appeals to parents reveal the Academy's unstated assumption that its entering students acknowledge parental authority; when a young man arrives at West Point, he is not striking out on his own; he is merely transferring custody of his person from the family to the Military Academy. Most parents are pleased with this arrangement, in part because it replaces their control with another established and respected authority, and in part because "having a son at West Point" not only may mean prestige in their communities but also removes completely the dreaded budget strains of a college education.[9] West Point not only costs them nothing but it also provides a monthly salary which covers their sons' personal expenses. And while registration day for freshmen at most colleges involves the sort of congratulatory and solicitously challenging message Professor Moynihan issued at Harvard, at West Point it is the "parents and guardians" who are made to feel "genuinely welcome." Their "July 1973 Orientation Program Itinerary" offered:

7:00 A.M.–10:45 P.M.	Shuttle bus service available between Michie Stadium, Cullum Hall and Buffalo Soldier Flats.
7:00 A.M.–3:30 P.M.	Reception and Information Desk open in Cullum Hall.
8:00 A.M.–12:00 NOON	Escorted bus tours of West Point originating at Cullum Hall.
8:30 A.M.–12:00 NOON	Continuous showings of West Point films in North Auditorium.
8:30 A.M.–4:15 P.M.	West Point Museum and gift shop open.
10:00 A.M–10:45 A.M.	Organ concert in Cadet Chapel.

11:30 A.M.–1:00 P.M.	Luncheon hours at West Point Army Mess and Hotel Thayer dining rooms.
1:00 P.M.–1:30 P.M.	Be seated in South Auditorium, Thayer Hall.
1:30 P.M.–1:45 P.M.	Superintendent's Welcome.
1:45 P.M.–2:15 P.M.	Cadet Honor Code and New Cadet Barracks Orientation.
2:15 P.M.–4:00 P.M.	Question and answer period.
4:20 P.M.–4:40 P.M.	Carillon Concert.
5:10 P.M.–6:00 P.M.	Observe Class of 1977 swearing-in ceremony.
6:00 P.M.–8:45 P.M.	Supper hours at the West Point Army Mess and Hotel Thayer dining rooms.
9:30 P.M.–10:30 P.M.	"West Point in Sound and Light" performance.
10:30 P.M.	2 July 1973 Orientation Program terminated.[10]

While the parents and guardians are being entertained by Academy officials, their sons are undergoing one of the most traumatic experiences of their lives. The ordeal they undergo is graphically described in the *Administration and Logistic Plan* for handling the new arrivals:

> 1. SITUATION:
>
> Approximately 1380 candidates will enter USMA on 2 July for New Cadet Barracks training in preparation for entrance to the United States Corps of Cadets.
>
> 2. MISSION:
>
> To indoctrinate, motivate, and equip each New Cadet so that he is qualified to join the Corps of Cadets and to further the leadership development of each member of the New Cadet Detail. [The New Cadet Detail refers to the upperclassmen who supervise the training of the incoming cadets.] [11]

The candidates first report to the Welcoming Center at Michie Stadium, the scene of legendary accomplishments by the Academy's football stars of the past. But there is no gridiron grandeur planned for this day; the *A & L Plan* tersely notes: "Candidates will use Michie Stadium as a place to say farewell." As the candidate's family members are put on buses that will carry them to various shows, speeches, and ceremonies, the prospective cadet begins "to process through each of ten numbered stations." He is about to learn why few West Pointers use the term New Cadet Barracks except with parents. For prospective cadets, upperclass cadets, and graduates it is "Beast Barracks." [12]

The ten processing stations begin a series of environmental changes which are calculated to demonstrate to the candidate that he has left the civilian world behind. He finds himself immersed in a total system in which uniformed upperclassmen and officers are omnipresent and in absolute control of his life on a minute-to-minute basis. Under the escort of upperclass cadets, the candidate reaches station one, where his baggage is taken from him and tagged; he is "instructed to remove money, immunization records, and any papers concerning . . . [his] appointment." At each of the next three stations, he is given an admission processing card which must be presented at each subsequent stop; he is "permitted to retain $10.00 and loose change, not to exceed $1.00"; the remainder is taken "for deposit in his account"; and, at the fourth processing point, he receives his Issue Book, which he must "carry . . . throughout the remainder of the Processing Week when he draws equipment from Cadet Store issue points." He is then measured by a tailor and "issued two pair of athletic shorts, three t-shirts, two supporters, and one barracks bag." [13]

For some young men, either station five or station six may be their last encounter with the Academy's initiation procedure. West Point may determine it does not want them; or the candidate may decide he is being swallowed up by a world which, in the jargon of his peers, is ripping him off at a dizzying pace:

> [STATION 5]: Candidates will turn in immunization records to an enlisted attendant and proceed to undress completely at the chairs

provided. Each candidate will be instructed to keep his barracks bag which contains his clothing with him at all times, except when directed to put it aside temporarily. Candidates will place their clothes in the barracks bag, put on one (1) athletic supporter and one (1) pair of athletic shorts, and report to a designated medical officer for a medical examination. He will then proceed to Station 6, carrying his barracks bag which contains his clothing.

[STATION 6]: As each candidate reports at Station 6, he will receive a numbered identification card which he will carry with him. This same identification number will be entered upon his admission card. In addition, a posture record containing the name and identification number of each cadet will be completed and retained by clerical personnel. Each candidate will then be directed to the stadiometer and the scale where he will be measured and weighed. Both measurements will be entered on his admission card. The candidates will take physical testing as required. The candidate will then report to the camera stations where he will remove the athletic shorts and be tested and photographed in that order. He will turn in his identification number at the camera station. Each candidate will then dress, wearing the issued athletic shorts, t-shirt, civilian socks and shoes, and report to Station 7.[14]

Some candidates who pass the medical exam and the physical testing and are found qualified to continue their processing conclude at about this time that the institution, which has just deprived them of almost all of their personal possessions and which is intent on charting their physical attributes and monitoring their every movement, is not the kind of school they had visualized. If such candidates desire to resign, then they, as well as those who are found to be medically disqualified, may be "processed to clear" West Point, provided they are identified to the appropriate officials by 4:00 p.m. on registration day. Those who train and supervise the new cadets want to get on with the business at hand. Keeping people around who are not willing or able is considered disastrous for everyone else's morale.[15]

Most candidates survive these first six stations and pass uneventfully through the last four, where they complete basic information forms, receive their company assignment—thereby changing their status from candidates to "new cadets"—and reclaim their baggage. After additional administrative processing they are moved to their assigned company area, where other items of individual identification are taken from them. Rings, identification bracelets, keys, and key rings must be surrendered and placed in the company safe. Cadets are allowed to retain their watches and religious medallions. An additional check is made to see that each cadet has no more than $10.00 in bills and loose change of $1.00. If he has violated this previous order, he will be corrected on the spot and his infraction will be reported to his tactical officer.[16]

In the afternoon of their first day, candidates meet the one upperclassman with whom they will have close daily contact in the weeks ahead—their squad leader. It is the squad leader's initial job to ensure that the seven men in his squad have received haircuts, an initial issue of uniform, and are in proper uniform for the Oath Ceremony which will make them officially part of West Point. With the gradual modifications that the Fourth Class System has undergone since the late 1960's, the squad leader's relationship with his squad is not as abrasive either in Beast Barracks or during the plebe year as it once was. West Point's notorious "bracing" (exaggerated form of attention) and such despised harassments as mandatory shower formations are no longer a part of Academy initiation rites.[17]

A PROFESSIONAL ATTITUDE

The commanding officer of the 1973 New Cadet Barracks was Colonel Hugh G. Robinson. His approach reflected a thoroughly pragmatic sense that "a lot of things which we accepted back then [i.e. the early 1950's] as okay, the youth of today would never begin to accept," and he also seemed determined that his own experience with the humiliations of Beast not be visited upon others.

Colonel Robinson recalled his "most humiliating experiences" as "shower formations where we stood down there naked and held our soap in one hand with a towel draped across our arm. We'd be ordered to do push-ups and pull-ups and all kinds of things and then we had thirty seconds to soap up and thirty seconds to rinse off and be out of the shower." As for food, "it was not unusual for us not to eat for two, three, or four meals in a row. I lost twenty-six pounds my year and I couldn't afford to lose twenty-six pounds." [18]

By most accounts the 1973 New Cadet Barracks continued to move away from the pattern of extreme harassment of earlier years. Cadets who held major positions in the New Cadet Barracks detail supported the official view that West Point was "more professional" in its treatment of new cadets. But there was still much emphasis on what First Classman Andrew Green called "the stress factor." While Cadet Green acknowledged that "there is a thing in upperclassmen's minds and a lot of officers' minds that 'to be a cadet' you have got to go through giving up eating your first few months here. But that has nothing to do with it. . . . The stress is being put on in other ways. Now it is more or less man on man. A man 'gets on' the new cadet and tells him right to his face what is wrong." In previous years verbal abuse was much more common; "dressing down" a cadet for five minutes in front of his peers is now discouraged.[19]

This shift in the method of applying stress did not, in First Classman Gary Coleman's view, reflect "a deterioration in the Army's standards, because one of the primary things we are trying to do here is to produce leaders . . . and you can lead a man by fear only so long. After that if you lose your base of authority you will be in big trouble." Cadet Coleman suggested that senior cadets must learn how to give orders in Beast Barracks, just as new cadets must learn how to obey orders. Although the new cadets are expected to obey orders without questioning, Coleman thought that the emphasis was on identifying mutual goals (e.g. a squad leader treats his cadets well if they proficiently carry out assigned tasks). Captain Stephen Lifrak, an Academy psychologist and Beast Barracks counselor, observed that "the Vietnam war has taught us something about leadership. You can't be out of touch with the people you are going to lead. In Vietnam if you gave an order that the troops didn't understand, they might say, 'Fuck you, Jack. I'm not going. See you around.' Someone who comes out of this place has to know how to deal with that kind of thing." But there is still strong resistance among many officers and the majority of cadets to "being overly reasonable" with their charges in Beast Barracks.[20]

Nevertheless, the current official party line on military training finds constant expression at the Academy. In academic matters, cadets frequently speak of "buzz words"—words or phrases which a particular "P" (professor), or frequently an entire department, reward a cadet for using. The buzz words for the New Cadet Barracks of the 1970's are "professional attitude" and "self-discipline." A cadet leader, such as Andrew Green, is well aware that he is echoing some of the most favored phrasing of both Colonel Robinson and the commandant, Brigadier General Philip Feir, when he speaks of "approaching New Cadet Barracks with a much more professional attitude." [21] To Colonel Robinson a professional attitude means that an upperclassman "never places himself in a position of looking like an individual who has lost control in some fashion. And this is what happens when they yell and scream and act in that manner towards new cadets." [22]

Even those who were among Robinson's staunchest supporters admitted that there were enormous difficulties in asking people who have gone through the harassment of "their Beast" to forgo the visceral pleasures of inflicting similar stress and discomfort on others. Michael Clifford, the cadet executive officer for the second NCB [New Cadet Barracks] detail, recalled, "You really have to think about it. Like there were sometimes when I'd really want to jump on the guy and I'd start thinking, 'Well God, Clifford, you can't do that!' And now you *do* hear guys saying, 'Man, pop out your chest!' or 'Walk straight, be professional!' When I was walking around in my NCB it was, 'Get your head in, Kraut!'; 'Hey, smackhead!'; and stuff like that." And when asked if the memorable language and bullying manner which have been a historic part of new cadet socialization have gone by the boards, Cadet Clifford answered, "It certainly hasn't gone completely yet. It happens in the barracks area when the squad leaders have their time [with individual new cadets]. Theoretically, yes, it should be gone; but, practically, no." [23]

Officers who genuinely support the new professional attitude also reported considerable problems with the new cadet detail as well as with their fellow tactical officers. A heavily decorated third-generation West Pointer who was one of Colonel Robinson's key staff officers during Beast Barracks said of the first classmen, "These kids here are very, very resentful of some of the people here in the Tactical Department who[m] they regard as 'Super Assholes.' They see the tac's as negatively oriented and think that all we are here for is to screw 'em out of their FCPs [first class privileges], screw 'em out of their weekends, quill 'em to death, and to reach in their goddamn laundry bags and squeeze around. These kids hate that; but, at the same time they are the greatest hypocrites in the world because they will turn around and practice the same goddamn negative practices on a new cadet." And the officer added, "To offset this thing is monumental." But he has made attempts:

> I don't know how many fired-up speeches I've given this summer about this. I said, "Look you sons-of-bitches, here you are—You're doing the same goddamn thing to plebes that you bitch about the tac's doing to you. You say, 'Sir, we can't screw over 'em in the mess hall anymore, can't screw over 'em in special inspections anymore. So you're taking away all the things where we can screw over the new cadets.' " And I said, "Let's just examine that. If I lead you in the same way you are attempting to lead them, you would regard me as a 'Super Asshole.' "
>
> So I think it's time for these guys, especially these guys across the hall [in the commandant's office], just to take a look at where we are headed. . . . What we need is a Jesus; we've got a lot of disciples;

> we've got four or five guys who are really disciples. But what we need is a Jesus who can show the success of this thing. If we can get off this real negative approach and make a guy lead like he has to in the Army, a man follows you out there in the military because of a great system of group dynamics. He doesn't follow you because of the goddamn flag, or motherhood, or God and religion. That son-of-a-bitch follows you because you are the man there that he deeply respects, a man there that is a leader of that damn group and you care for him and he deeply senses and feels that you care for him. If you can be caring, if you can be sensitive to another man's needs, if you can satisfy his gut level of expectations, and, if he has got the sense of that, then you can turn pivots on his face and he will follow you.[24]

Both General Feir and Colonel Robinson have characterized the leadership training of the New Cadet Barracks of the 1970's as a substantial departure from the past; but the changes are essentially superficial: the elimination of much of the hazing and the insistence on more decorous behavior from upperclassmen. Neither of these changes made Beast Barracks a qualitatively different kind of experience for new cadets. Even the implementation of minor changes were dependent on the personalities of the two commanders, who will move on to new assignments and hope that their successors will retain their reforms. General Feir talked constantly about "self-discipline"; but officers and many cadets frequently viewed him as single-minded and inflexible. Many believe that "self-discipline" is really a code word for "doing things Feir's way," rather than for a substantive change in policy. Robinson had a very different temperament. His dealings with subordinate officers were informal and relaxed; he was firm but friendly with cadets.[25] As President Lyndon Johnson's Army military aide for three and a half years and with an excellent military record in the field, he is regarded as one of the Army's young super-stars.[26] However, the central administrative fact about these two officers was that, like over 90 per cent of all faculty and staff officers, they were in transit. Whether or not their successors will effectively emphasize self-discipline and a professional attitude depends on the personal idiosyncracies of the future commanders. And if they are officers eager to leave their mark on Academy policies, they may seek to reverse the changes of the early 1970's and return to "a more traditional Beast." But even as the names and personalities change, the socialization process which new cadets undergo remains essentially the same.

STRESS AND SURVIVAL

Since the qualities that Beast Barracks is intended to develop are the same soldierly qualities that the Thayer System was designed to develop, the changes introduced in 1973 worry some officers, who are fearful that the Academy is entering "an era of permissiveness." Since over 70 per cent of those charged with the military training of cadets are West Point graduates, the reflex to measure the new reasonableness of the early 1970's New Cadet Barracks against the practices of past decades is very strong. Colonel Frank Kobes, the Academy's director of physical education, reflected the concern of older graduates who worry that the current members of the Corps of Cadets have it easier than they did: "We tell cadets that they've got to make it, but it's just not as true today as it once was. I've talked to enough cadets to know that the general feeling they have is that it's just difficult to get thrown out of here." Kobes described himself as "a conservative type who would like to go back to the old ways," but admitted, "I don't know if the Academy could afford that luxury." [27]

In addition to serving as a rite of passage, a Darwinian process which identifies those most likely to survive in the Regular Army, the rigors of Beast Barracks are remembered by many West Pointers as traumatic rituals which profoundly affected their personalities. Substantive criticism of the procedures followed in Beast Barracks, or reform of those procedures, are understood by thousands of graduates as challenges to the values associated with military service. However, others charged that the constant harassment in Beast made West Pointers inefficient "nervous nellies." A 1962 graduate argued, "I've never seen anybody who could equal a West Pointer in jumping through his ass. West Point turns out guys who are the biggest nervous nellies over the littlest, tiniest, most miniscule things." A classmate, an infantry major, disagreed. He acknowledge that the Academy "does turn out guys who sweat everything; they are trained to sweat everything. But in sweating everything they can still function and get it done. A lot of people who didn't go through Beast also sweat everything, but they sweat it so much that *they can't function.*" Until the early 1970's, the officer recalled, new cadets frequently went through a series of Keystone Kops antics involving the rapid changing of uniforms on the orders of their cadet superiors: "It was these clothing formations that suddenly made me settle down and relax. To me Beast Barracks started getting better when I suddenly realized what I couldn't do. I couldn't really change clothes in thirty seconds and I was up there trying like hell to do it. I really was. Suddenly in making the mental trade-off under real stress, because I was going to get my ass reamed either way, I suddenly said, 'Why beat myself to death?' And I think everybody went through that." The lesson the officer learned was invaluable to him in later combat situations: "At West Point and then later in Vietnam, it wasn't that you quit humping, but that you came to terms with your limitations. At first they ran you continuously so that your brain wouldn't even function; and, after awhile, your brain could begin to work under this sort of phenomenon." [28]

In the view of many West Pointers the end result of the harassment and unreasonableness of what they invariably called Beast Barracks was the ability not only to manage time but to make rapid decisions in moments of extreme stress—to prepare men to perform in ways which few untrained civilians could duplicate. A nongraduate lieutenant colonel, who had a tour of duty at West Point, emphasized how this linkage between managing time and making split-second decisions under extreme pressure was essential for military leaders: "The people who leave West Point without graduating are more times than not people who won't or can't manage time. In my experience with the military, one of the things that I think is true, basically true, is that we're usually working against some kind of deadline. And starting with Beast Barracks, cadets are trained for what they will be doing for thirty years in the Army." To illustrate the importance of being conditioned for reflex action under extreme stress, the officer drew on his experience as a battalion commander in Vietnam:

> I had a real bright young lieutenant, an ROTC graduate from some eastern college, who was an unassuming type, not very active, a sensitive English major type. He happened to be in charge when a helicopter pick-up zone got mortared. His personality was such that he usually thought carefully about everything he did. But when you've got mortar rounds falling on top of your men, there's not enough time to think; it's time to do something and do it very quickly. Well, he didn't do it very quickly. As a result of that action, I called out twenty-four casualties. Some of those guys would probably be alive now if the lieutenant had been a different kind of person. But, he wasn't and, as a result, he was relieved. At West Point, cadets are forced to make the kind of decisions that prepare them for those kind of combat situations. They're forced to make judgments about all kinds of things that most college students never have to face.[29]

Most graduates and Academy supporters like to emphasize the "can do" attitude and the "combat readiness factor" which they feel is inculcated during Beast Barracks and the plebe year. These benefits are especially welcome because they present opportunities to invoke examples of decisive and heroic decision-making on the battlefield.[30] But there are more pedestrian lessons, such as learning "how to survive." West Pointers do not use this phrase only to mean survival in combat; "survival" also means making it through West Point and having a successful career in the Army. And learning how to survive involves learning to accommodate oneself to the parameters set by an institution and its authorities.

A graduate from the late 1950's remembered that his classmates "were not wave makers. I don't think it ever entered our minds to make waves. We had come to West Point at a time when, nationally, West Point was still considered much more of a challenge than it is now." Although entering cadets were already inclined to follow institutional restraints, the officer recalled that "this place forced me to shape myself to fit into its mold. All institutions do that to some degree, but West Point is an extreme case. The intriguing thing about the process was the way it caused us to see the whole thing as a challenge." The officer explained how his own self-confidence grew as he learned to accommodate himself to the Academy's standards:

> My first time in PE [Physical Education] class they told us to get on some parallel bars and do some exercises; and, I thought, "Oh, my God, I'll never be able to do them." And I couldn't do them. I thought, "This is the end." But, of course, I was able to do them eventually and the only other time when an incident like this occurred was the first couple of days in Russian when I failed to understand how completely we were supposed to have mastered some of the initial things the instructor asked us to do. In the Russian class we were told to learn the alphabet, and I guess I didn't understand what learning the alphabet had to do with because there are different characters for the alphabet in the Russian language. And when I went to class the next day, the instructor said go to the board and write the alphabet; and when I went to the board I was unable to write the alphabet properly. With the exception of these two instances, there was never any question in my mind that I would succeed at West Point; but, I didn't know how well I would succeed. And I think that most people got used to measuring their own abilities against the demands of the system.[31]

For most new cadets in the 1970's, the initial week at West Point serves, as it has for many decades, to test the motivation of those who enter. The testing continues to be carried out through a combination of physical stress and mental stress and there is considerable disagreement about which factors are most influential in causing new cadets to "select out" (resign). "Most of the Beast Barracks program is physical conditioning," argued one officer. "The guy who can't hack it in Beast Barracks is the guy who can't take the physical punishment. It is not any great intellectual challenge in Beast Barracks." But another graduate insisted: "I don't agree with that at all. I think the challenge of Beast Barracks is almost entirely mental. You have got to get through a physical program, but the real battle is making it in your head. The pressure is almost all mental. The first week they rip you apart physically and then after that they start building you up again physically, but they are always tearing you down mentally." [32]

The continuing presence of physical and mental stress in the Beast Barracks of the 1970's is clearly set forth in *Bugle Notes*, a book given to all entering cadets: "The first eight weeks of a cadet's service at West Point are devoted to the intensive basic training of the soldier. This is the period in which the cadets are equipped and given the preliminary training that is necessary before they join the Corps." A young man is not officially admitted into the Corps of Cadets until after he has been socialized as a soldier. This chronology is crucial because the new cadet is required to submit to an intensive military indoctrination process before he begins what the Academy calls his "academic year." Although Beast Barracks may be an appropriate training ground for future military leaders, it is also a "breaking process" that systematically represses the entering cadets' capacity for unfettered intellectual inquiry. Beast Barracks functions as an institutional filter converting civilian students into cadets. The new cadets are conditioned to measure their educational expectations against West Point's unique educational standards. *Bugle Notes* stresses the primacy of "exactness of execution; strict, but just disciplining; development of instant, ready, and willing obedience; and careful physical hardening and development. The new cadet's waking hours are completely controlled. His every activity during the day is carefully supervised." And, "If this training has been successfully conducted, it will have resulted in a new class whose members have received proper initial training, have learned the standards of West Point, are proud to be members of the Corps, and are ready to uphold its customs and traditions." [33]

This training is run according to a schedule which, even on weekends, allows little time for contemplation:

5:50 A.M.	First Call
6:20 A.M.–6:50 A.M.	Reveille/Physical Training Formation
6:50 A.M.–7:15 A.M.	Recovery
7:15 A.M.–7:45 A.M.	Breakfast
7:45 A.M.–8:15 A.M.	Preparation for Training
8:15 A.M.–12:20 P.M.	Training/Classes
12:40 P.M.–1:10 P.M.	Lunch
1:10 P.M.–1:45 P.M.	Preparation for Training
1:45 P.M.–3:40 P.M.	Training/Classes
3:55 P.M.–5:10 P.M.	Mass Athletics
5:25 P.M.–6:15 P.M.	Classes or Parade
6:35 P.M.–7:05 P.M.	Supper
7:05 P.M.–7:25 P.M.	Preparation for Training
7:25 P.M.–9:05 P.M.	Training/Classes
9:15 P.M.–10:00 P.M.	Maintenance Time—Taps [34]

For most cadets, the goal is simply to survive each day.[35] During the 1973 New Cadet Barracks there were 682 periods of scheduled training; these periods were divided into "Fixed Subjects" and "Variable Subjects." West Point's *Operations and Training Plan* explained that the "time available for the training program is based upon a twelve-period training day multiplied by the total days allocated to New Cadet Barracks. A training week is considered to be Monday through Sunday. A training period is . . . 50 minutes, except for period eight [3:55–5:10 P.M., Mass Athletics] . . . and PE [physical exercises] which is 45 minutes." [36]

Among the "Fixed Subjects," tactical training consumes the most periods (157). There is particular emphasis on the fourth class bivouac, a five-day field exercise at the Academy's Lake Frederick training site where new cadets undergo squad tactical training. There are also two company bivouacs which involve "training such as night firing & tactical dispersion . . . and field sanitation & tactical feeding." One of the company bivouacs occurs during the thirty-two-period cycle of M-16 rifle marksmanship training, when the new cadet receives "practical work . . . in detecting, locating, and hitting combat type targets." Substantial periods of time are also devoted to marches, which are described as "foot marches over varied terrain to teach . . . the techniques & methods of conducting a march," and to bayonet training—"Practical Exercise periods to familiarize the New Cadet with the basic positions and movements used to employ the bayonet as a weapon & to introduce the spirit and aggressiveness required in unarmed combat." [37] The intention of bayonet training was further explained by Colonel Hugh Robinson:

> The first classmen are the ones who actually conduct the bayonet training. We want to emphasize the expertise of the first classmen in all aspects of training. We want to show the new cadets that that is what they are going to become is experts in everything. . . . We had bayonet when I went through here twenty years ago. It is primarily intended now to build a man's confidence. . . . It produces a certain attitude and mental toughness which is what we are really interested in when you start talking about the training of potential officers. We want him to have confidence in himself. We want him to feel tough, whether he is or not.[38]

One of the major concerns throughout Beast Barracks is not only "to indoctrinate, motivate, and equip" new cadets but also "to further the leadership development" of the first classmen who constitute the "New Cadet Detail." While "on-the-spot corrections" of a new cadet by an upperclassman normally occur dozens of times daily, upperclass errors are not corrected in front of new cadets for fear of undermining command authority. The *Operations and Training Plan* insists: "Under no circumstances will Detail Members be corrected [by officers or their classmates] in the presence of New Cadets." [39] It is in the thirty-four periods devoted to ceremonies and cadet drill that the mistakes made by detail members in the presence of new cadets are most common and most visible. Colonel Robinson stressed that these ceremonial activities were important training devices because the new cadets "are impressed with the discipline and ceremonial aspects of being in the military" and with the "idea of being able to form a coherent unit and do things as a unit. We stress that a lot in New Cadet Barracks. Even when the upperclassman makes an obvious blunder, we want the new cadet to learn to follow the fellow's order." [40]

The reception and processing of new cadets on the traumatic first day, the tightly controlled schedule and the rigorous and regimented training the cadets undergo during the first two months at West Point constitute a remarkably intensive and successful form of professional socialization. Professor John P. Lovell, a West Point graduate who returned to the Academy to study the way it indoctrinated and institutionalized young men, emphasized the thoroughness of the process "by which members of a profession learn the values, attitudes and behavior appropriate to their roles within the profession." Lovell suggested that West Point was a good example of what sociologists call a "total institution"; that is "a place where all phases of one's daily activity are carried out under a prescribed routine, in the same place, in the company of others required to conform to the identical routine, and under one common authority; the routine emanates from 'a single overall rational plan purportedly designed to fulfill the official aims of the institution.' " [41] At civilian colleges and universities the academic environment is deliberately structured so as to give students latitude for individual choice and personal preference. There, on the assumption that the decision to pursue a particular career can be made more sensibly after the student has explored his own interests and values, professional training follows undergraduate education. In reversing the process West Point has considerably reduced the indecision and uncertainty that frequently characterizes the civilian student population elsewhere; it has also restricted the cadets' potential for intellectual development.

Despite the disagreements among West Pointers about the elimination of some forms of harassment in recent years, there is ample evidence that Beast Barracks still shapes new cadets along the desired lines. And many of those who worked closely with the 1973 New Cadet Barracks, such as Captain Harold Jenkins of the Office of Military Psychology and Leadership, doubted that "there is really all that much difference between what new cadets are experiencing now and what I experienced twelve years ago when I went through. There may be differences in the way things are done," Captain Jenkins admitted, but the really crucial fact is, "No matter what happens, a guy is coming into a new world. He's got so much to learn and so much to do . . . and there is really not that much time given to him to do everything." Captain Jenkins felt that new cadets in the 1970's have made discoveries and adjustments similar to the ones he made in the early 1960's. "Somewhere about the second or third week," he recalled, "I discovered that there wasn't all that much to be scared of. And exactly what did it? I don't know. But my roommate used to say, 'I wouldn't take a million dollars for the opportunity to do this, but you couldn't pay me a million dollars to do it again.' So, you know, it is *that kind* of experience." [42]

The paradoxical note in Captain Jenkins' recollections is reflected in the attitude which many officers have about the nature of their "educational" experiences at West Point; Beast Barracks was the experience which began to make them into the soldiers they now are. It opened up their options as military men at the same time that it closed other options. To perhaps the majority of West Point graduates, Beast Barracks provided the most forthright and accurate indication of, in the words of one officer, "what the Academy is *really* all about. West Point," he said, "is not a college. It's a greenhouse for career Army officers." Most West Pointers are soldiers with a commitment to the military socialization process begun in Beast Barracks and continued when the new cadets enter the Corps of Cadets and come under the influence of a company tactical officer and the Tactical Department. "The TD feels that they are running, insofar as possible, the best, or close to the best, military show there is," a young major said. "I mean West Point sets the standards. Other institutions who are trying to set up similar programs come here. When they set up the Air Force Academy, West Point people in blue [Air Force officers] and also in the Army were involved. If you want to set up a new academic institution, you sure as hell wouldn't come here. But for a military institution, there is a sense of expertise." [43]

GETTING OUT AND STAYING IN

Although the Academy's ingenuity in military socialization is considerable, there are many young men who decide after arriving at West Point that they do not want prolonged exposure to what West Point has in mind for them. About 15 per cent of the entering cadets in the early 1970's had resigned within the first three months of their entrance. Many cadets "stick it out" during Beast Barracks just to prove they can take it or to see if Beast is an institutional aberration inexplicably disguising a college or university. After Beast Barracks is over those who stay only to prove they could take it usually resign. They are soon joined by those who are stunned to discover that, when classes start, they are still very much in a military academy where priorities are determined according to the values represented by Beast Barracks.[44]

Most resignations during a class's first year at West Point occur during New Cadet Barracks. In Colonel Hugh Robinson's experience, "There are three main reasons why cadets resign in NCB.

One, they came here because of parental pressure. That is the biggest single group. Then there is the group (which also includes some from the first group) that came in with a hip-pocket college acceptance. . . . They came to try it out. They came here with no commitment either to themselves or to their family. They already had a college acceptance from the place they will go to if they decided to leave. Those men become potential resignees the first day." The first-day pressures make for what Colonel Robinson called "a very, very trying day. What they go through in that day in being converted from long-haired civilians to people in a military unit who march down to Trophy Point and take the oath of office is phenomenal. Because it is such a trying day, nobody likes it. . . . And then it goes downhill all that whole week." [45] The third group Robinson identified is represented by "the guy who comes here feeling inadequate. He doesn't understand how he got here in the first place. He applied but he thought he would never be accepted and all of a sudden he is here. And so he starts off with the defeatist attitude, feeling very out of it." Ironically, the cadets in this third group are the ones most likely to be persuaded to stay at the Academy.[46]

Unless a new cadet resigns within hours after he arrives, the resignation process may take a week to ten days. A cadet is counseled by a wide variety of peers, upperclassmen, and officers, one of whom is likely to discover that the cadet is suffering from the delusion that the West Point of the 1970's is asking, "Are you good enough?" when what it is really asking him is, "Are you willing to persevere?" Contrary to a popular national legend, which is sustained by television reruns of movies such as *The Long Gray Line*, resigning from West Point is no simple matter.[47] In part, this is the result of a socialization process which strips young men of almost all vestiges of their civilian past and encumbers them with an incredible variety of clothing, supplies, and other paraphernalia of cadetship. But it also reflects the institution's understandable reluctance to streamline a process which undermines its source of manpower. Colonel Robinson explained the New Cadet Barracks resignation process in these terms:

> Well, if we are convinced that he really wants to leave, he can get out. If he is one of the first ones, he can get out in about four days. He doesn't have as much stuff to turn in so it doesn't take as long, that is one thing. But we end up getting a big backlog through the second and third week and a guy who gets stuck in that jam may be here ten days waiting to get out. Not because we are holding him up, just because our physical processing procedure for getting him out of here doesn't allow us to get him out of here any faster. The hospital physical is the bottleneck. They can handle at the most ten or twelve a day.[48]

Even those new cadets who behave in ways that West Point officials regard as bizarre may be counseled to stay. In the early 1970's "the God Squad group" constituted what one official described as the "biggest single weird group" of potential resignees. "God told them that they have got to leave," Colonel Robinson reported. "These are the kids who come in and say that they have got the Word now. They have got to leave and there is nothing anybody can tell them because God has already told them that they have got to leave. They have got to perform their ministry in another arena than West Point. And I say, 'Well, how did God manage to get you into this arena?' " Sometimes other West Point agencies come to the assistance of those officers responsible for holding down resignations in New Cadet Barracks. Colonel Robinson recalled that during the Beast Barracks of 1973 one of the Protestant assistant chaplains, "not because we asked him, but coincidentally, gave a sermon—'Do Your Work Where God Put You!" Robinson reported that the chaplain told the new cadets, "God wants you to do your work where He put you. He seldom removes a man from trying circumstances and says, 'I am going to make it easier on you' or 'You'll work over here in an easy environment.' Usually He gives His support where you are and in the trying circumstances in which you find yourself." The chaplain's interpretation of God's message to cadets pleased many officers. "Of course, it was a kind of inspiring sermon for new cadets," added Colonel Robinson. "And it did slow down the ones who were leaving 'because God wanted them to.' "[49]

For those cadets who stay on through Beast Barracks, the effect of their first two months at West Point on their remaining time as a cadet is impossible to quantify. What can be identified are the predominant patterns of a military socialization process. Professor Lovell's analysis of the process as it existed in the early 1960's has continued to hold true in the 1970's. It begins with "the moment" in July when the entering cadet first comes "within the purview of the first upperclassman, whose austere demeanor, erect posture, and immaculate uniform command a strange mixture of respect and fear." From that first day, the new cadet is "totally enveloped in a new world—an impersonal world of multitudinous rules, of impossible demands, and of endless days. . . . The self, deprived of previous sources of emotional support, becomes increasingly dependent upon the satisfactions provided by responding to the rewards and deprivations of the system."[50] Major Francis E. Conrad, psychiatric counselor during several Beast Barracks summers in the early 1970's, also emphasized that the essential purpose of the training was to instill reflexive obedience to established authority: "There's nothing specific that they learn out there or are supposed to learn. It's the process, learning to subordinate their personal hopes, aspirations, desires, whatever, to the group. They could achieve the same results if they taught them how to do Sanskrit or how to brush their teeth. It's the process of being taught rather than what's taught that's important."[51]

By the time cadets are ready to enter the academic classrooms each September, they are preoccupied with what one faculty member bluntly called "the wrong sorts of standards, standards which have been deeply internalized by the Tactical Department and the upper classes in the Beast Barracks experience." Whether the attitudes of the plebes are right or wrong in any absolute sense is a debatable philosophical question. They are the kind of attitudes that a military man will find invaluable. They are not the kind of attitudes normally associated with critical or imaginative thinking. But few of the new cadets who have survived the summer ordeal are predisposed to speculate about the implications of their experience. They are eager for "the college part" of West Point to begin. For each of them, as one faculty member noted, "the same principle holds: He's been here at West Point for two months and he hasn't gone to class yet." [52]

Chapter Four

★★★★★★★★★★★★★★★★★

THE CADET AS STUDENT

There is one basic assumption upon which the whole system rests and that is that somebody knows the right answer. In the case of the academic environment, the "P" knows the right answer. The name of the game is to flood this kid in his courses with a lot of information and make him come up with what's important and see if he has hit it on the head the next day. . . . But, how do you gamesmanship a problem when there may not be an answer? What do you do? Being oriented, being geared toward quantifiable solutions is totally useless. Right? . . . So maybe we push somebody out of here who is much too sure, much too confident about situations which don't deserve any sense of one's feeling confident about.

A West Point Major (1972)

The cadet lacks determinative power over most areas of his life: the questions of when, where, what, how, and even whether he eats; when, where, and how he sleeps—to stick among the more basic life functions—are all determined for *the cadet. . . . The central, ironic paradox of Academy life is that the institution attempts to build leaders by denying them room for individual choice, thought and initiative. . . . Under the present system, the most effectively socialized cadets are also the dullest, the least independent, critical, and creative—and the most addicted to a regulations book approach to life.*

Cadet Donald D. Cantlay (1971)

★ ★ ★ IT would be difficult to overestimate the importance of Beast Barracks in the development of dominant cadet attitudes. Official Academy literature explains that what is called New Cadet Barracks is "designed to instruct the members of the new class on how to be cadets and soldiers." Yet, although it has no formal academic purpose, Beast Barracks defines the parameters of cadet life in a way that drastically affects academic life for the remaining four years at West Point. While it accounts for only about 5 per cent of a cadet's time at the Academy, it has an impact that belies statistics and percentages.[1] Both officers and cadets recognize this fact and frequently trace distinguishable class characteristics back to Beast Barracks (i.e. "the class of '76 had a rough Beast, and their high leadership potential shows it"). In the only book-length study of the cadet socialization process, John Lovell concluded "that by mid-plebe year, the cadet has formulated attitudes which are consistent with subsequent indoctrination and information received." Lovell speculated that either the Admissions Office had selected young men whose attitudes already fit cadet role requirements, or these young men pre-selected the Academy, or Beast Barracks had done a remarkably thorough job of transforming adolescent civilians into cadets.[2] But whether the computer-assisted selection process of the Admissions Office, a self-selecting pool of candidates, or the rigors of Beast Barracks is the cause, the effect is the same: the plebe who walks into a West Point classroom in September has already been conditioned to behave in ways that distinguish him from his peers in civilian colleges.

According to one graduate of the class of 1972, the most conspicuous characteristic of cadets as students is "a rather sardonic attitude toward their academic work, as well as their personal relations and their lives." He described his introduction to this attitude in Beast Barracks:

> On the first evening during Beast Barracks, following the formal oath ceremony, we were all marched to Room 104 Thayer Hall and there reiterated in writing what we had said that afternoon. It was there that we agreed that we would give five years minimum to the Army upon graduation. . . . The upperclassmen who had marched us to the room stood around, arms folded across their chests, chuckling, knowing looks upon their faces, and told us of the awesome consequences of what we were doing. "You are now signing away nine years of your life. Nine years!" The significance of that fact escaped most of us, I think. We were seventeen and eighteen years old. . . . We didn't realize that we could be trapped, deceived, cajoled for however long it took the school, the Army, the mystique to take hold and keep us there "for the duration." The upperclassmen did. And when allowed to view the beginning of the process, they sensed the significance. Yet they reacted without compassion, empathy, or even sympathy, but with a cruel sort of laughter. They had had it done to them. We would have it done to us. Future classes, future generations, would have it done to them.[3]

Any effort to understand cadets as students must take into account the pervasive cadet tendency to view their Academy experience as "something that is being done to them." Although some new cadets look forward to classes as a haven from the harassment suffered during the summer months, most reflexively bring the values acquired in Beast Barracks to their academic classrooms. Classes, like military training, are perceived as requirements, as something to endure. "It is my feeling that plebes come into a class the first day," said one tenured professor, "thinking there are certain things they can say and certain things they can't say. . . . And to get the cadets to go outside those parameters is very difficult. They think a certain standard of behavior is expected of them." [4] Another officer added that cadets adopt a sardonic attitude toward everything during their Beast Barracks experience, but that much of their cynicism should not be taken literally:

> First, you shouldn't believe everything cadets say. They're young and they like to make you think they don't give a damn about any-

> thing. Second, they come over here to the classroom after two months of god-awful treatment. . . . In Beast it's a matter of survival and they tend to impose the same attitudes on their course work. They tend to see academic requirements as obstacles that they should run through with the least expenditure of energy, because they know there will be more obstacles to leap tomorrow. They begin to view the curriculum in much the same way as they view military training and they begin to view life in much the same way as the curriculum.[5]

It would be difficult to believe everything that cadets say about academic life at West Point because they say a variety of different, even contradictory, things. Cadet First Captain Joseph Tallman insisted that the Academy provided a rigorous academic environment in which the vast majority of his classmates exerted themselves to become "what West Point is looking for, the well-rounded guy." A senior officer suggested that the Academy attracted students with a wide range of academic commitments, but that unlike civilian colleges, West Point offers little encouragement to students who might desire to spend the bulk of their time in academic pursuits. According to this officer, West Point offers encouragement to cadets who discount intellectual activities. "You tell a cadet he should take a more lively interest in the historical issues raised by studying the Treaty of Versailles, and, so often, he just comes out and tells you he doesn't care about the Treaty of Versailles," said one instructor. "There's a prevailing sense that he's not supposed to care except insofar as it will affect his GOM [General Order of Merit]. And if his [military] aptitude is high, he knows he's going to get cadet rank as long as he stays 'pro.' "[6] In the same way that many students at civilian schools claim to be less capable at physics or mathematics than history or political science, many cadets claim to be less capable at or interested in academic subjects than the military activities they are required to master.

Although few cadets are avowedly indifferent to academics, the values of the cadet subculture reinforce those who claim, often hypocritically, that they "never crack a book" and discourage cadets with genuine intellectual interests. "If somebody takes seriously the material you are discussing in class," explained one former member of the faculty, "and actually demonstrates a certain enthusiasm, that guy is regarded as a fool. Or at least he has to demonstrate that there are other things about him that make it okay. If he is a jock or a company commander or a Pete Dawkins [a 1959 graduate, football All-American, and Rhodes scholar] type, well, that makes it okay. But still it's just only okay." [7] Most cadets think it permissible to work at academics in order to maintain a high grade-point average, because this represents a form of triumph over the system and brings rewards like increased privileges. It is "bad form," however, to express a personal enthusiasm for things intellectual. As a woman student from an eastern college put it: "When I talk to cadets about my interest in my courses, they think I'm ridiculous. And if I tell a cadet I'm into a book or writing a paper and can't go out, he thinks I'm feeding him a line." [8]

One faculty member in the humanities, himself a second-generation West Pointer, readily acknowledged, "If you are going to judge this place from a purely academic frame of reference, it is going to be found wanting. We don't produce contemplative people because they never have time to be contemplative. Kids don't come into class now and say, 'I see where Edmund Wilson died yesterday and the *Times* ran an obituary that reviewed his life and work. I wonder if we could discuss the issues Wilson addressed in *Patriotic Gore.*' " But, the officer insisted, the cadets are not anti-intellectual: "It is not that they don't want to read associated books. Assuming they had ready access to paperbacks in their field, they just don't have the time to read them. The goals that are in effect here are not conventional academic goals. They are essentially military goals, which don't really leave much time for the pursuit of academic excellence. Cadets just don't have the time. And the powers-that-be don't forget that. They recognize that these kids are drinking out of a firehose." [9]

The common cadet perception of West Point as an eighteen-hour-a-day hassle to be survived rather than mastered is exemplified in graduation exercises each year. The loudest cheer is reserved for the last-ranking member of the class. To many he represents a special triumph over "the system" because he has played the game most skillfully; he has graduated while expending a bare minimum of energy in academics. He joins George Armstrong Custer, last in the class of 1861, and other notorious graduates in the Long Gray Line's "goat brigade." Since 1968 he has received a paper bag containing hundreds of dollar bills contributed by his classmates.[10]

Few cadets actually aspire to finish last in their class. But most do have more in common with the "goats" in their class than with the "star men," those cadets who wear stars on their collars as evidence of high academic rank. There are academically motivated students at West Point, as the Academy's Rhodes scholar figures demonstrate, but they are the exceptions.[11] The cadet with academic promise usually learns very quickly that academic survival is preferable to academic excellence, because it allows time for other duties and for oneself. For many the watchword is "2.0 [the minimum passing grade] and go," which one cadet defined as "get the minimum grades that give you privileges and don't do anything more."[12]

Nevertheless, West Pointers respond hostilely to suggestions of anti-intellectualism. Since there is no conscious intent to encourage such an attitude, cadets and faculty deny its presence even while acknowledging its pervasiveness. A first classman explained: "It's true, the vast majority of cadets don't care, but most of them aren't anti-academic or anti-intellectual. They just don't think about their education. You don't get any hard-core anti-idea types. . . . They just don't feel it's right to get excited about course work."[13] A recent graduate contended that some cadets are academically inclined, but that "you get so bogged down, you have to kiss off the subjects you're interested in. I so often found myself specking some laundry list [memorizing unrelated facts] for the next day's class in thermodynamics and being unable to read what I was really interested in that I threw the thermo book across the room. . . . After a while you learn not to have intellectual interests 'cause they just get in the way." [14] One of the most discerning critiques of cadet attitudes toward academics in recent years came from First Classman Donald Cantlay, who addressed his comments to the dean in an open letter: "In my opinion, the academy product has been cheapened; if I were to sketch an emerging type, characteristics such as—'extremely hedonistic,' 'brooding but basically unthinking,' and 'motivated only toward survival in his game environment' would be central to the picture. You would have to look far down the list indeed to see any mention of 'idealistic,' 'mature,' or 'dedicated to the pursuit of knowledge and truth.' Or, for that matter, dedicated to anything." [15]

FUNCTIONAL ILLUSIONS

It would be easy to explain prevalent cadet attitudes toward academics if the young men admitted to West Point were third-rate students who had never in their lives taken academic work seriously. Of course, they are not. The college board scores of entering plebe classes have declined somewhat over the last ten years, but they are still far higher than the national average. The young men who come to the Military Academy are not of the same academic caliber as students in the Ivy League; nor are they quite as academically gifted as students at elite schools like Oberlin, Stanford, and Middlebury. They are the kind of students who easily gain admission to most state universities.[16] And over 80 per cent of most plebe classes rank in the top quarter of their graduating high school class, indicating that West Point attracts "over-achievers" whose academic performance outstrips their tested academic potential. A surprisingly large number of entering cadets, about 70 per cent, plan to pursue advanced degrees, another clear indication of academic commitment. In fact, when new cadets were asked why they decided to come to the Military Academy, over 85 per cent indicated that they were most influenced by "the academic reputation" of West Point. This represents a dramatic change from post-World War II years, when most cadets said they came because of their "desire for a military career." And perhaps most ironic of all, since the 1960's an increasing number of cadets have described the chief attraction of West Point as "the quality of the education." [17]

Such expectations about West Point are carefully cultivated. In its approach to prospective cadets, the Academy stresses, "the academic side" of West Point life. The in-depth Barron's profile of the Military Academy sent to each applicant contains information which encourages the aspiring cadet to regard West Point as, first and foremost, an academic institution. He is told that West Point is interested in fostering "intellectual stimulation" and "an investigative and probing mind." The Academy is described as a "college community" with an academic philosophy that emphasizes "a broad education in the arts and sciences." The bulk of the Barron's profile is given to a description of the academic program, along with the explanation that "the vast majority of academic courses are conducted much as they are at a civilian institution. Military instruction is confined to a few courses and the intensive summer training sessions." [18] High school guidance counselors who visit West Point are given more precise information. For example, they are told that during the nine-month school year, 83 per cent of a cadet's time is spent doing academic work and only 17 per cent is occupied with military training.[19] Finally, there is the official mission-statement of the Academy, which asserts that West Point strives "to provide a broad collegiate education in the arts and sciences. . . ." [20] Small wonder that most investigators concur with a reporter for the *Washington Post*, who concluded that the Academy is "little more than another university, albeit one where everyone has been to the same tailor." [21] It is also understandable that entering plebes regard admission to West Point as admission to a college, since that is the central message of the admissions literature. After four years of free college education, they reason, they will pay back the government with five years of military service. There will be a few drills each week and summer vacations will be interrupted by military exercises, but the chief business during the four years will be academic.

Unfortunately for academically minded cadets, the officers who run West Point do not share this impression. In their minds the Military Academy is not a college. It is a professional school designed to produce officers for the Army. "The only reason this school is here is to prepare a guy to be an officer in the Regular Army," said the academic dean, General Jannarone, "and if people come here with other views, with other ideas, then I can understand why they might feel that they would like to be studying more social sciences or more mathematics or more English." [22] A similar conception of the relative significance of academics was reflected in the jaded view of a junior faculty member when he observed, "If this place has anything that is good about it, it isn't academics. In terms of international and national prestige, it is not academics, but the ability to carry out a long-term military socialization program. This is what it does. And it does it very well." [23] And another member of the Academic Board, Colonel Edward Saunders, stressed: "We're an expensive place and the only way we can justify our existence is by doing what we're getting paid for doing. And that's to *produce* professional *Army* officers. . . . Not to train physicists, not to train English majors, or what have you. That's sort of incidental. It's nice to have but by no means essential. . . . Guys like me assume everybody understands . . . but it's not always obvious to the people who should know." [24]

An officer in the English Department extended this sense of the primacy of West Point's military mission by recalling from his cadet days "the residual feeling that this is the way it has got to be because we were getting paid. I mean, *it is a freebie.* Right? And you are getting paid a salary to boot; so, if you've got twenty-three minutes to read a book, you are fucking off. Seriously, I have felt that to do the Ivy League thing with a pipe in your mouth and your feet on the table is not what [Uncle] Sam is putting you through here to do. The government is not putting you through here to read novels." [25] These sentiments were echoed by the commandant of cadets, General Philip Feir, when he observed: "A person goes out into the Army and fails not because he can't diagram a sentence or because he can't write the equations about some free body in space. He fails because, in four years here, he has not developed . . . sufficiently soldierly qualities . . . to be a successful troop leader." [26]

Although the desire to produce troop leaders, or "people who can lead men in ground combat," and the desire to provide cadets with "an education equivalent to that given by our leading universities" are not mutually exclusive goals, neither are they especially compatible. As the comments from members of the Academic Board make clear, when the two goals conflict, there is no doubt about which one has priority. This does not mean that cadets are yanked out of the classroom to practice the manual of arms. Nor does it mean, as one officer in the History Department phrased it, "that if you could show that three hours of English literature is not essential to the development of an infantry officer, they'd throw out English." [27] In fact, there are few direct conflicts between the academic and military sides of the Academy, primarily because the academic departments are staffed almost exclusively by Regular Army officers, over 70 per cent of whom are Academy graduates. Many are convinced from their years of experience in the Vietnam era Army that the purely academic side of West Point life contributed very little to their survival and success after West Point. And few of them would argue with General Feir's blunt declaration about the nature of cadet-faculty relationships:

> I make the point with the people over in the academic departments that their responsibility here at the Military Academy is to

> the Army and the institution first and to the Department of Mathematics or the Department of Electrical Engineering, or whatever it might be, second. If they accept that hypothesis, then . . . every officer here is first and foremost a tactical officer. And secondly, he should face up to his specific responsibility as an academic instructor. . . . I think that where an instructor . . . places his academic objectives first he does a disservice to the institution and to the Army. . . . He fails in terms of accountability, a very important thing here. And therefore he fails to do the service to the cadet that we think is appropriate in terms of that cadet's development.[28]

A CADET DAY

At 5:50 each weekday a World War I howitzer booms in the morning at Trophy Point just north of the Plain. A few minutes later a small contingent from the West Point band marches up to the barracks and plays reveille. At exactly 6:05 a plebe appears in every barracks hallway, announcing that there are ten minutes until breakfast formation, specifying the uniform for the day, and providing all listeners with the breakfast menu. The minute-caller reappears at 6:10, 6:12, and again at 6:13, when he shouts "This is the last minute to be called for this formation. Do not forget your lights. Two minutes, sir." The cadet first classman usually sleeps through the cannon boom and the morning music, but is up at 6:05 and fully dressed by 6:10. He makes his bed, places his wastebasket in the hall for the janitor, and surveys his room. He assures himself that his uniforms are properly arranged in the closet (from left to right: full-dress coat, dress coats, blazer, gray jacket, class shirt, khakis, fatigues, civilian clothes), his toilet articles are in keeping with regulations governing the medicine cabinet (from top to bottom: brush, soapdish, razor; toothbrush, toothpaste; shaving cream, deodorant; water glass.) The window and shade and the shoes under the bed must also be aligned correctly. As a "firstie" he is sufficiently adept at cadet minutiae that his final check of the room requires only seconds.

He marches to breakfast at 6:25. By 6:40 the first warning light in the dining hall goes on, allowing first classmen to leave, so he returns to his room for another hour of sleep. After 7:30, however, regulations prohibit a cadet from lying on his bed unless he is a member of an athletic team with a scheduled intercollegiate activity that day. It is time to get up anyway, because he has an eighty-minute class, The History of the Military Art, at 8:25. The lesson for the day involves the strategy of the Continental Army during the American Revolution and has required a reading of three pages from volume one of *The West Point Atlas of American Wars* and a ten-page article from a supplementary text prepared by the History Department. The class ends precisely at 9:45.

He now has fifty minutes of that most precious cadet commodity, free time. He can go to the library to study, but probably will not, unless he has a writ (test) scheduled for his next class. More likely, he will go to Grant Hall, where he can chat with other cadets, drink coffee, and read the newspaper. Depending on his rank in the cadet chain-of-command, he will spend a portion of his free time performing specified cadet duties. If he is a regimental athletic officer, for example, he must draw up schedules for the intramural basketball season, assign officials for the games, and ensure that cadets whose athletic aptitude is below the established par are given additional instruction. If he is a battalion supply officer, he must supervise laundry pick-ups and handle complaints from cadets who did not receive their copies of the *New York Times* that day. If he is a company commander, he is certain to be occupied with room checks, weapons checks, regulations checks, and counseling sessions with delinquent cadets. By 10:35 he has completed his duties, whatever their nature, because he is due back at Thayer Hall for his class in comparative political systems. After a seventy-minute discussion of the impact of the Cultural Revolution on Chinese foreign policy, he heads back to the barracks. He has just enough time to read his mail before the minute-caller calls the minute and apprises him of the menu for lunch, which is at 12:15.

After lunch he has back-to-back classes from 1:05 to 3:15. These are his electives, two of the six courses he has been allowed to choose on his own while at the Academy. On this day the cadet finds himself translating eleven pages in Military Readings in Portuguese, then analyzing Melville's chapter "The Whiteness of the Whale" in American Literature of the Nineteenth Century. Class dismissal at 3:15 leaves him fifteen minutes to return to the barracks and dress for either a drill and practice parade or for intramurals. Now is the time when the Plain is filled with a regiment of marching cadets, the athletic fields become "fields of friendly strife," and the sidewalks become lanes for joggers and for formations of football, lacrosse, soccer, or rugby players marching double-time to their mini-wars. The parade and the games go on until 6:00.

Two days of the week, however, the cadet is not required to participate in athletics or drill. But military duties have usually built up during the day, so he spends a good portion of the two and a half hours of free time filling out forms on cadets found deficient in military aptitude, updating rosters, checking equipment or whatever else his cadet duties demand. The early completion of his duties allows time for sleep or a pick-up game of basketball.

Once again there are minute-callers, this time for the evening meal, which is from 6:15 to 6:45. There may be a football rally outside the dining hall at 7:00, liaison sessions for cadet commanders in the regiment, meetings of the cadet activities council, conferences with tactical officers. Or a good movie might be showing in the auditorium at Thayer Hall. Contingent on these various diversions and duties, as well as his mood, academic aspirations, course load, and the proximity of term-end examinations, the cadet allocates part of the evening for study. At 8:00 he has Evening Call to Quarters, during which time he will study two or three hours, punctuating his work with barracks horseplay, letter-writing, last-minute cadet duties or listening to his stereo. Between taps at 11:00 and 1:00 a.m. he may do his most serious studying since he is confined to his room, except to use the latrine. At 1:00 a.m. regulations require that lights go out.[29]

The cadet's schedule imposes the most important single constraint on his academic development. Put simply, the structure of a cadet's day and the pressures generated within that structure make it impossible to devote the requisite energies to intellectual pursuits. In an absolute sense, of course, there is time for study. All one need do is eliminate the extra naps, the "barracks bullshitting," and the hours spent day-dreaming about members of the opposite sex. Barring a revolutionary change in the mentality and physiology of American youth, any plan based on the absolutely efficient student is a fantasy. As long as the cadet encounters the present number of required classes, military formations, and other duties, he cannot be expected to devote the same energy to academic work as does a student in college. On average, he will spend five more hours per week in the classroom than the student at a civilian school, but he will spend only a fraction of the time studying and reading outside the classroom as his peers at Cornell and Georgia Tech.

It is not only the relative lack of time devoted to study that inhibits academics at the Academy; it is also the piecemeal character of the time that is available. "There are potentially outstanding students at the Academy," according to one tenured faculty member, "but very few of them ever attain that status. Why? Because physically and psychologically the other pressures make extended study impossible. Their time is so divided that they don't have time to read books." [30] Most of the faculty members are aware of the cadets' problems—most of them were once cadets themselves—so they adjust their academic sights in order to accommodate the fragmented study schedule. "In the classroom we present the cadet with pre-packaged increments of bite-sized knowledge that he can digest within the constraints of the system," one officer has remarked, "because we know that's the only way he will be able to handle the material." [31] This faculty attitude also influences the study assignments. Most departments have an informal ceiling on the number of words or pages per lesson that can be assigned a cadet. As a result, arguments within academic departments often take the form of a debate between advocates of the specific discipline ("How can we hope to have an intelligent discussion on the New Deal when they've only read twenty-seven pages of a textbook?") and advocates of the cadets ("Look, you know he doesn't have time to read Leuchtenburg's *F.D.R. and the New Deal*, so why assign it?"). In the end the latter group almost invariably wins the argument, because the men who run West Point are soldiers who work within a system that gives priority to military training.

The very duties and requirements occupying so much of the cadets' academic year are considered essential parts of his "professional military education"—West Point's primary mission in the view of the Academic Board. And most faculty members have no delusions about what this mission includes. "The one thing we do know to be true is that cadet life is time consuming," said one officer. "A cadet might go through here without ever having a period of time when he can put on Beethoven and just think about what he's doing, just as a Yale undergraduate will never have a tac asking him to display his dress uniforms. . . . We understand that the cadet lifestyle denies the possibility of contemplation . . . but then who wants a platoon leader who always contemplates the order to take that hill? " The same officer offered an extended example of the crowded character of a cadet day in order to support his contention that comparisons between academic life at West Point and civilian colleges are ludicrous:

> I don't know how an above-average student at Yale goes about completing an eighty-page reading assignment, but I suspect that he is not going about it in the same environment as a cadet is, with the phone ringing, a tac knocking on his door, somebody coming to see if his desk has dust on it, and with three or four other requirements coming to a head. And if he's a cadet who holds a position of responsibility, he is also an administrator. If some plebe has a problem, it is

> as likely as not that his phone is ringing with some major on the other end wanting to know from this cadet, "Why?" This is while he is on page forty-three of the assignment from Herman Kahn and the tac wants to know why the hell Mr. Smith is deficient in French. And that just does terrible things to the continuity of your educational experience. So that when this guy gets back to page forty-three an hour later, he finds that he has eight minutes to read the other thirty-seven pages.[32]

Academically gifted cadets who develop a critical attitude toward the system also learn to live with the constraints, in part because efforts to make changes eventually take more time and energy than compliance. Cadet Philip Linder told of his attempt to challenge a regimental policy requiring that all cadets keep their windows opened halfway when they were out of their rooms. Linder drafted a lengthy memorandum, arguing that the policy did not promote regimental uniformity, since there were always some cadets in their rooms, so some windows were always closed. "Plus I had both a northern and eastern exposure, so I had a little whirlwind in there. Being from the South, I was also susceptible to upper respiratory infection." Linder's cadet commanders disapproved of the memorandum because it implicitly criticized the regimental tactical officers, but forwarded it up the chain-of-command. When it produced a change in policy, they were grateful. But even this meager reform effort demanded a great deal of Linder's time and energy; and it also cast doubt on his military aptitude. "You have a certain amount of political capital to expend here," he explained, "and if you blow it all in one place, you're lost." [33]

Donald Cantlay was another academic "hive" critical of regulations; but Cantlay decided that discretion in a noble cause was tantamount to cowardice. He drafted a lengthy critique of the entire academic atmosphere at West Point. He also ignored the regular chain-of-command and sent his comments directly to the dean. Moreover, his comments went beyond description to offer an analysis of the widespread cadet apathy toward academic pursuits and to locate the wellspring of cadet attitudes in Beast Barracks and the regimented cadet schedule:

> The notion of "survival" at West Point is central to understanding cadet motivation. On the infamous first day of Beast Barracks that word ascends to preeminence in the cadet's vocabulary—a position from which it may never descend. All during Beast (and later, plebe year) the new cadet is constantly impressed both by the powerlessness of his own position and the related necessity of doing what he has to in order to get by—to survive. In this highly pressurized situation two major bad effects are most noticeable: the cadet experiences a substantive maturative regression that in many ways can be likened to the "samboization" of the American slave that Stanley Elkins discusses in *Slavery;* and the cadet begins to gear his thinking to "budgeting his time," which often translates realistically into a search for the easiest way to survive. . . . He learns, among other things, not to stand out; he is told, time and again, to stay in the 'safe' middle—and being conditioned to mediocrity by a respected authority figure is bound to have a severe effect. . . . In my own more cynical, Machiavellian moments I am almost forced to conclude that the Academy has so little faith in the life it is selling that it feels it necessary to resort to a debilitating, self-vitiating socialization process in the co-option of future military leaders.[34]

Not all cadets agreed with Cantlay's analysis; and, even among those who did, there was a marked tendency to react in a way that confirmed his description of the cadet as "sambo." "We agree with what he says," explained a former first classman, "but what a stupid thing to do. He's a first classman. He has all his privileges now. He's putting all that on the line. Look what he stands to lose. What a stupid thing to do." [35]

Donald Cantlay's comments constitute one of the more eloquent critiques of academic life at West Point ever written by an "insider." Although Cantlay's self-conscious eloquence was, in part, a studied effort to attract the attention of the dean and, in part, a vehicle for the release of his own pent-up intellectual frustrations, his view of West Point academics as socialization rather than education cuts to the heart of the problem. His analogy between cadets and black slaves was a dramatic device designed to convey what he perceived as the negative, even immoral, character of the socialization process at West Point, but it did not take into account the fact that cadets will eventually be "freed" and that their four years at West Point are intended as a preparation for future professional life. In the view of Academic Board members, the course work required of all cadets is not and should not be structured to emphasize the development of intellectual curiosity in young students; like the military training, academic work is intended to mold young men into soldiers. The crowded daily schedule of the cadet is an essential part of that process. A highly decorated former member of the faculty explained the rationale: "Their training at West Point prepares them for what they will be doing in the Army. They won't have time to contemplate. They'll have to do jobs instinctively, especially those jobs that get thrust upon leaders in combat situations. Usually, the only incorrect response to any combat situation is to do nothing while you contemplate the options. The correct response is to *do something*, oftentimes almost anything. . . . You won't find that kind of thinking coming out of Princeton or Yale. A lot of the requirements might seem absurd, I guess, and some of them are; but, they have to be understood in the context of what cadets are being prepared for." [36]

THE ENGINEERING APPROACH

Like a sanctuary, an academic classroom is commonly perceived as a hallowed place closed off from the rest of the world. At most civilian colleges, when a professor enters the classroom and closes the door, those inside feel insulated from outside interventions. There is no prevailing institutional mission, no uniforms displaying rank and accomplishments, no complex rules of deference and decorum to condition what is spoken and written. Yet even at West Point, where academic freedom is often subordinated to military doctrinal conventions, where senior officers regularly observe younger instructors in the classroom, and where the omnipresent visiting dignitaries are often ushered into classes that have a reputation for vivaciousness, it is difficult for an outsider to know what actually goes on, or does not go on, inside the classroom. A visitor inevitably becomes an intruder who alters the pedagogical situation and inspires a more formal lecture, if not a theatrical scene. But since the classroom is the center of an undergraduate's academic world, any effort to explain cadets as students without exploring the other side of the classroom walls would be like explaining American military history without taking West Point into account.

Physically, a West Point classroom looks like a seminar room in a new university that has not been forced to cut back the maintenance budget. Most rooms come equipped with a television that has closed-circuit capability, a view graph, maps, a set of the books used in the courses that meet there, blackboards on all four walls, and four different colors of chalk. The student desks, made of metal and a hard plastic-like material, sit in a U-shaped formation with the open end facing the teacher's metal desk. Between thirteen and seventeen cadets are in their assigned desks by the time the second hand sweeps past the twelve on the classroom clock. In most classes cadets are seated according to their current academic ranking in that course, so that the grade-point averages descend from the instructor's left to his right. When he enters the room, all cadets stand at attention; the first ranking cadet, called the section-marcher, salutes the instructor and reports absences. The instructor returns the salute, gives the command "Seats," and the class begins.

The instructor is, with but few exceptions, a male career officer in the United States Army. During most of the year he is wearing a dress green uniform, highly shined black shoes, a name tag, and the combat and service medals he has been awarded during his military career. Most heads of departments attempt to recruit well-decorated officers for three-year tours on their faculty, because they contend that each instructor is not only a teacher but also a career model for the cadets. And cadets do notice the details of an instructor's uniform. "I can remember many days being bored in class," one instructor and former cadet recalled, "and sitting there looking at the instructor's ribbons and saying, 'What is that yellow and red and green thing he's got down there? I ought to know what that is if I think about it hard enough. It must be the Korean Order of Merit. . . .' It was something to pass the time." For other cadets such reflections quickly escalate into complex inquires. Another graduate remembered "day-dreaming on 'How is it that one guy has only this [ribbon] and last hour I was in a session with the guy's classmate and he has about four of them. Or here's a guy who is class of '52 and he obviously escaped Korea; he's only got an ARCOM [Army Commendation Medal] and a National Defense Medal.' " And then by the way of explanation, he added, "If the class is boring, and you know how much there is to look at around West Point, you just run a trip on a guy's uniform. You know, trying to work things out." [37]

Although the classrooms, uniforms, and military rituals are standardized for all classes, the conduct of the class discussion varies according to department and instructor. Of the forty-eight academic courses a cadet must take in order to graduate, forty are "standard courses." These constitute the prescribed part of the curriculum, are slightly weighted toward the hard sciences and tend to subscribe most closely to the goals of the Thayer System. The most time-consuming and influential of all the standard courses is plebe math (MA 107–108), which meets five days of the week for eighty minutes per session. "When you're a plebe here, man, it's math and math and more math," said one graduate. "Then you go over to a swimming pool and tread water for a while and come back to the classroom for more math." [38] A first classman concurred: "Plebe math is the big introduction to academics at West Point. Everything else gets pushed aside and, later on, in other courses, cadets approach the material in the way they learned from plebe math. It's the main course I can remember from plebe year." [39]

The Mathematics Department has a faculty composed of seventy officers, most of whom are needed to teach the fifteen-man sections in the plebe math course.[40] One of the more commonplace stories in West Point folklore is that one can walk down the corridor in Thayer Hall in the morning and observe math instructors in their classrooms turning on the view-graph, picking up their pointers, and explaining the same diagram at the same time. And math classes do follow essentially the same format. After the section-marcher reports the absences and the class has been seated, the instructor asks if there are any questions about the previous night's homework. Departmental guidelines emphasize that questions should make reference to a specific problem or theorem. After answering specific questions the instructor then gives the command "Take boards." Each cadet goes to his particular section of the blackboard, which is assigned, like seats, according to class rank. He is authorized to take with him the problem book, a slide rule, and a book of mathematical tables. He portions off his board, draws a line down the middle, and draws a box in the upper right corner for his name and problem number. All lines must be drawn with a straight-edge.

The instructor then gives the even-numbered problems to every other cadet and the odd to those remaining. Almost always, the problems come from the homework assignment. After about twenty minutes, the instructor gives the command "Cease work." Cadets must immediately put down their chalk and return to their desks. Designated cadets remain at the board to explain their solutions, using a different colored chalk to mark any changes made after they have ceased work. Each cadet must stand on the left side of his board, hold the pointer in his left hand and the problem book in his right hand, and begin his explanation "Gentlemen, I was required to prove. . . ." A cadet can expect to recite every other day. Procedural errors are customarily treated as seriously as matters of substance. The instructor assigns grades, announces the homework problems for that evening, and dismisses the class. If the physical appearance of the cadets or the neatness of the problem boards has not been satisfactory, the instructor may announce that tomorrow's class will begin with an inspection.[41]

Colonel Charles P. Nicholas, former head of the Mathematics Department, emphasized the cumulative impact of this kind of instruction on the cadets: "when his mind undergoes this experience during every day . . . it is bound to develop along the lines induced by that experience. Each day's preparation by study is a military responsibility." [42] Although Nicholas' comment comes from an article published in 1967, Colonel Somers Dick, his successor in the Mathematics Department, confirmed that Colonel Nicholas' comments "express pretty well our philosophy in the way that we teach the math." Clearly, the plebe math classroom is devoted as much to military training as it is to academic learning. The concern for procedure, decorum, and detail enforces habits believed to be of constant value to a platoon leader. "Our system," explained Colonel Dick, "puts the boy on the mat, you might say. . . . Our primary goal, as far as the cadets are concerned, is to develop in them those attributes of being able to stand on their own two feet and being confident that they have got the moxie to come up with a solution. . . . We don't feel that it is our mission to make them masters of the theory, the foundations of mathematics. I think in the military man it is the application of mathematics that's really important." For those cadets who criticize the classroom stress, Colonel Dick has a ready answer: "There is a feeling by some that it puts too much pressure on them. Well that's a difference of opinion. I think an Army officer is always going to be under pressure and I think it's one of the things we see in all areas of the Academy—we are training the boy to withstand it. It's better to find out now." [43] For those cadets who dispute the need to spend so much of their time with mandatory mathematics classes, an assistant dean, Lieutenant Colonel James Hall, indicated that it also has a military function: "There is an important learning point in having the cadets choose to take courses they would not choose to take. When you get out in the Army, there are a lot of things you have to do which are not nice things to do and which you will not enjoy doing much of the time. You're going to have to learn to take the job you are assigned and do it to the best of your ability. So there is a certain *discipline* there; that's the best word for what is involved, I think." [44]

In fact, plebe math tries to inculcate more than just the tidiness, orderliness, and practical discipline required of an army officer. It is the cadet's introduction to a way of thinking that will be reinforced in engineering, physics, chemistry, economics, and even history and literature classes throughout the next four years. Cadets call it the "engineering approach"; Colonel Charles Schilling, head of the Department of Engineering, calls it "iterative decision making"; people in social sciences call it the "systems-analysis approach"; in English they call it the "argumentative method." Despite the different names, the particular thought process is similar in each case; the goals are analogous—to produce proficient and efficient decision-makers for the Army; or, as Colonel Nicholas put it, "to shape the cadet's mind into an effective instrument of military leadership." [45] In the hands of some instructors at West Point, this problem-solving technique can become a refined version of the scientific method or a sophisticated form of rational inquiry. Colonel Olvey of the Social Sciences Department can defend what he calls "systems analysis" quite ably, arguing that it is simply a way "to approach policy questions on a rational basis. And if that makes me a 'military mind' or whatever, then I suppose I am one." Colonel Schilling has also contemplated the implications of iterative decision-making and drawn up elaborate charts that attempt to describe the logic of the methodology. But for most officers and cadets the engineering approach is more an instinctive habit of mind than a gracefully defended and well-understood intellectual process. It is the way one is supposed to think.[46]

Anyone who has read an army manual, observed a Pentagon

briefing, or watched a cadet at the boards in plebe math has some familiarity with this "mechanistic" or engineering approach. First, the methodology is not intended to develop critical thinking but to solve inherently soluble problems. The problems are "given" (to derive a theorem in MA 107; to prepare the platoon for inspection; to close with and destroy the enemy). In mathematics, applied engineering, and the vast majority of military situations the method has great utility because the problem either is self-evident or someone else (the instructor, the commander, the elected or appointed civilian leader) has defined it beforehand. Second, the method assumes that every problem has a solution, usually only one correct solution. The ramifications of this assumption are profound and cause both immediate and long-range problems for cadets and officers. In the humanities, especially in history and literature courses, capable instructors have difficulty sustaining cadet interest in questions to which, quite obviously, there is no commonly acceptable answer. Similarly, in military situations rendered ambiguous by complicated political or cultural developments, officers addicted to this methodology have trouble constructing an "operational equation" that does justice to the non-military "factors." But in mathematics, the hard sciences, as well as most situations in the Army, the assumption that there is a correct solution receives reinforcement (in MA 107 there is an answer book; in field engineering there is a manual that provides the approved techniques for constructing pontoon bridges; in the Army there are field manuals that specify the proper way to draft an operations order or assault a fortified position). Third, the method is inherently reductionist, that is, it encourages the belief that all problems are reducible to smaller, more tangible problems susceptible to technical analysis in which the solutions become self-evident (to derive the theorem by resolving it into several parts, each of which is explainable in terms of other theorems; to break the M-16 into its components to discover the source of the malfunction; to translate the amorphous military mission in Vietnam into kill-ratios, measurable in terms of enemy bodies). Finally, the solution of the larger problem follows naturally from the solution of these smaller problems.

Although cadets moan about the rigors of plebe math, by the end of the academic year they have usually assimilated its methodological assumptions. They tend to approach their academic work and their other classes with the operational skills acquired in their fourth-class year. There is little reason to question the applicability of the method, since it works quite well in their mathematics, engineering, and science classes and provides the answers for most tests in the social sciences and humanities. There is even an "approved solution" room in which cadets can find the answers to essay questions on history exams. And when a history instructor refuses to organize his course on the American Revolution in such a way as to fit with the methods of the engineering approach, cadets turn in evaluations that say, "This is all very stimulating and all that, but what's the right way to see these developments? What's the answer?" [47] It gives them a ready-made format for the expository essays they are required to write in English courses; cadets call it "the M1-A1 theme" and it consists of an introductory paragraph that defines the topic (the problem), a body in which each "part" of the topic is discussed in detail, and a conclusion based on the preceding discussion. What this "Euclidean style" lacks in grace, say English instructors, it makes up for in clarity and precision.

Outside the West Point classroom, in the barracks area, the hypertense organizational approach with its emphasis on defining priorities and marshaling the resources to accomplish assigned duties is especially pervasive. Cadets employ this method to arrange their lives on a day-to-day basis, to decide what duties or requirements are most pressing, and to break their daily schedule into goals capable of realization. And on those occasions when they confront civilian students at a symposium or open seminar, it gives cadets "an intellectual backbone," an argumentative style that seems to combine the confidence of a mid-1960's McNamara whiz kid with the casuistry of a Jesuit. Lieutenant Richard M. Saunders, a 1973 graduate, explained, "We would go down to Manhattanville to talk about race, marriage, the energy crisis and so on. But it was difficult to have reasonable discussions because the cadets tended to be logical, but dogmatic and very sure of themselves, and as a result the girls down there would get overpowered by the argumentative method and self-confidence of the cadets. . . . The other students would be more value-oriented and more emotional, while cadets would be more factual, logical and close-minded." [48]

The habits of mind developed in plebe math and reinforced throughout the academic life of a cadet are much in evidence in the Army. "It's unconscious, but it's a way of thinking that is pervasive," said one senior officer. "Even in an area like race relations, which everybody knows is unbelievably complicated, a commander has a tendency to say, 'OK, so we've got a race problem. Give me a program which will solve the problem . . . , give me somebody who can develop a good program to solve it. If the program involves training people in race relations, then we will train people in race relations.' " And the inevitable scenario was that "a program is developed and the commander says, 'OK, it's a good program and it *will be* successful.' And if the commander is not able to declare the completed program a success, if we still have racial problems on post, then most commanders say, 'it is the fault of the goddamn people who developed the program. They didn't do the job. If they had done the job and developed a good program, then we wouldn't have a race problem anymore.' It is as simple as that. That is the way they tend to look at it." [49]

This reflex of "shaking down problems," which so frequently involves distorting the problem so it can be dealt with in "manageable increments," may be functional in a firefight and in bureaucratic gamesmanship, but it seldom results in a comprehension of the context in which "problems" occur or in the development of more than temporal responses. And yet, operational skills are in great demand, especially in America's defense establishment. If the former cadet does well in the Army, well enough to become a National Security Council adviser or a member of the Joint Chiefs of Staff, his operational philosophy can prove invaluable. One former officer in the Social Sciences Department recalled policy-making conferences during the Vietnam war. "You put a West Pointer up against a State Department guy who sat on the Southeast Asia desk and who has spent his life studying the history and culture of Vietnam. And the West Pointer didn't know dogshit about history. But when the NSC [National Security Council] types, the Bundys or the Kissingers, asked for a recommendation, all the State Department guy had was complexities, nuances, more problems. The West Pointer did not analyze things as deeply, but he had solutions. And the guys who needed solutions said, 'Hey, here's a guy who's got solutions.' Frequently the solutions didn't work but it always took awhile to find that out and by then the NSC guys had new problems they wanted answers to." [50]

THE APPEAL OF ANSWERS

Although there are some powerful West Point alumni and professors who believe that absolute uniformity is a desirable commodity, no one at West Point seriously argues that the young men who graduate from the Academy each year think or act as if they were automatons manufactured on the same assembly line. Upon graduation the approximately eight hundred members of a class will have taken the same prescribed courses. Their transcripts will show that they have earned at least one hundred and forty-one academic credits, plus about thirty-five credits in specifically military courses.[51] They will have endured and, in turn, imposed on others, a great deal of harassment. Depending on one's calculations, each cadet's education will have cost the American taxpayers somewhere between $65,000 and $120,000.[52] Taken as a whole, they will have shared more common experiences and developed stronger ties with their classmates than any other group of college graduates in the country.

Yet while West Pointers share much in common in their approach toward their profession and in the way they carry out their assigned duties, they are eager to demonstrate their individuality in off-duty hours. Among the West Point officer corps are some of the Army's best informed and most devastating in-house critics. Yet they are very reluctant to "go public" with their criticisms because, lacking alternate career options, they are more dependent on the skills and status that a West Point degree provides and thus not inclined to jeopardize their own careers by "running down the image" of West Point or the Army in public.

In-house criticism invariably ranges from blunt pronouncements, such as that of a 1972 graduate who reflected, "Maybe the appreciation will come later, but right now I think a lot of stuff was just garbage," to probing self-analysis.[53] For instance, there are the melancholy observations of a newly commissioned second lieutenant on the seductive dangers of being a reasonable in-house critic while waiting for a turn at setting policy. "You go through twenty years in the Army, and you tell yourself, 'I'm just layin' low, wearing this mask. When I get into a position of power, I'll rip this mask off and really accomplish something.' But after you've worn that mask for so long it becomes part of your face." [54] West Pointers also make fun of themselves and their attachment to the engineering approach. "Can you imagine, we would go through Plato and try to distill his philosophy down to two or three sentences so that we could say, 'these are Plato's solutions.' " [55] And many recognize the comic consequences of the Academy's attempt to provide tangible guidelines for the length of sideburns: "For awhile there was anarchy . . . but then someone discovered the part of the ear called the traegus. That's what we needed. Now it's defined: 'No sideburns below the traegus!' Poof. It's absolute." [56]

Perhaps it is just the perversity of youth, the instinctive refusal of some young men to accommodate themselves to the mold. Whatever the cause, each year West Point turns out a small minority of officers who have rebelled against, but remained within, the West Point system. Ironically, they have received a liberal education of sorts; they have refined a personal value system by testing it against other values. They have developed their reflective and probing intellects, in large part because they have continually challenged and questioned the academic values at the Academy. They have been able to satisfy, some even to exceed, the prescribed West Point requirements as they have developed intellectually and spiritually through their constant straining against the system. For perhaps as many as 10 per cent of the recent graduates, the Academy has been an intellectual and psychological isometric exercise in which West Point has been the stationary object.

But for the vast majority, the West Point education is what it is meant to be—a socialization process. Most cadets have been trained rather than educated because West Point has not provided them with the time or the incentive to develop their own ideas and convictions. For those who generalize the engineering approach into a philosophy of life, West Point has developed in them a quite remarkable capacity, in the words of one instructor, "to work fast, to get things done. At West Point the pressure is to sort things out *now*." [57] A 1963 graduate noted, "The West Pointer is trained to get things done to a certain specific standard under a pressure situation. . . . It is very difficult for me to get something done which is three months away in the future. I find that I work much better when the heat gets on. For instance, in Vietnam, I had a tremendous number of actions crossing my desk all the time under great pressure and I was really having a good time. I wasn't really worried about what I was doing, just about getting all these things done and to a standard which I felt was high and my boss did too." [58]

For professional Army officers, who are required by regulations and motivated by command pressure to be mission-oriented, an operational perspective on their life and work has both a professional and personal utility. Not only do officers who get the job done usually have the satisfaction of pleasing the boss, they are also freed from the frequently troublesome chore of deciding for themselves what is worth doing. The act of performing an assigned task in such a way that it can be declared accomplished has enormous appeal, especially at a time when many Americans seem to be wandering aimlessly in search of fulfillment. One of the most attractive features of a military career is that it allows, often demands, that an officer structure his life to meet tangible goals and provides him with jobs which, because of the very way they are defined, are accomplishable. Although John Dewey would cringe at the prospect, the world of the military careerist provides an almost perfect arena for the application of his pragmatic or instrumentalist principles. And at an even more general level, the highly structured world of the military man allows for a confidence and kind of personal commitment that recalls a mythic view of an earlier, younger America in which national and personal goals were commonly agreed upon and pragmatism seemed to work. Yet nostalgia is tempered by the awareness that the very assumptions that give the engineering approach its utility and appeal are difficult to sustain in modern America. As one West Pointer put it, "how do you gamesmanship a problem when there may not be an answer? What do you do?" [59] Such questions provoke an uncertainty fundamentally at odds with the kind of confidence Americans have come to expect and admire in their soldiers.

At West Point unanswerable questions are anathema. Cadets learn to gain satisfaction from giving answers to problems which have been constructed to be soluble and from completing assigned tasks and pleasing superiors. Thus, in academics, a sense of accomplishment is derived from successfully hurdling requirements rather than from developing a sense of competency in a particular discipline. And the pervasive feeling of the Academic Board is that to allow the cadets to control their choice of courses, if only to the point of majoring in a specific discipline, subverts the Academy's mission. By historic design, fulfillment is gained much more from satisfying institutional requirements than from one's sense of personal development. The emphasis is on "what West Point has to offer" rather than on creating a context for individual growth. When Cadet Cantlay expressed his conviction that "making West Point a better academic institution will concomitantly and necessarily make it a better military academy," he was challenging the fundamental assumptions of the members of the Academic Board.[60] For they believe that the kind of academic environment in which a free exchange of ideas can flourish would undermine the military "qualities and attributes essential to his [the cadet's] progressive and continuing development as an officer in the Regular Army." And inculcation of those qualities, they correctly observe, is the stated mission of the Military Academy.

What the bulk of the graduates get from West Point, then, is not an education in the usual sense of the term, but the ability to carry out specific and often unpleasant tasks more effectively than others. "I have a secret and dangerous mission," General George Marshall purportedly said. "Send me a West Point football player." Morris Janowitz, the most prominent sociologist of American military institutions, has observed that the twentieth-century military leader is, more and more, a man who must possess the requisite managerial skills normally associated with junior executives in large corporations.[61] West Pointers invariably have these skills, as well as an adroitness at organizational maneuvering that makes them powerful players in bureaucratic in-fighting. As a recent graduate, now serving as a lieutenant, put it: "We are very good managers. Given eight things to accomplish, and no time to do them, a cadet will get them all done and turn them in on time. While such an attitude would repel someone interested in enlightenment and serious academic work, West Point strives to produce good managers, not philosophers, scientists or historians." A history instructor said it most succinctly: "They meet requirements efficiently. They get the job done." To Americans who do not regard the post-World War II military establishment with equanimity, such assertions are hardly reassuring. However, West Pointers' dedication and energy in carrying out assigned tasks is probably unique among alumni of

American schools and has contributed significantly to their being in great demand in government, industry, and education as well as the military. And in the view of some Americans this energy and dedication have often won them promotion to positions in which their limitations have become national problems.[62]

Chapter Five

★★★★★★★★★★★★★★★★★★

THE SOLDIER AS SCHOLAR

A West Pointer is a guy of absolute conviction, who, almost without question accepts a certain way of life that requires that he be masculine, dominant, certain. He expects immediate obedience to his values. He tolerates criticism, but not the critical attitude. He is a serious person.

He has accumulated a great deal of aggression in response to the multiplicity of renunciations, deprivations thrust upon him. When he feels he has right on his side, watch out. He'll turn his buddy in for honor, send men up Hamburger Hill, or destroy a career with a bad "ER."

Now I couldn't do that. I can't even get these enlisted guys around here to do their job. I'm just not a hard-ass. But you can bet that a guy who graduates from here wouldn't be worried about the things that worry me.

Major Francis E. Conrad, M.D. (1973)

West Point turns out all kinds. I don't think there's any such thing as the West Point type. Edwin Walker is one for example. John Kennedy said to me one day, "Jim, what the hell do you teach people up there at West Point?" That was the day [in September 1962] after which Ed [Edwin A.] Walker was on the monument down at Oxford, Mississippi, harassing the students to go after the Federalists. . . . I don't know what made Ed Walker like that. West Point turns out all kinds.

Lieutenant General James M. Gavin (ret.) (1973)

★★★ OVER 90 per cent of the officers on the West Point faculty are transients, but unusually successful transients. Most are captains or junior majors on the Army's "high road" with the expectation of retiring with at least the rank of colonel and, with the right breaks, perhaps even a star or two. They arrive at the Academy with six to twelve years of active duty behind them, usually fresh from a two-year stint in a university master's degree program. For their families West Point offers the luxury of a three-year uninterrupted tour; few officers are involuntarily reassigned out of West Point unless they are guilty of "gross misconduct" or some other extraordinary circumstances arise.[1] The guaranteed stability of the tour and the professional prestige associated with the assignment to "Staff and Faculty, West Point" make competition for the "faculty slots" very keen.

Competition starts years before the assignments are made. In fact, it starts when the future instructors are still cadets and receive regular ratings on their "instructor potential." The Electrical Engineering Department, for example, maintains a rating card on every cadet. As Colonel Elliott Cutler described the process, "The officer has the card of the cadet while the cadet is in his section, but they don't get very elaborate ratings. They just rate them as potential instructors—superior, excellent, satisfactory, or not recommended. This rating is given to all cadets and then we take the top-rated cadets and stick them in one box and put the other cadets in another box." Such ratings normally cover about six weeks of classroom observation, since most cadets are resectioned three to four times every semester. After a cadet leaves the Academy, he is rarely considered a prospective instructor unless his ratings are consistently high, or unless a permanent faculty member takes a special interest in him. According to Colonel Cutler: "We would not be looking for a cadet in the other box unless he wrote in and had a good story, or unless somebody wrote in to recommend him, and then we would move him up to the other box." [2] Almost every department head has his favorite anecdote about a former cadet who subsequently demonstrated he was "in the wrong box" by insisting on "proving his mettle in graduate school" and "coming back here and making . . . a really fine instructor." Such stories are frequently decades old and are sometimes passed down from a retiring professor to his successor as a part of the official lore of the position.[3]

The elaborate system employed by the Academy to keep track of its own contributes substantially to the high percentage of graduates who make up the faculty. Over 65 per cent of the non-tenured faculty, all but two of the twenty-one tenured full professors and all but nine of the thirty-one tenured associate professors, are West Point graduates.[4] These figures are particularly striking when one considers that there is no other university of West Point's size or prestige in America, including its two major sister academies, with comparable figures on employing its own graduates. In fact, one has to go to zealously insular institutions such as Bob Jones University in South Carolina to find analogous figures.[5] And such a comparison is appropriate because both schools are mission-oriented and are firmly persuaded that there are unique advantages to having people "on board" who have been baptized "on the grounds" in the institution's traditions and policies.[6]

For the "non-graduate" faculty member the route to the Academy is normally circuitous. Most department heads believe that a prospective candidate should be a Regular Army officer and a military careerist. He should also be recommended by a West Pointer who has himself taught in the department. "We may not know everything in the world abut him," Colonel Somers Dick said, "but those who are recommended to us by the people we have here are what we're looking for; our former instructors are pretty good judges of what we want—participators, good appearance, good Army record, any number of attributes." On some occasions an officer may be suggested to West Point by his branch, or he may write in on his own. If an unexpected vacancy occurs and the officer has a master's degree, he may be selected. But even among those professors who would welcome more non-West Pointers, there is a seldom acknowledged but quietly cherished conviction that the Academy intimidates non-graduates. "I would like to have more non-grads in my department," Colonel Gilbert Kirby contended, "but part of the problem is that the perception out in the Army is that the only people who come to teach here are graduates. . . . Others simply don't feel that they can come; so, they never say anything." Colonel Elliott Cutler expressed similar initial sentiments, but with a differing final emphasis: "I would like to get more non-graduates, or at least have a chance to get more than I do now; but, the problem is, how do you find out about them?" Colonel Cutler noted, "Sometimes a branch, when asked [by West Point] for nominations, will nominate non-graduates to come to the Academy, but *we* would like to know something about people *before* they come here." Whatever the explanation for the failure to recruit non-graduates onto the faculty, the result is clear: With the exception of a few sectarian schools, West Point is the most inbred educational institution in the country.[7]

Most members of the Academic Board prefer that their instructors be West Pointers or at least "West Pointer approved in the field." This policy was somewhat strained in the 1960's and early 1970's when regular officer commitments to Vietnam combined with the expansion of the Corps of Cadets (and hence of the faculty) to produce not only a shortage of graduates for West Point but a shortage of all regular officers. Colonel Dick recalled that "we experienced two or three times during the sixties what I call 'the crunch.' And we had to take a few officers who dropped out of the files down at the personnel office in Washington. They were math majors or reserve officers coming on active duty who had been teaching." But Colonel Dick's most troublesome year was "about '67 or '68, when Vietnam was going fast and furious; and, it took

[away] all of our instructors that had been here two years. We also had our normal three-year group leaving and that meant thirty-eight new instructors had to be brought on board that year. . . . I just didn't have sufficient grist to say to Washington, 'Well, this is what I want.' They wouldn't give it to me anyway, because they had places they were putting kids fast and furious. But I did have shaken out of the hopper down in Washington about four or five reserve officers who had only about a year or less on active duty." [8]

Senior faculty members viewed this sudden influx of reserve officers with considerable apprehension. Although few in number, these reserve officers, called "obligated volunteers" or "OBV's" in the Army vernacular, represented a major break with Academy tradition. (In a very important sense, they represented a partial return to the practices of the Thayer era, when department heads were civilians.) It was precisely because these OBV's were virtual civilians that they became a source of institutional anxiety. Not only were they non-graduates; they were not careerists. In addition, many of them had Ph.D.'s or had completed considerable graduate work beyond the master's level. This combination of inferior military training and superior academic achievement disturbed Academy officials because it contradicted the established priorities for selecting West Point instructors and thus undermined the principle that West Point was a school for soldiers which should be run and staffed by soldiers. As Colonel Dick said, "I do get requests almost weekly from math majors in ROTC programs at other institutions and what I always tell them is, 'I've got no doubts about your ability to teach mathematics; but, this being a military school, we want our officers to be able to give to the cadets a little injection of their experiences in the Army. You put in two or three years of active duty and have a little troop service, and perhaps a staff assignment, and then I'll consider bringing you back as an instructor depending on how you perform out in the Army.' " [9]

Most members of the Academic Board concur with Colonel

Dick's view of faculty recruitment. In their view West Point is first and foremost a professional school for future Army officers. And from their perspective the faculty ought to be composed of first-rate soldiers whose academic competence is less important than their role as military models. Although there are a large number of highly capable academicians looking for teaching jobs, the product of massive overproduction by American graduate schools in the 1960's and 1970's, there is little interest at West Point in considering people from this group for even interim faculty appointments. With the exception of the Law Department, there were less than a half-dozen OBV's on the faculty by 1974, and those few department heads who seem receptive "to having them around" agree with Colonel Olvey of the Social Sciences Department, who contends "the source has simply dried up." Olvey admits that "they raise the voltage a little bit and they're useful to have around. But I'm very pessimistic about being able to get people like that."[10]

Colonel Olvey's pessimism is rooted in his own conviction that his colleagues on the Academic Board have a strong argument in insisting that civilian instructors, or OBV's, are ultimately "counter-productive." A Rhodes scholar and a Harvard Ph.D., Olvey is less vulnerable to the criticism that is often directed at other department heads, namely, that intellectually committed instructors make them uneasy. (The most popular Olvey story at West Point has to do with his performance at Oxford. When Olvey entered the examination room to take his orals, the dons simply rose, applauded, waived his examination, and awarded him "a first.") Olvey liked having OBV's in his department because they "tended to be people who went on to academic careers, and it greatly facilitated our ability to stay in touch with civilian universities." He readily admits, however, that OBV's are "different":

> Now I think where they are different is that they are much more questioning about the local institution. They have been some of our

> best in-house critics. And there is something to be said for having people who are inclined to take issue with traditional ways of doing things rather than to accept them as a matter of course. But one of the minuses is that we do take very seriously that part of our mission, which is to try to cause young men to look favorably on a military career. And I think there is some cost there. It's the sort of thing which no systems analyst should try to measure, but it is there. And I think that's one of the major reasons there is no more official support for doing this sort of thing than we have had.[11]

The prospect of employing civilian instructors is all but inconceivable, even to a faculty member like Lieutenant Colonel Thomas E. Blagg, a former associate professor in the English Department who was particularly solicitous of reserve officers during his time at the Academy. Blagg, whose tours in Vietnam involved heavy combat as a green beret team leader in 1965 and as one of the last combat battalion commanders in Vietnam in 1972, was highly respected by reserve officers for his forthrightness and his willingness to engage in open discussions and to take seriously views contrary to his own. On the issue of civilian instructors, Colonel Blagg observed:

> Civilian instructors would certainly improve the quality of the English instruction, the classroom performance. John Milton would be better taught. Even *John Brown's Body* [a traditional plebe assignment] would be better taught if done so by a 'teacher.' . . . There is an advantage in having instructors and professors who are academically qualified. People like me can't possibly be as qualified to teach English literature or parts of American literature as somebody who has made it their life's work. And it's absurd to even suggest that. But the question is, "Does it need to be done *here?* In terms of *the purpose* of the institution? Do you need to have that quality of professorship?" [12]

In short, Blagg also endorses the view that the mission of West Point makes the academic competence and commitment of the faculty less important than its military competence and commitment.

"In terms of their preparations for a military career," Blagg insisted, "there is an advantage in having people here who have had experience as platoon leaders, as company commanders, as staff officers; people who have been in combat, who have been to Ranger School and other professional schools. If I stand up there at 6 foot 3, 230 pounds, with ribbons and telling them, and sincerely meaning it, that there is a value to an Army officer in understanding the English language and in understanding and having an interest in literature, it's going to have a greater impact on the cadets who are there than it would if a civilian were to tell them." Blagg underscored the paradox by adding, "and what I'm saying is true, although that civilian is probably a lot more qualified to talk about literature than I am, or most of the other faculty is, particularly in terms of his total understanding of what he is talking about. But the fact is, the credibility of the curriculum is enhanced by having it taught by people in green suits." [13]

Blagg's observations are reinforced by the experience of other faculty members. A junior member of the History Department recalled being ordered to wear his combat decorations on a day when he had escort duty for visiting Japanese dignitaries: "I had been told that I must put on all this trash. So I came into the classroom with it on. And the cadets said, 'Gee, we didn't know you had been in the war!' And then several of them stayed around after class and talked about that. I had been teaching these guys for weeks and that day I learned those ribbons did mean something to them. It changed their image of me enough so they thought that maybe they had better go back and review their view of this clown. Maybe he did know something about European history." [14]

Few cadets believe that their academic development suffers because of the Academy's uniformed faculty. In fact, the presence of civilian instructors at Annapolis is commonly seen by cadets as a proof of the Navy's lack of professionalism.[15] And the West Point instructors are generally more competent than the one group cadets are likely to compare them against, their high school teachers. Most instructors have a master's degree; their apparent control of subject matter is enhanced by their ability to establish "command presence" in the classroom. Furthermore, a cadet's experience predisposes him to accept the notion that an instructor who has never had a course in philosophy can, on command, "get up" a course surveying centuries of Western thought. Cadets and faculty share a methodological bias, a belief in the engineering approach, which predisposes them to regard all subjects as soluble problems and emphasizes the necessity of breaking a problem into component parts for convenient study. Devoting successive lessons to Nietzsche, Epicureanism, Stoicism, Aristotle, and Kant is, therefore, functional for teacher and student, even though neither party may develop an understanding of Western philosophy, because the course systematically moves all participants through a one semester introduction "to the main currents of philosophic thought from Socrates to Camus." [16]

Cadets frequently remind instructors who begin to make excessive academic demands of the relatively low priority accorded to academics. A second-year instructor in the History Department reported:

> Today I was dealing with one of my cadet company commanders, who is doing about a D- with me and hurting bad. And I had him out in the hall and I am saying, "You know, if you don't pass the final exam you are in deep trouble." And he said, "I will, no problem." And I said, "What has happened in this course? Why haven't you done worth a toot?" And he said, "You know I'm not very good in academics. But I'm very good in athletics and I'm very good in [military] aptitude and I think I'll make a very fine officer but I just don't have too much talent in academics." And I started to tell him—"you dumb shit, you just told me you were dumb!" [17]

While the instructor's indignation would win a sympathetic reaction from most civilian professors, at West Point this particular incident drew a matter-of-fact response from an infantry major. "The best guy I ever worked for," he said, "was as dumb a son-of-a-gun as you'd ever want to run into." Then he added, "Let's face it, at West Point there is a sort of mystique that you don't have to be very good at academics because it is really [military] aptitude and those other things that count." And, as a related irony, one of the most important lessons learned inside West Point classrooms is that intellectual pursuits must be undertaken on rigid time schedules or things "can get out of hand," throwing instructors and cadets irredeemably behind in their weekly assignments and interfering with the many other responsibilities of faculty and cadets.[18]

WATER WALKERS IN THE PIPELINE

The language the department heads at West Point use to describe the recruitment of faculty reflects a blend of bureaucratic jargon, military acronyms, and Academy idioms which usually perplex the uninitiated. But references to instructors as "P's" or to graduate schools as "pipelines" or to the process of faculty selection as "shaking the hopper" are features of a language which allow the senior faculty to cope with a massive organizational problem in terms that are meaningful and inoffensive to most military men. No civilian college or university has comparable recruitment problems every year because no civilian college or university loses almost one-third of its faculty annually.[19] Every year departments at West Point must replace those officers who are returning to "the real Army" with officers who are emerging from graduate schools. Meanwhile, the departments must negotiate with the different Army branches in order to "get the warm bodies to occupy the slots in the graduate schools and keep the pipeline filled." The constant shuffling to and fro has several consequences, one of which is that the Academy faculty has an average of only one year of teaching experience at the start of an academic year. The planning and organizational machinery required to keep the Academy staffed with instructors also creates a bureaucratic atmosphere in which an idiom such as "water walker" (an exceptionally accomplished officer) becomes an attempt to stylize an inherently bureaucratic process. And through it all there is the awareness most career officers have learned to live with; namely, that they may be able to influence but cannot control where they will be stationed. This absence of autonomy makes the recruitment of academically motivated officers even more remarkable, because, as recently as the late 1960's, a regular army officer who wanted a faculty tour at West Point had little influence over whether or not he would receive such as assignment, or which department he would go to, or where he would go to graduate school, and what academic discipline he would study.[20]

These decisions were made for the officers by department heads. As Colonel Cutler explained it, he and his colleagues "put ten names in for every slot we had open. This was done the fall preceding the time they would be assigned here or the fall preceding the time they would be going to graduate school. Then there was 'a grand slave market,' as we used to call it, where all the department heads would get together and where there was a multiple conflict, they would flip a coin." Many officers did not know their futures were being bartered away. The man who attempted to influence the Academy's choice by writing to a specific academic department, requesting personal consideration, faced the possibility that the Department of the Army was likely to intervene, denying his request for the West Point assignment on the grounds that "other tickets had to be punched first." A year or two later, when the officer became available, there might be a need in the English rather than the Mechanics Department, for example, and he would be passed over again. At present attention is given to an officer's background and interests; departments now try to learn of an officer's availability before requesting his assignment to the Academy and try to take his academic interests into account. But the needs of the Army and the needs of the Academy still take priority over personal desires. Only about one in ten of the officers whom West

Point requests are made available by the Department of the Army. Many of those who are available accept departmental assignments primarily as a road back to West Point, not because of any special interest in that department's subject matter.[21]

Since all the department heads and most of the permanent faculty members are West Point graduates (and all are Army officers), they perceive West Point's current faculty situation in terms of how much of an improvement it is over those of the past. One faculty member recalled the traumas in the 1960's when his department was ordered on a year's notice to offer a new course in geography. He remembered that "half the faculty would teach topography in the morning and load up in cars and go down to Columbia five days a week for a special program we had set up to teach 'em geography. And this went on for a full academic year and a summer. It was really a hump." Others recalled making it through graduate programs in English by specializing in linguistics, which their scientific background made far easier than the study of literature. The need for a department to develop a sudden "expertise" or for an officer to get through his master's program by taking peripheral courses is no longer commonplace, but the conviction that each officer must be willing and able to serve as a multi-purposed part in the Army bureaucracy—"to meet the needs of the service"—still guides faculty selection. An officer's personal interests must be sufficiently malleable to allow for schooling in fields as disparate as physics and French. Those who are less flexible, it is argued, do not really want the assignment.[22]

An officer's willingness to meet institutional needs does not mean that he has no preferences of his own; certain departments at the Academy are far more popular with prospective instructors than others. As in most vocations, Army officers view their assignments in terms of their potential for career advancement. Although teaching at West Point is attractive for family reasons and is a pleasant way "to have your instructor ticket punched," the assignment is not beneficial professionally unless it produces high efficiency reports. The very fact that many of one's colleagues at West Point are what careerists call "five percenters"—officers in the vanguard of their career group—means that the competition for high ratings is severe. Every department has its share of stories about one-time five percenters whose careers suffered because of a series of less-than-outstanding efficiency reports at West Point. Most prospective faculty members seek to avoid assignment to departments with a reputation for not accepting the practice that efficiency reports at the Academy should be inflated in order to take the elite character of the officer group into account. The "best" departments are those known to have elaborate alumni networks that facilitate choice assignments after the West Point tour.

The best three-year assignments are generally considered to be in the Department of Social Sciences. The least attractive assignments are usually those in the humanities, which at West Point include only the Departments of English and Foreign Languages. The History Department, unlike its counterparts at Annapolis and the Air Force Academy, has carefully avoided association with the humanities and operates principally with Social Sciences under the heading of "National Security and Public Affairs." [23]

Unlike some of the other departments, Social Sciences is able to recruit from a pool of officers who genuinely want to serve in the department. There is no departmental concern over how prospective instructors will do in graduate school, since most were top students at West Point or elsewhere. Colonel Olvey explained: "We are overwhelmed with an abundance of riches. There are far more very talented people from West Point who want to come to teach for us than we can take. So we can afford to be very selective. Not only do they have very impressive academic credentials, but they also have very impressive military credentials. We consciously pick them on that basis." Colonel Olvey is not inclined to exaggeration; his department is stocked with water walkers. As a tactical officer said of them, "Some of those guys could breeze right by Jesus Christ like he was in a rowboat and they had hydroplanes for shoes." Olvey is reluctant to publicize the superior credentials of his instructors because he is well aware that many faculty members resent the department's status among prospective instructors and throughout the Army. But when pressed, he acknowledged: "Of the group in the department who had the opportunity for an early promotion, over 40 per cent received it. This was on the basis of what they did before they came to the department and that puts those guys in the top 5 per cent among their contemporaries. . . . They've all been taken on the basis of a pretty intensive search, interviews, and personal knowledge of myself or other officers who have been in the department. So they are an extremely select group." [24]

For most other departments, to greater or lesser degrees, the chore is to get the people they need on line and into a graduate school and out within eighteen months to two years with a master's degree in hand. And in many cases special arrangements exist at selected graduate schools where fellow Army officers and sympathetic professors assist the new student in selecting his program of study and in his initial adjustment. Frequently the problem is simply getting the man into a respectable graduate program. Colonel Gil Kirby argued: "My criteria are whether or not a guy would make a good instructor. I get a lot of flack on this from my colleagues, but I think they are wrong. Some departments won't take 'em unless they stood very high in their class and others like them to have had high cadet rank, which I think is ludicrous. We don't look at either one of these things." Kirby's detractors contend he is "just blowing smoke" to cover a lower level of officer interest in his department; but he is not deterred. If former cadets have high ratings as potential instructors, Kirby then checks to see "whether or not they are too low in the class for me to negotiate them into a school." In fact, this is the plight and subsequent procedure for many department heads, but few are as outspoken about it as Kirby. If Kirby is called upon to negotiate, as he frequently is, he banks on the fact that previous West Pointers with marginal qualifications have succeeded. As Kirby described the scenario: "I talk to the schools and I tell 'em, 'Say, look Glotz, I've got a guy who stands a little low but I'd like him to come, how 'bout taking him?' And they take them and they invariably do well." [25]

By most accounts prospective West Point instructors, especially those who are graduates, do well in various types of graduate programs throughout the country. Perhaps the major reason for their success is "attitude." Assistant Dean James Hall spoke of "how well prepared, in terms of attitude, they were for graduate study. They impressed, usually, their civilian professor at the graduate level in their attitude toward their work. They really jump in there without much dillydalling around. . . . you give a guy a master's thesis to do; and—*wham*! Boy, he's in there working at it. He's cranking that thing out. And, in general, in half the time that a lot of civilian students would take to do the same job." The source of this attitude, in Colonel Hall's view, is that "our graduates are so mission-oriented." A West Pointer "has this constant idea—give me a job; tell me what you want me to do and point me in the direction; and I'll get it done." One faculty member at West Point remembered overhearing a retired Caltech engineering professor say of West Pointers, "Yeah, I remember when I used to have those guys in class. You know, they weren't very smart, but they worked like hell." Such remarks are even more common from civilian professors who taught West Pointers in the humanities, especially in English, because until the early 1970's most graduates who completed English masters programs in strong departments such as those at Pennsylvania, Indiana, and Columbia had never taken advanced undergraduate courses in English. One former instructor summed up his graduate school survival and his West Point teaching in these terms: "I'm reminded of a little anecdote about Jayne Mansfield. She was playing the piano, playing very badly, but when questioned about it she said 'isn't it remarkable, given my circumstances, that I'm playing at all.' " [26]

While the remarkable industriousness of West Pointers is undeniable, they also have considerable advantages in graduate school. Perhaps the most substantial advantage is their discovery, as senior captains or junior majors, that their salaries and benefits as master's candidates usually exceed those of most professorial faculty who teach them. Another benefit is the prearranged communities into which many officers move. For instance, Colonel Dick reported that "We send most of our candidates for being instructors off to RPI [Rensselaer Polytechnic Institute] only because we have had an arrangement with them for years. . . . We've got an arrangement for housing, we've got the program all laid down, they know what we want, we know what they want and so forth. So administratively it is easier and they get a good education." The prospective instructor also knows that his future employment is dependent only on his ability to pass his course work, and this gives him an enormous psychological advantage over fellow students for whom marginal grades may well mean unemployment as teachers.[27]

These advantages do not appear to have encouraged West Pointers to coast in graduate school, even though by the mid-1970's many prospective instructors will have benefited from their participation in the modest electives program while they were cadets. The characteristic graduate school routine for West Pointers represents an attempt to impose a rigorous daily military schedule on the civilian environment. A 1965 graduate recalled: "Classmates whom I've talked to about graduate school frequently describe it as the experience of getting up in the morning and going to the university at 7:30, attending the required classes and then spending a good portion of the day in the library and returning home at the end of the day. Most of their free time is spent with people they have known in the Army and they continue to use the facilities of a local Army post." When prospective West Point instructors have serious problems in graduate school, they frequently turn out to be Regular Army, non-graduate officers. And their problems usually arise because they lost sight of what is called "the attack arrow." [28]

A 1958 graduate explained: "The West Pointer's graduate school approach is very easily identifiable. It's oriented toward the goal you have to achieve as opposed to learning as much as you might be able to learn. The attitude is—if 'x' reading is not important to achieving my immediate goal, I won't read it; and if 'y' reading is important to achieving my goal, I will read it. This is the approach taken. Follow the attack arrow and don't veer off course. And you know what? It works!" As a case in point, he cited a successful Army officer, a non-graduate, who "had a lot of trouble at [the University of] Massachusetts because he attempted to read the world. He reasoned, 'I'm an English student and I'm going to read the literatures of the world.' And it took a long time for our guys to squeeze him hard enough so that he'd follow the direction of the attack arrow." And so, in addition to being somewhat older, more mature, more financially and professionally secure than civilian graduate students, most officers *know* why they are in graduate school: they are there to get a degree. The degree is an end in itself, not necessarily a symbol of some deeper and more personal intellectual development. Career officers already have a clear sense of their own priorities. "You can bet your sweet ass that I knew what would happen to me if I didn't get that master's degree," explained one West Point instructor, "especially after [Uncle] Sam picked up the tab. My military career would have been over." Colonel Frederick Smith, head of the Department of Mechanics, also affirmed that "a West Pointer going to a university has a built-in whip. He can't go back to the Army and say he failed. Remember, if he is singled out for graduate school and he has stars in his eyes he is thinking about how it will get him ahead in his profession. There is a strong motivation there." In the same way that cadets learn to use the operational skills developed in plebe math to order their lives at West Point, so potential Academy instructors apply these same sure-fire skills, which have continued to prove extremely useful in the Army, during their two years in graduate school.[29]

Despite indignant claims to the contrary, most of American higher education is quite susceptible to this "attack arrow" approach. "One of the things that came to my rescue in graduate school," admitted one West Pointer, "was the hypertense organizational approach to assignments that I learned as a cadet—getting rid of what's not important and trying to figure out what is important. . . . And the P's I worked for at Columbia fell all over themselves saying that I had a really great approach. All of us at Columbia, that is all of us who were Army officers, felt very inadequate in that environment, and of course we were academically inadequate, but the ability to recognize what was essential for the degree got me off on a good footing." Although the organizational approach and the accompanying ability to break complicated tasks into tangible and more accomplishable jobs did not always produce the desired results in Vietnam (where body counts and "pacified" zones did not yield a series of unqualified successes), the problem-solving techniques that West Pointers begin to master in plebe math do work quite effectively when success or failure is determined by superiors.[30] And in graduate school, success is usually determined by a few civilian professors, who are often frustrated by the inability of their civilian students to establish priorities, meet deadlines and maintain steady work habits. The general success of West Pointers in graduate school, then, is not just the result of their ability to perform these workmanlike chores, or their considerable talent at pleasing superiors; both of those invaluable assets are direct consequences of a mission-oriented attitude that allows them to set aside ambiguous, value-laden questions that drain off intellectual energy and to concentrate their efforts on the most visible and tangible tasks at hand. An officer who described one of the underlying reasons for the Army's frustration in Vietnam was simultaneously describing the reason for West Pointers' success in graduate schools: "Their reflex is to accomplish the mission . . . and once you define their parameters and send them out they'll bust themselves trying to carry out the job they've been given. They do it because that is what they were sent there to do."[31]

ANSWERS AND RATIONALES

Perhaps the inclination to do the job given them also helps explain why most Army officers take up their West Point faculty assignment with high initial expectations. Despite the fact that for most graduate school was following the attack arrow, sticking close to Army people (or, for the water walkers, cultivating key civilians for future reference), these men frequently leave graduate school with a sense of themselves as young educators; not because they necessarily feel they have developed intellectually, but more because of their new master's degree and secondary MOS [Military Occupational Specialty], "West Point Instructor." They have been out in the civilian world ("earned their spurs in academe," as a senior Academic Board member expressed it), and in the best Army tradition they report to the Academy eager to accept the mantle of their civilian-endorsed expertise.[32]

In the West Pointer's world, the graduate school experience can represent a vicarious triumph over a secret terror—"could I hack it in civilian life?" Graduate school has been their first extended foray into the civilian world since high school, ten to fifteen years before. As graduate students they entered a more ambiguous world of infinite variables where relationships were not well defined and eccentricity was encouraged. Most officers are usually relieved to return to the orderliness of the Academy and to the more familiar life patterns of a military post, but they also bring enthusiasm and ambition to the task of demonstrating how well their civilian master's degrees have prepared them to teach academic subjects. For many officers this attitude is undermined by "new instructor meetings," which are held shortly after they report for faculty duty. In orientation periods in individual departments and in briefings from representatives of various Academy agencies, the new instructor learns what will be expected of him. A non-graduate careerist remembered this period as particularly jolting. When he reported to West

Point in the early 1970's, his most recent educational experience had been as a doctoral candidate at a prestigious university. He recalled the culture shock:

> When I came to West Point we had an orientation program for the new faculty. We had a briefing one day from a man from MP and L [Office of Military Psychology and Leadership]. And the briefing was to tell us what cadets were like and what we could expect from cadets in the classroom. And he said, "Be firm in the classroom because cadets expect you to be firm in the classroom. Cadets expect you to know what you are doing in the classroom. They will be very uncomfortable if you don't have the answers. And you are up there because you *do* have the answers." And I asked "What if cadets ask questions to which there are no answers?" He did not answer the question but he said, "Then they will wonder, if you do not have the answers, what you are doing up there. Because you are not suppose to be up there unless you *do* have the answers. And they will wonder why you are up there, if you are not qualified to be up there." [33]

As officers soon discover (for graduates it is a rediscovery), such instructor guidance is readily comprehensible when one comes to appreciate that the classroom is, in many respects, intended to function as a military training ground. The willingness to entertain unorthodox ideas, the ability to engage students in a dialogue—difficult when most cadet comments must be concluded with the word *Sir*—and, most important, the commitment to an inheretly critical mentality are all at odds with what most officers associate with soldierly characteristics. Major Francis Conrad, a psychiatrist at West Point, described the typical Academy officer as "a guy of absolute conviction, who, almost without question, accepts a certain way of life that requires that he be masculine, dominant, certain. He expects immediate obedience to his values. He tolerates criticism, but not the critical attitude. He is a serious person." [34] Of course, not all West Point faculty members fit this description, but most successful career officers come rather close because success in the Army usually requires that one possess such characteristics. And the Academy's preference for instructors who have outstanding military records ensures that the martial virtues will be well represented in the classroom. Commandant Philip Feir exhibited the certainty and absolute conviction associated with successful soldiers while reiterating the essentially non-academic functions he expected West Point instructors to perform. Feir emphasized that he "taught Electricity here in the early sixties and here I am as com[mandant]. So I know exactly what goes on over on the other side of the street. And I know precisely what goes on here as well." Armed with his certitude, Feir's counsel to incoming faculty is unflinching:

> I point out to them that it's important for them to understand what those standards are which we are setting here in the Department of Tactics for cadets. Once having found out what those standards are, it's important that they give full support to seeing to it that cadets measure up to those standards because after all a cadet spends a lot more time on an average day with an academic instructor than he does with a member of the Tactical Department . . . .
>
> Now I'm not asking academic instructors, obviously, to have a quill pad in their hands constantly and to be writing cadets up. That's not the point, because I fully recognize that that could destroy, or at least disturb, the rapport that has to exist between instructor and student in order for knowledge to pass in an efficient way. I never had any difficulty with that personally, as an instructor, but I know that many do and I respect that.
>
> But, on the other hand, I don't think that that kind of rapport is in danger by virtue of on the spot correction. I think that academic instructors should insist that cadets should come over there wearing trousers that are reputable and that they come over there with their shoes shined properly and that they come over there with their hair cut to standard and they they come over there shaved properly . . . and that their belt buckles are polished and all those other things which I see as the basic soldierly qualities and which, as a matter of fact, are expected of privates in the back rank out in the Army. I just don't think that's too much to ask. I don't think that academic in-

> structors should put up with cadets falling asleep in classes and I know they do. I never did. I just told them to, "Get the hell out." And sometimes report to his tac and sometimes not. But in any case, the cadet got a zero for the day. Because I just believed that it was his responsibility to stay in there, to listen, and to learn.[35]

The most remarkable feature of General Feir's articulation of policy is its candor. Feir's successor is not likely to be as straightforward, because the pressures on the Academy to present itself as a first-rate academic institution as opposed to a military school will increase throughout the 1970's. It is especially ironic that Feir's reign can be represented in Academy publications as uniquely progressive—he was the architect of major revisions in cadet regulations. But the central fact of cadet life is that they are still governed; the socializing intent of that process has not been substantially altered. It was clear that Colonel R. L. Gruenther, head of the Office of Military Instruction, was reinforcing Commandant Feir's sentiments when he observed that every faculty member should constantly ask himself "how does what I am doing impact on the goal of producing people who know how to make guys fight wars?" [36]

Although most officers do not ask themselves that question each time they enter the classroom, they usually do inspect their own shoes, brass, and haircuts to assure themselves of their own propriety. Since most teach only one course, but teach it to four different sections (two on one day and two more repetitions of the same material on the next day), instructors have a fairly good idea of what to expect in the classroom by the time they teach the fourth section. Before they teach most instructors have read the material assigned for that class and perhaps attended a meeting of all instructors, called a lesson conference, in which the course director in charge of the instructors and responsible for the course reviews the main teaching points, suggests questions to ask the cadets, forecasts likely cadet questions, and establishes administrative procedures for all the sections. These lesson conferences tend to be run like military staff meetings; the designated senior officer, regardless of his academic competence, is in command. One of the instructors is frequently ordered to do background reading in the subject to be taught that day and to provide relevant information to his fellow instructors. He might give a half-hour briefing on the use of imagery in Ralph Ellison's *Invisible Man*, the mathematical theory necessary to understand certain fiscal and monetary policies, or the psychological models underlying different types of military leadership.

There are few direct constraints imposed on a new instructor once he leaves the lesson conference and enters the classroom. "You can go in there and spout Lenin or talk about Army's linebackers or follow the guidance of the course director and pass out the poop," said one former instructor, "as long as you get your cadets ready for WPR's [Written Partial Reviews] and exams." Although there are few regular checks on an instructor's classroom behavior, new instructors soon discover that the cadets expect teachers to dispense information rather than to ask open-ended questions. "One of the reasons why cadets expect you to have all the answers," explained one instructor, "is because they tend not to ask questions for which there isn't an answer." In fact, the new instructors who might experience frustration at the limited range of cadet questions and thoughts are a distinct minority, since most instructors have only a limited interest in and knowledge of the subjects they teach and little desire to go beyond the required dispersal of "testable information." [37]

Still, some new instructors—it is difficult to know how many—were genuinely fascinated by their academic courses in graduate school and wish to communicate that excitement to their classes. The intellectual indifference of most cadets hits them hard and the departmental priorities that get in the way of inspired teaching are often the fatal blow to their aspirations. For example, it quickly becomes clear to new instructors in the English Department that the correction of cadet essays *must* follow a departmental guideline that places heavy emphasis on essentially mechanical skills. One learns, in the words of a former English Department officer, "to determine what the departmental priorities are. And if it is terribly important for you to catch all of the spelling and comma errors on a theme, then you set out to do that better than anyone else in the department. And whatever time you have left over after accomplishing these, or other departmental priorities, you can use to pursue what you think is important." [38]

A junior major in the department puzzled over this dilemma: "People don't come to the English Department anxious to emphasize the comma and the spelling. And the fact they end up having to emphasize such matters along with format and a very arbitrary theme organization is a fundamental tragedy of the English Department. And perhaps all departments at the Academy. People come enthusiastic about teaching cadets. They come enthusiastic about exploring their particular subject matter and they are not permitted to do it because they must put themselves in a specific mode of working. . . . You can structure things and still give people freedom of choice. To say that you lose all sense of structure when you give people freedom of choice is just not true." The frustration in this officer's words is commonplace among first-year instructors at the Academy. They soon discover that their departmental status as new instructors means that they are as much candidates for instruction as the cadets. They are constantly cautioned, "Remember, you haven't been through this block before." The pressure is constantly "to learn how we do it around here." And in the experience of many instructors the emphasis is not so much on the subject one teaches, but on the complex testing policies, the departmental SOP (Standard Operating Procedure), the way the department works as an efficient academic-military unit.[39]

There is no need for instructors to immerse themselves in their supposed field of academic competence. Like cadets, they are expected to regard knowledge as information or "facts." One goes over the assignment, factors out the unimportant (non-testable) facts and dispenses the remainder to one's classes, draws up exams to test cadets' retention, grades the exams, and calculates the scores to produce an "order of merit." Classes are usually resectioned in accord with the order of merit and the process begins anew. Since an instructor's interest in his subject plays no essential role in this pedagogic routine, Academy officials expect him to be bored or "burned out" within three years. As the head of the Math Department put it, "In the first year they are in the learning stages of being an instructor. While I don't think there is any question about their ability to put the material across, it's a question of their ability to carry a class on to a certain extent. The second year they are here they have improved on that and the third it's the maximum and they are gone. I think that sometimes when we keep the chaps for a fourth year they get a little stale. Now we keep them a fourth year in many cases because they have to then become a course director. It is the working with the program rather than the teaching of it that is important for a fourth-year man. And that is where they contribute rather than in their enthusiasm for teaching." [40]

Perhaps the most striking fact about this account of the instructor tour at West Point is how drastically the basic rationale differs from that of civilian schools. There it is assumed that three or more years may be required before a young teacher develops satisfactory control of his subject and confidence in his classroom ability; in the Academy's view an instructor's experience after his third year has reached the point of diminishing returns. Most of the officers at West Point do not regard the Academy's attitude toward faculty tenure as unusual or deviant, because they do not think of themselves as uniformed civilian academicians. They are soldiers serving a tour at a military post that also happens to be a school. They expect to move into and out of Army assignments every two or three years. They accept the Army policy that requires officers to be reassigned soon after they have mastered the job at one duty station. And West Point officials are reluctant to admit that the academic proficiency necessary to teach college-level courses is qualitatively different and takes longer to develop than the kind of skill an officer must master when he assumes command of a battalion. Much of the emphasis on organizational considerations and departmental procedures, in fact, performs the useful function of shielding Academy instructors from an awareness of their academic limitations. Teachers who do not have to grapple with their academic inadequacies complain about the bureaucratic horrors of their respective departments without realizing that their own pedagogic and scholarly inexperience, as much as these administrative horrors, prohibit competent college-level teaching. Like the cadets, the Academy faculty members are protected from damaging insights by the very institutional practices they decry. Life as a faculty member at West Point, like life on most Army posts and in most corporate or governmental bureaucracies, assumes the form of a daily grind. The innumerable petty details of the regular routine deflate soaring ambitions just as they discourage self-scrutiny. In-house complaints about the absurdity of what is called daily administrivia are considered therapeutic as long as "you don't make a big thing of it on the outside."

In such a context the energetic new instructor, especially if he is a West Point graduate, may experience an acute sense of *déjà vu*. Like his vision when he came to West Point to get a college education, his vision when he goes back as a teacher is based on false, and he may shamefully admit, foolish, hopes. "Very little has changed since I was a cadet," acknowledged an associate professor, "and I think instructors coming back to the Academy realize that things are essentially the same." Thus, an instructor with a master's degree from Harvard may be back where he was as an advanced placement cadet from St. Mark's School. His job is to do what he is told. His life, while hectic, will again be organized in discernible increments. The Academy experience becomes once again an obstacle course with the instructor's lesson blocks as his current obstacles. And the lesson blocks, as a former instructor recalled, are composed of smaller blocks or lessons that the cadet will negotiate in preparation for his career, eventual graduate school, and perhaps future faculty status: "The History Department tends to teach that understanding the French Revolution involves breaking it down 'as a social problem' which can be covered in 'the French Revolution lesson block' in, say, five lessons. For these five lessons the instructor has to affect expertise in 'the way it happened.' The implication is that you can break it down into a number of component parts in the same way that a M-16 rifle can be broken down. You study each part, and then having understood each part you put it back together again and you understand the problem. Then you move on to new and different problems in the next lesson block." [41]

Most candid faculty members would not quarrel with this assessment. But the same officers would insist that critics of the academic atmosphere at West Point, like critics of the military in general, "don't have the big picture. They don't understand the constraints we have to work in." One West Pointer explained how the mechanistic, incremental approach to teaching and to one's faculty duties is simply a sensible response to the way things are at the Academy:

> When each department briefs its instructors in the fall, it takes great pains to point out that the student doesn't have three hours a night to do your subject. Please remember this. Please don't take the position that he can go home and read Carlyle. How are the instructors going to react? They are going to react by saying, "What we have got to do, since this guy is so overloaded and has so many things to do and such a short amount of time in which to do them, is to present him with prepackaged, little increments of learning which can be digested periodically. And in the end, hopefully, they will be assimilated so that he can see the whole from the parts we have been giving him." And the new instructors soon see that an incremental approach like this is the only practical one to use.
>
> So there is a bias. The bias is probably analytical; it says that things have to be broken down. And when you do things like that it tends to simplify them. And the cadet tends to look at them and say, "Yeah, that makes sense, that incremental part of the whole is some-

> thing I can certainly come to grips with on Tuesday." And on Wednesday he moves to the next part and the first thing you know he feels he's a master of the entire discipline because he has mastered component parts on Monday through Friday.

The officer warned, however, that "this tends to suggest that cadets are mechanistic and positivistic; in fact many of them are not. . . . A couple of years after graduation a man who has had experience realizes that problems are not handed out incrementally." And, the officer added ruefully, "He loses his head of steam and his sense of order in the world begins to disintegrate." But the difficulty for a military man is that, having mastered the ability of appearing to be on top of the problem, he is very reluctant to set his legerdemain skills aside and admit he doesn't understand the problem.[42]

While the officer's account of the way things are is transparently sensible, it is also reminiscent of *Catch-22.* Certainly it is accurate to recognize that the daily cadet schedule rules out the possibility of extended study or contemplation and that West Point instructors shape their teaching to fit that academic reality. And from there it is but a short step to the recognition that West Point graduates, who also endured the inexorable pressures of cadet life, are best equipped to understand and cope with cadets in the classroom. It then also follows that fully developed academic competence is unnecessary for Academy instructors, since cadets would not have the time or inclination to assimilate undiluted classroom presentations even if they were available. However, there is a circularity to all these deeply entrenched rationales which is similar to the claims made by some Academic Board members that they would like to hire more "non-graduates" for the faculty—only they do not happen to know many. Underlying such rationales are two crucial, but usually unstated, assumptions: first, that West Point's academic and military goals are inherently compatible; second, that any conflict between academic and military priorities at West Point must never be resolved in a way that compromises the military mission of the Academy. What frequently goes unnoticed at West Point (it is unnoticed, not willfully concealed) is the extent to which these assumptions undercut the academic integrity of the faculty and the institution.

ADMINISTRIVIA AND EVALUATIONS

Within some departments it is fashionable to deride the academic quality of the West Point instruction, to sneer at the engineering approach to learning, to talk about "getting out and working toward my Ph.D. so I can teach at a place where people appreciate ideas." But even in those few cases in which such talk is more than rhetoric, there is little chance that officers will translate their words into action. Most West Point instructors have wives, children, better incomes than the average college or university professor, and eight to ten years before they are eligible for retirement. In June 1972 the *New York Times* reported that a large number of Academy faculty were resigning en masse, an indication that West Point and the Army were losing some of their brightest and best officers. Although Academy officials were upset at the unfavorable publicity, they realized that the story misrepresented the faculty situation. They knew that most West Point instructors were, in the words of one officer, "locked into a pretty good deal. They aren't going to throw all that over for a garret in graduate school and, if they're lucky, a low paying job at some junior college." At some point during their West Point tour the vast majority of officers, even those who come to West Point with intellectual pretensions and who develop a caustic attitude toward the intrusiveness of military requirements, recognize that they will soon be going back to "the real Army." Their future military careers, they know, depend on their ability to impress those superior officers who write the annual officer efficiency reports. And this recognition rekindles their interest in departmental duties for which they sincerely claimed to have contempt.[43]

The watchword in most departments, which few Army officers

need to be reminded of, is administration. "The single most obvious way a West Point faculty member can come to grief is to screw up on administrative responsibility," reported a former faculty member. "If you do foul up on an administrative matter, it comes to the attention of the tenured faculty member who is writing your efficiency report. He is an administrator and he is concerned with administration. And his job goes smoothly or poorly depending on how well the administration is done." Although quite aware of the limitations of such a focus, the officer added, "I am all for good administration because a great deal depends on it." But, he cautioned "in most academic departments it has gotten way out of hand." [44] In short, form and procedure frequently take precedence over academic substance.

Instructors are required to spend a good portion of each day on essentially administrative matters. For many of them very little of their duty time is spent in the classroom or on the subject matter they are ostensibly there to teach. An average day in a department with afternoon classes involves reporting for duty by 8:30 a.m., attending a lesson conference for a discussion of the recommended methods, presenting the day's lesson, then taking care of the daily administrivia. By mid-morning an officer has probably had a couple of cups of coffee, read the daily departmental and Academy information memos in his in-box, and spoken at least a greeting to the other ten to twenty officers who share his office. (Most officers work out of large rooms where individual desks are separated by four- or five-foot-high partitions, with the supervising officer occupying a desk at the head of the room.) At 10:30 or so many officers go to the gym for a workout before their noon lunch at the Officers' Club. Their two sixty-minute classes are normally taught back to back at 1:05 and 2:15 and the rest of the day might be spent talking to a deficient cadet in a small counseling cubicle, filing the appropriate report on the session, grading cadet papers, or processing the paperwork which is an inevitable part of West Point classes.

The relentless routine of such typical days with their departmentally imposed patterns of uniformity is the principal source of instructor indignation and disenchantment at West Point. In most departments officers work under the "unwritten requirement" that they be in "their office" if not at the gym or the club for lunch. Some departments even have sign-out boards and expect officers to indicate their whereabouts during duty hours, even if they are only going to the latrine. A typical ploy in dealing with officer frustrations over such practices is cited by a junior officer:

> One of the things that struck me when I came in here was the fact that if anything was wrong you blamed it on the Dean and the Academic Board. I came in here with ideas about things which I thought ought to be different and we had the "New Guys' School" where we sat around for hours and talked about how to fill out grade books and things like that. And I kept saying, "Why do we do this?" And they said, "Well, the department doesn't like it, but the dean's office requires it that way."
>
> And finally we had a chance to go in and talk to the associate head about these things, and everybody was going to go in, but I was the only one who stuck with it. And his response was, "Well there's nothing the boss can do, it's beyond our powers, it's the Academic Board." And I have not yet had a satisfactory answer as to why a bunch of people who don't know a goddamn thing about our subject can tell the colonel how to run his department. There is a lot of collective responsibility, in the good old Soviet sense of the word here at the Military Academy, which really limits innovation, just as it does in the Soviet system. A real unwillingness to take responsibility and say, "Look, I've got a Ph.D. and I've been working my ass off in this field for fifteen or twenty or thirty years or whatever. So you run your department and I'll run mine." [45]

Few officers who retain any hope for an Army career would confront their departmental superiors so directly. Like most bureaucracies, West Point's academic departments could not operate efficiently if the obvious inadequacies and inconsistencies of the organization were constantly subjected to scrutiny. There is an unspoken recognition of this fact of bureaucratic life in all Academy departments, even those regarded by insiders as conspicuously, if not excessively, committed to a muted version of academic freedom. Frustrated instructors have a keen sense of their powerlessness and are usually able to persuade themselves that they are "keeping their powder dry" in order to maintain their credibility for future and more crucial confrontations, which seldom materialize. More realistic instructors recognize that the department heads and tenured professors to whom they might complain are not scholars who have been working in some academic speciality for decades. They are career soldiers who are most sensitive to the need for team players and most wary of boat-rockers. A close observer of this mentality who has had two academic tours at West Point remarked matter-of-factly: "The people at the Academy in positions of power and authority are by definition in management positions. Consequently, they want to manage people who are manageable. They are not able to manage people who are really competent scholars. The really competent scholars are a source of anxiety because the managers don't understand them. And, if they had one [scholar] around all the time, they would be afraid to talk to him because they don't trust their own academic abilities, and with good reason." [46] A former reserve officer who taught at West Point in the early 1970's and who emphasized, "I very much enjoyed my tour," said of the permanent faculty in the humanities:

> Almost none of them appear to read books. They may read the *Times* reviews and other superficial sources in order to have an apparent currency in their field; but, if you stay around them, you soon discover that their level of currency is strictly on the surface. The point is that those guys, because of the nature of their jobs and the constraints of time, are not really able to do much reading. At a civilian university, a faculty member knows that if he takes an administrative position, serious reading in his field is almost impossible. This becomes more ironic at West Point because Army people believe in a concept which to many civilians would be perfectly incredible. They feel that when someone goes to graduate school and gets a Ph.D. he thereby reaches a level of "expertise" which he will

> then have for all time. When these people come into the department, they are regarded as "resident experts."
>
> Many of the brighter academics at West Point genuinely believe that the very presence of Ph.D. faculty members creates a situation in which they are providing "great input" to the temporary instructors because of their alledgedly "expert" level. But what these permanent faculty members are really doing is overseeing the work of temporary faculty members. This is almost exclusively an administrative job. And since they write the efficiency reports of the temporary faculty, there is little relaxed and candid communication between the junior officers and those who are writing their efficiency reports.[47]

The tenured members of a department, who are the raters for instructors' efficiency reports, spend only a fraction of their time teaching courses. "They are all-consumed with administrative tasks," admitted one officer. "We don't really have tenured teachers at the Academy. We have tenured administrators." Whether or not an officer will have a career (and in a period of reduction in force the question is posed this starkly) depends on how well he has impressed his tenured superiors. Although the selection of tenured faculty is inevitably accompanied by a good deal of bureaucratic beard-pulling, the criteria for selection are essentially administrative. The ideal choice for an associate professorship, for example, is an officer senior in rank to the instructors he must command, a man of proven organizational ability who is not sufficiently gifted to usurp the power of the deputy head, who is heir apparent. When such men sit down to write the efficiency reports of their instructors, they naturally look most closely at the instructor's ability to administer efficiently. Not only are they most comfortable evaluating the kind of abilities they themselves know best, but they are skeptical of instructors who consider academic competence more important than more practical and team-oriented virtues. "If a great chemistry teacher comes to the Military Academy," argued one tenured officer, "and teaches better than anyone else, you would expect, just on the face of it, that the man would receive a maximum efficiency report. But efficiency reports are also marks of one's potential as an Army officer. When you mark an efficiency report for a West Point faculty member, you're concerned with the kind of Army officer you think he is. So he may be a hell of a chemistry teacher and still get a poor efficiency report if you have reservations about what kind of Army officer he would be outside of a chemistry lab." Like cadets, the instructors at West Point expect, in some cases even need, to receive regular evaluations of their work. But the institutional schizophrenia that influences so many parts of Academy life also affects dutiful soldiers who insist on trying to become scholars as well. They feel torn between their dual goals and, eager to succeed in both roles, become confused about what is expected of them. "It is a source of many of the anxieties here," confessed one instructor. "People are uptight because they don't know how well they are doing." [48]

Chapter Six

★★★★★★★★★★★★★★★★★

DUTY AND HONOR

Encourage us in our endeavor to live above the common level of life. Make us to choose the harder right instead of the easier wrong, and never to be content with a half truth when the whole can be won.

From the "Cadet Prayer"

The old man had listed hundreds of the truths in his book. I will not try to tell you all of them. There was the truth of virginity and the truth of passion, the truth of wealth and of poverty, of thrift and of profligacy, of carelessness and abandon. Hundreds and hundreds were the truths and they were all beautiful.

Sherwood Anderson,
Winesburg, Ohio *(1919)*

★ ★ ★ ANY discussion of honor and the Honor System at West Point seems destined to proceed in two different directions at the same time: upward to metaphysics and downward into an abyss of legalistic jargon. Neither direction is satisfactory. On the one hand are generalizations devoid of specificity, the Academy officials sounding like Hegelian philosophers, the strings of abstract nouns that, at best, convey the sincere but amorphous official conviction that the West Point Honor Code embodies noble ideals. On the other hand are the details devoid of significance, the lawyers and cadet honor representatives sounding like theologians debating the infinitesimal differences between degrees of sin, the petty if not picayune facts that constitute the actual operation of the Honor System.[1] After all the oblique philosophical posturing and complex legalistic ruminations, many of the considerations which influence the meaning of honor in the daily lives of cadets and officers remain unexplored. Recent events associated with the lives of three graduates—George C. Patton, Samuel W. Koster, and James J. Pelosi—offer resonant dramatizations of both the theoretical and practical questions concealed by the rhetoric of West Point's motto—"Duty, Honor, Country."

QUESTIONS OF MORALITY AND MORALE

Patton: In the winter of 1970 the film *Patton* made a special appearance in Thayer Hall at the Military Academy. George C. Scott's performance in the title role had already attracted critical acclaim; south auditorium was filled with cadets and officers. The Patton they saw at the start of the film looked remarkably like the bronze statue of Patton the cadets passed by as they approached Thayer Hall—the eccentric Army general, wearing a polished helmet liner, a pair of ivory-handled revolvers, and a defiant expression that dared his listeners to challenge his audacious appearance. The opening scene, in which Scott's Patton stood on a stage in front of an enormous American flag and lectured the troops (and the theater audience) had a certain irony, since from this West Point audience might come America's future Pattons. The cadets yelled the loudest when Patton promised them: "We won't just shoot the sonabitches. We're going to cut out their living guts—and use them to grease the treads of our tanks." [2]

Scott, who was to win the Academy Award as best actor of the year for his performance, gave the audience a Patton of great power, but also a Patton afflicted with egomania, if not lunacy. He was an avid student of military history, but also a mystic who heard the sounds of past battles and saw the ghosts of dead Roman warriors. He was a hardened professional soldier, but also an officer whose uniform was a parody of regulations, whose tactics were unorthodox, and who publicized his desire for personal glory. He was, in other words, a romantic embodiment of several antithetical values. Above all, he was an ambiguous heroic character, a twentieth-century Sir Galahad who donned his combat gear like a knight preparing for a tournament. Near the end of the film he mounted a white stallion and wondered out loud if the automated wars of the future would allow room for military heroics.

This was not a question of interest to most cadets. They were absorbed in discussions of the film's authentic and accurate use of World War II equipment (i.e. the director did not make the usual mistake of using M-60 machine guns; he used the correct M-1919 A1). Other cadets spread the false rumor that Armor officers at West Point had scheduled the film just before first classmen made their branch selections, hoping to produce a massive rush to Armor, Patton's old branch. A counter-rumor insinuated that Infantry officers planned to retaliate with a special showing of *Sergeant York.* Other cadets discussed Patton's "goat" image at West Point (it took him five years to graduate) and the proposition that goats made better generals.

A small group of officers from the Social Sciences Department, intrigued by the film's depiction of Patton, gathered in the Officers' Club afterward and discussed the possibilities of a man like Patton making it in the Army of the 1970's. There was a consensus that a modern-day Patton would never advance beyond the rank of lieutenant colonel.[3] One officer argued that Patton was an anachronism even in World War II, a man who said the saddest day in his life was the day his Cavalry unit stacked its sabers and changed to tanks.[4] Patton was a throwback to pre-modern warfare, a vestige of the feudal era, the last surviving Crusader. Wars could no longer be international jousts; they would be either nuclear holocausts or limited, brushfire operations, neither of which permitted large armies to clash in dramatic battles with generals orchestrating grand strategy. Others recalled that Patton would go forward to the front lines in a jeep, then return to the rear by plane, so his troops could never see him retreating.

By acknowledging that Patton relied on modern conveniences to sustain his notion of chivalry, the West Pointers appeared to affirm that even in World War II the profession of arms was decades beyond its "aristocratic phase," when contestants paced-off like gentlemen at a dawn duel. Perhaps war had never been an honorable affair; and certainly in the nuclear era the chivalric myths appeared unsupportable. Nevertheless, many of the cadets in the 1970's were enamored with the Patton image and still believed that wars could be heroic conflicts between men of honor. This was a functional illusion, the officers contended, for it attracted young men into military service and even sustained them through difficult or unpleasant tours of duty. Eventually they would learn that soldiering was a job, a career, a profession. Soldiers did their job, they argued, and those who did it most efficiently got the best efficiency reports and promotions. Leadership was primarily a matter of precise calculation, expertise, and rational decision-making, and only incidentally a matter of "psyching up the troops with that 'follow me' shit." "We in the military are simply the bullet in the gun," is the way one colonel put it later, "and the gun is the whole American society and the trigger is pulled by the President and Congress. So *they fire us.* They decide what we are to hit. We don't worry about the target and we don't pretend we're heroes. . . . A high degree of professionalism means you don't question your target and you send the heroes to the rear." [5]

The group of officers did not address certain questions which seemed to follow naturally from their analysis of the differences between Patton and the modern military leader. If the Army officer was primarily a professional, paid to do his job well, how was he distinguishable from a mercenary? Had not a conviction about the honorable character of their cause given American soldiers of the past a rationale that justified actions which, without that conviction, were unjustifiable? Was the conviction that modern career soldiers were military managers, technicians of violence who eschewed Patton-like posturing in favor of cool, objective calculation, an adequate rationale for warriors? If military honor was dead, how were the cadets going to explain their jobs to themselves?

Koster: Other questions of honor were raised by events in March of 1970 when General Samuel Koster, superintendent of West Point, resigned his post because of alleged complicity in the cover-up of the My Lai massacre. A 1942 graduate and a strikingly handsome officer "in the Westmoreland mold," Koster later served as an Academy tactical officer until his tour was cut short by the Korean War. After directing the Eighth Army's guerrilla warfare effort against North Korea, he continued a distinguished career that eventually carried him to the command of the Americal Division in Vietnam and back to the prestige of the superintendency at West Point. Yet, when he stood in front of his quarters with his wife and returned salutes as the Corps of Cadets paraded by in a final review, he was the focal point for some of the most distressing moral questions raised by the Vietnam war.

Until 1970 the national debate over the war had barely breached

West Point's walls. Thousands of West Point graduates had served in Vietnam. Only a few graduates, such as Richard Steinke (class of 1962) and Louis Font (class of 1968), had refused orders to go to Vietnam.[6] Even at the height of the student movement none of the anti-war groups had selected West Point as a target for peace demonstrations. In 1969 about two hundred women from Vassar College entered the Academy grounds, handed daffodils and apples to cadets, and departed singing "America The Beautiful." One journalist reported that the cadets used their superior military knowledge and their proficiency in the argumentative method to humble the Vassar women in a debate on Vietnam.[7] As cadets remembered it, most of them insisted they wanted to make love, not war; but a football player hastened the exit of the women by devouring a handful of flowers offered as a token of friendship.[8]

The Koster departure was a more solemn occasion. After press releases had made it clear that he would be called to testify before the Peers Committee, which was investigating the killings at My Lai in 1968, Koster decided to announce his resignation. At the noon meal on March 17, he stepped onto the balcony overlooking the dining hall and addressed the Corps of Cadets:

> I have been informed by my superiors that action has been initiated against me in connection with my performance of duty in the Spring of 1968 while serving as commanding general, Americal Division, in Vietnam. I have therefore requested reassignment in order to separate the Military Academy and you of the Corps from the continuing flow of public announcements or any other connection with the alleged events which took place in Vietnam involving elements of my former command. . . . I wish to say that throughout my military career the cherished principles of our motto—DUTY, HONOR, COUNTRY—have served as a constant guide to me. I shall continue to follow these principles as long as I live. . . . Don't let the bastards grind you down.[9]

This last sentence had a special meaning to cadets. Koster was telling them that he was a hapless victim of circumstance, a loyal military professional trapped in a tangle of regulations. He was not guilty of war crimes, but he was going to accept responsibility in order to appease the press, the politicians, and the civilian bureaucrats (i.e. bastards) who demanded a high-ranking sacrifice. Since cadets so often see themselves as the victims of nefarious regulations against which they must fight a rear-guard action, most of them were particularly receptive to Koster's message. They gave him a standing ovation and later draped a banner in front of Washington Hall saying "Don't Let 'em Get You Down." "Everybody was caught up in the emotion of it," said one cadet. "Everybody seemed to sympathize with the general." [10] In describing this day, Thomas F. Fleming depicted the cadets as "so stirred that they leaped onto their chairs, cheering and clapping, and then, without waiting to be dismissed, rushed out of the mess hall to hold further demonstrations in support of their indicted commander." [11]

Yet some cadets claimed that their support for Koster was neither intended as approval of his role in the alleged cover-up of My Lai, nor as support for the officers who ordered the massacre of Vietnamese civilians, nor as support for the American involvement in Southeast Asia. The enthusiastic reaction of the Corps of Cadets, and the orderly parade in tribute to Koster, made most cadets appear to endorse all these propositions; and reporters interpreted the affair accordingly. Instead, many cadets explained that they sympathized with Koster because they understood that large military organizations were structured in such a way that the officer with over-all responsibility for the unit was not always aware of what junior officers were doing. Moral culpability and command responsibility, in other words, were often separated by layers of bureaucracy. The increasingly stratified structure of military organizations made moral judgments increasingly problematic. "The stories in the papers made us all sound like we supported war crimes," said one second classman. "All we were doing with Koster was saying that we understood what it was like to get caught in the bowels of the system." Although the discrepancy between Koster's purported sacrifice to the bureaucrats and the mass slaughter of scores of Vietnamese made Koster's unfortunate plight seem trivial by comparison, many cadets were acutely sensitive to the superintendent's dilemma and virtually numb to the moral questions raised by the massacre itself. "Such an outstanding career," sighed one cadet, "all ruined to appease the media." [12]

A handful of cadets questioned the propriety of the final parade in Koster's honor. "Everybody said that that procession past Koster's house was voluntary," explained a first classman. "Well, the cadet chain-of-command may have requested it, but you can be almost certain that they were ordered to request it." [13] Another recent graduate remembered that "there were some guys who said that Koster was charged with war crimes and that they were not going to pay him the honor of a final salute. But there was heavy pressure for everyone to march, mostly from cadet commanders. . . . Some guys marched, but didn't do the 'eyes right' thing." [14] "I asked myself why I had to violate my own conception of honor by marching past Quarters 100 [superintendent's house]," recalled another cadet, "and I decided it was because I didn't want to spend that spring walking punishment tours." [15]

Koster moved on to Fort Meade, where he was reduced one grade in rank, then to Aberdeen Proving Ground, where he conducted an unsuccessful campaign to salvage his reputation. He retired as a brigadier general in November of 1973 when the secretary of the Army and fellow West Pointer, Howard H. Callaway, rejected his appeal to retire as a major general. At West Point the issues that Koster symbolized lingered on in conversations and were revived again when the Watergate scandal posed similar moral problems in a civilian context.[16]

It was the perennial moral dilemma of the military man, which the unpopular war in Vietnam seemed to pose more acutely than at any time since the Civil War: how was a soldier to choose when, in terms of the West Point creed, duty and honor conflicted? If Koster knew that the emphasis on body counts encouraged hostile attitudes toward the Vietnamese civilian populace, should he have refused to obey the directives from his military and civilian superiors back in Washington? Should the cadets who opposed the parade in Koster's honor have refused to participate? Was not West Point a place for training young men who could be counted on to regard orders as moral imperatives (i.e. duty = honor)? If not, if officers and cadets were encouraged to regard themselves as autonomous moral agents always measuring their orders against some personal ethical standard, did not the entire chain-of-command break down? What happened to officers who expressed their disapproval of orders? Answers to that question had troublesome moral implications. "About the time my class began to make captain," one West Pointer remembered, "I think we started to come out of our naïve shell and we came to the realization that a lot of times, when we took a stand against what we thought to be injustice, we were also taking a stand against somebody who was a pretty powerful son-of-a-bitch. He didn't care about your ideals. He cared about his ol' fanny. And you re-trench very quickly when that happens." [17] "Can you tell your commander that you are filing a report that disagrees with his judgment?" asked one cadet rhetorically. "If you do, you may as well resign. Or spend twenty years as a captain." [18]

For many Americans, My Lai represented the futile and dishonorable character of the war in Vietnam, and General Samuel Koster epitomized the central role of the military, especially West Pointers, in the perpetuation and extension of the dishonor. And while at West Point there was much conversation about the Army's Vietnam blunders, there was also a widespread conviction that civilian agencies had made the critical policy decisions to involve the United States in Southeast Asia. "The Army is being set up to take the rap for something that it is only partially guilty of," said one major.[19] And the conviction that the military was being used as a scapegoat caused some West Pointers to reconsider the meaning of honor among soldiers. Was this not the time to band together and make loyalty to uniform the highest form of honor? Yet, in the view of some observers, such as Mary McCarthy, this banding together was already too prevalent. She believed that officers in the Americal Division, many of them West Pointers, "from General Koster on down acted like the three wise monkeys: see no evil, hear no evil, speak no evil." McCarthy contended, "they [Army officers] knew the score in Vietnam. It could not puzzle them to find civilian corpses lying around: sometimes the boys got rough. A smart commander did not criticize every little thing. When Ernie Medina [a non-graduate] saw some bodies, he did not stupidly start *thinking*. He promptly attributed them to gunships or maybe artillery fire—a military response as automatic as a kneejerk. . . ." [20]

The belief in the need for solidarity among soldiers, rather than any indifference toward My Lai, substantially contributed to the cadets' support of Koster. Yet such overarching sentiments could quickly result in the sanctioning of cover-ups like those with which Koster was charged. And the widely held cadet rationale that "the civilians got us into that mess and then wouldn't let us fight to win it" was frequently used to muffle criticism of the Army's performance in Vietnam. But if civilians were the principal engineers of our Vietnam policy, why had military men not banded together in order to oppose the nature and extent of American involvement in Vietnam? Why was it that, in this war, not one high-ranking West Pointer had resigned in opposition to allegedly civilian-imposed policies?

Pelosi: In September 1971 the Honor Committee at West Point ruled that Cadet James J. Pelosi was guilty of cheating in an electrical engineering class. Reports of the case, published over a year and a half later, indicated that Pelosi had been found "guilty of completing an answer on a quiz after the examiner had given the order to stop writing." Despite the apparently technical character of the violation—it seemed more a matter of tardiness than outright cheating—and although Pelosi "denied the charge and produced witnesses on his behalf," the Honor Committee determined that he was guilty of an honor violation.[21] The West Point Honor Code appeared to allow no room for mitigation—"A cadet will not lie, cheat or steal or tolerate those who do." [22] The twelve cadets who comprised the Honor Committee for Pelosi's case had decided that he had cheated. Since there was only one prescribed penalty, dismissal, Pelosi would have to leave the Academy.

But Pelosi did not leave. Instead, he elected to have a board of West Point officers hear his case and sought counsel from Captain David W. Hayes of the Law Department faculty. At the initial hearing in mid-October, Captain Hayes argued that the Honor Committee's findings should be invalidated. He contended that an officer in the commandant's office had attached a note to Pelosi's file (*before* it was sent to the Cadet Honor Committee in September) expressing his personal opinion that Pelosi was guilty. The president of the board then ruled "that this [unauthorized opinion] was beyond the scope of instructions issued to the board and it should be resolved by the Superintendent." General Knowlton subsequently decided that since the Honor Committee members who ruled on the Pelosi case had seen the officer's note, the case was prejudiced by improper "command influence." On November 3 he dismissed the board of officers and reinstated Pelosi as a member of the Corps of Cadets.[23]

But the superintendent's actions were not accepted by the Corps. Instead, the full forty-four-man Honor Committee convened and reaffirmed its judgment that Pelosi was guilty of cheating. Since Pelosi refused to resign, and since the board of officers was unable to dismiss him, the Honor Committee voted to "silence" Pelosi. A referendum of the entire Corps of Cadets supported this decision, which required that Pelosi live and eat alone and that all cadets converse with him only in the course of official duties.[24]

Pelosi endured the ostracism until his graduation nineteen

months later. His diary, portions of which were published in the *New York Times*, recorded some of the abuse he received from the Corps of Cadets:

> Friday, 10 December/1971/: I inspected my gym locker as part of my preparation for the next day's inspection. All my articles of clothing had been thrown in the shower, soaked and then dragged around the floor of the latrine.
>
> 5–7 May/1972/: Ring Weekend for the class of 1973. On Saturday, 6 May I received a telephone call in the F-1 orderly room. The unidentified caller said, "Pelosi, we're going to get your ring if we have to cut off your finger to get it." On Monday evening, 8 May I received another phone call. The caller said, "Pelosi, you wear that ring and you're dead."

But he stuck it out and graduated with his class. "When you're right," he told a reporter for the *New York Times*, "you have to prove yourself." [25]

By mid-June 1973, newspapers and national magazines had taken up Pelosi's cause.[26] He became a symbol of what many felt was the injustice and inhumanity of the West Point Honor System. Even the *Army Times* expressed outrage in an editorial entitled "Chicken Cadets":

> We've always (well, almost always) contended that there is no such animal as "the military mind" in the sense that it compulsively ignores principles of justice and humanity whenever they get in the way of military expediency. . . . But our beliefs on that score were set back grievously in the case of Cadet James J. Pelosi. . . . he was forced, in effect to live in isolation at the Academy. Why the superintendent, during this period, did not reassert *his* authority in the matter is a mystery to us. The fact remains that Pelosi had the guts to endure the hassle and get himself graduated. As for us, we are beginning to suspect that there is such a thing as a "military mind" and that its breeding starts early at USMA.[27]

As the adverse publicity about West Point continued, Pelosi received offers from publishers, film producers, and talk-show hosts.[28] During this same time six cadets convicted of cheating on a physics exam appealed their case to a federal court, arguing that the procedures of the Honor System had deprived them of their constitutional right to due process. The notoriety created by the Pelosi case had helped to inspire them to challenge the legality of the entire West Point Honor System.[29]

The implications of the Pelosi case were expanding far beyond the question of the apparent injustice done to one cadet. But Pelosi's guilt or innocence was the one issue cadets were most eager to discuss. "I am convinced that he did what the Honor Committee said he did," one cadet insisted, "and that's not what the *New York Times* said he did." Academy officials had only minimal official comment and expressed private concern over "the avalanche of bad publicity generated by Pelosi." [30]

The Academy's official silence was particularly puzzling because inquiries among members of the Honor Committee revealed that Pelosi's case had been somewhat misrepresented in the press. The charges against him involved more than the failure to obey the command to cease work at the end of a test. He was accused of changing his answers on a self-graded quiz after the approved solutions had been posted on the board. One cadet witness, as well as the class instructor, testified that they had seen him commit the offense. The evidence and testimony seemed to confirm the decision of the Honor Committee that Pelosi was guilty of cheating. Since public sympathy for Pelosi's nineteen-month ordeal depended in part on the belief that he was innocent of any wrong-doing, his heroic image had, at best, a shaky foundation.[31]

Yet the more one probed beneath the surface of the Pelosi case, the more serious the questions about the West Point Honor System became. The public outcry against the harassment of Pelosi caused officers and cadets to re-examine the wisdom of silencing. When the cadets returned to classes the following September, there was a good deal of pressure exerted on the cadet honor representatives to consider abolition of the silence. In September 1973 the chairman of the Honor Committee announced that a referendum of all cadets had indicated widespread disapproval of the policy. Future silencing would no longer be sanctioned by the Honor Committee.[32] But Academy officials were still concerned about the legal questions that the Pelosi case and other cases raised: most important, were the deliberations of the Honor Committee subject to the rules of due process that governed regular judicial proceedings?

If the "civilian concepts of due process" were applicable, most seniors officers at West Point agreed with Colonel Olvey of the Social Sciences Department: "I frankly don't see how we are going to comply and yet maintain the [honor] system in its traditional form." [33] And yet the Academy's official position seemed simply an abdication of responsibility. The operation of the Honor Committee was entirely a cadet affair, they insisted. Therefore, Academy officials could do nothing about the absence of constitutional guarantees in an honor trial (i.e. the right to confront one's accuser, the right to cross-examine witnesses, the right to remain silent). And the officers' review board was always there, Academy officials explained, to review Honor Committee decisions and right the wrongs done a particular cadet defendant. That, of course, was precisely what the officers' board had tried to do with Pelosi. And his fate continued to attract national interest. Even though the Corps of Cadets abolished the practice of silencing, reports in the *Army Times* and elsewhere revealed that Lieutenant Pelosi, who was attending the Infantry Officer Basic School at Fort Benning in the fall of 1973, was still being shunned by many of his one hundred and fifty West Point classmates also enrolled in the school.[34]

As if in proud defiance of the continuing uproar over Pelosi, many officers and cadets argued that the Honor System was above the law and not susceptible to lawyerly nit-picking. "We are trying to instill standards here which are higher than national standards," claimed a graduate, "and we ought to be doing that, because military leaders need to have a higher sense of honor. But how can we maintain the honor of the Corps if legal loopholes allow guilty cadets to go free?" [35] Several members of the Academic Board expressed similar opinions, adding that the emphasis on a defendant's rights were part of an "era of permissiveness" that the Academy would have to endure.[36] All of which raised the question in one young officer's mind whether "the Military Academy might be encouraging cadets to develop contempt for the Constitution they were pledged to serve." [37]

Finally, and most ironically, the initial silencing of Pelosi had a very limited effectiveness, because a considerable number of cadets (perhaps as many as 30 per cent of the Corps) openly approved of his "victory over the system." Although their approval ebbed considerably when Pelosi became the subject of national attention and the cause of widespread civilian ridicule of the Corps of Cadets, the fact that a sizable minority of the Corps initially welcomed Pelosi's legalistic triumph suggested that many cadets had come to regard the Honor System as just another one of the various regulatory agencies designed to constrain their freedom. "The Honor Code has become something other than a set of ethical standards," one cadet explained unhappily. "It has become part of a system you are trying to outsmart and outmaneuver." [38] Pelosi benefitted from this growing hostility toward the Honor System and its enforcers, the members of the Honor Committee. "For a while, he became a folk hero in the Corps," recalled one recent graduate. "It was regarded as a certain amount of status to be seen with the guy." [39]

There is no doubt that Pelosi's silence at West Point was partially effective; many cadets refused to recognize Pelosi's existence and others took advantage of his predicament to harass him.[40] Still, Pelosi's ability to survive for nineteen months becomes more comprehensible when one learns he had a rooting section in the Corps.[41] It is also clear that the bulk of the pro-Pelosi faction was not registering support for legal guarantees of due process; most of them were congratulating Pelosi for beating the system.

DUTY-BOUND

Neither official nor self-appointed spokesmen for West Point provide answers to the difficult questions about honor among soldiers and cadets. They do insist, quite convincingly, that the Military Academy takes questions of honor seriously. In fact, several members of the Academic Board contended that the inculcation of high standards of honor is West Point's primary mission. Most academic courses at West Point are very general, if not superficial, they admitted; but cadets catch up with their civilian peers in graduate school. And the military training is likewise only the beginning of professional schooling which for many will include an initial Army branch school, Ranger School, a career course in a branch school, the Command and General Staff College and the Army War College.

But honor was different. If cadets left West Point without it, they were not going to pick it up later on. One tenured professor speculated that many of his colleagues would resign their positions if the federal courts ever forced the Academy to alter the Honor System in its traditional form.[42] "It's the critical system around here," contended General Feir, "the critical code. It's the thing that sets this place apart from other schools, in my opinion. I feel so strongly about it that, if we lost it, I'd just as soon accept officers into the Army from ROTC or OCS and forget about this place. It's that critical." [43]

Distinguished Academy graduates have articulated the reasons why they believe that West Point is an essential moral training ground. In his autobiography, for example, General Maxwell D. Taylor cited former Secretary of War Newton D. Baker's observation that "men may be inexact or even untruthful, in ordinary matters, . . . but the inexact or untruthful soldier trifles with the lives of his fellowmen, and the honor of his government; and it is, therefore, no matter of idle pride but rather of stern disciplinary necessity that makes West Point require of her students a character for trustworthiness that knows no evasion." [44] All incoming plebes receive sixteen hours of instruction on the Honor System in which this point is hammered home:

> The tale is told of an officer who was responsible for reconnaissance of a specific area. When asked by his Regimental Commander about the area, the officer reported that enemy strength there was slight, although in fact he had made no reconnaissance at all. The Regimental Commander then committed a battalion of men into the area. Because enemy strength in the area was much greater than indicated by the false reconnaissance report, the entire battalion, three companies and the battalion headquarters, was lost. [45]

Most West Pointers believe that the Academy, more than any other institution, has over the years provided officers with a uniquely high code of honor; they are the men who set and maintain standards of honor for other soldiers. "From Thayer's time to today," argued General Matthew B. Ridgway, "West Point has been the inexhaustible reservoir of high-principled integrity inculcated through its graduates in our officer corps, and by it transmitted to our NCO's. I know of no substitute for that high moral force. It must not be diluted by any concession to any lesser codes of society." [46]

Ridgway's reference to "lesser codes of society" reveals West Point's elitist ethical self-image as well as its corresponding fear of corruption from either civilian or military groups less imbued with high moral standards. General Knowlton echoed General Ridgway's sentiments in his remarks to the Board of Visitors in 1971: "The Honor System is the wellspring of all that we strive for at the Academy and our cadets fully understand the importance of holding firmly to a system that never will be compromised or diluted in order to appease the whims of those who do not—and perhaps never will fully comprehend its meaning or purpose." [47] Despite their self-righteous ring, such comments follow quite naturally from the West Pointer's belief in the special moral requirements of his profession. And most graduates endorse the notion that they disseminate their Academy-developed sense of duty and honor throughout the Regular Army Officer Corps. Such beliefs undoubtedly provide a sense of status and prestige which help to compensate for the family separations, the boredom of garrison duty, and the physical hardships associated with a military career. It is chiefly because of their defensiveness about Vietnam, their sense that both the Academy and the Army have suffered a drastic loss in prestige, that Academy officials are so eager to reassert West Point's moral mission and the Army's special moral requirements. Paradoxically, it is also Vietnam that has made visible the impossible moral task the Academy has set for itself and the dual and contradictory obligations America has imposed on its military men.

Put simply, it is unrealistic for Americans to look to West Pointers for "moral leadership" at any time, and to do so during wars in which there is not widespread public agreement on the wisdom of American policies is an ominious national delusion. Historically, initial public apprehension about American involvement in most wars has ultimately given way to national unity as the propaganda machinery of governmental agencies throughout the country took effect. Vietnam, unlike most wars but like the American Revolution and the Civil War, did not follow this pattern. Cracks and strains in the American consensus widened into chasms as American military involvement increased. In this kind of situation West Pointers, and American military leaders in general, should not be expected to provide moral guidance for a fragmented nation. "The Academy obviously benefits from the unanimity with which the country views its foreign commitments," one West Pointer observed. "And when there's not unanimity, or at least consensus, we have trouble." [48]

Perhaps more than any other group, the military is victimized by a divided allegiance: on the one hand, they are charged with carrying out the dictates of the elected or appointed civilian leaders; on the other hand, as the Americans most intimately acquainted with the implementation of our military policies, they are the most likely to have personal qualms about the effectiveness of these policies. When caught in this moral dilemma, most West Pointers are conditioned to perceive their obedience to lawful superiors as the highest form of duty. Such a perception is regarded as the essence of military professionalism, for it involves putting personal considerations beneath service, duty above self. When there is a conflict between what a West Pointer calls duty and honor, then, he is likely to have no ethical answers. Or rather, he is trained to answer by equating honor with duty. Colonel Sumner Willard, a Harvard-trained foreign language specialist and one of the two tenured professors who is not a West Point graduate, described this syndrome:

> You don't waste your time shouting about it or fretting about it. You don't strike about it. You don't write letters to the [New York] *Times* about it. You don't protest about it. This is inconsistent with service to the United States government. . . . In civilian life you never take things lying down. You issue a protest against something even though you know the decision has been made because it's instinctive in a democracy not to accept what has been put out. . . . [But in the Army] you suppress or arrest your personal feelings over a beer in the club, or when you're retired over a scotch and soda in the privacy of your living room. You may sound off, and officers often do, in these private circumstances. I'm not saying the officer corps doesn't have strong private opinions. It does. But publicly and officially these private opinions are not expressed. And so, this is what it's all about.[49]

Just as military considerations shape academic policies and pedagogy at West Point, they also shape the meaning of honor. In the *Honor Instruction* booklet distributed to all plebes during Beast Barracks the examples intended to delineate honorable from dishonorable behavior do not involve conflicts between honor and duty.

Most of the examples are drawn from situations in which a military superior is misled by a junior officer's lack of candor, a cadet lies to another cadet to cover up a violation of regulations, or a cadet cheats on an exam to enhance his own grade at the expense of other cadets.[50] (Cheating is defined as "the intentional taking of an unfair advantage over another" rather than a violation of conscience.)[51] There are some humorous examples, usually relating to truthfulness with "girls": "you cannot tell a blind date that you are Cadet-in-Charge of Quarters when in fact you are not. . . . You had better think of a better way of getting rid of this girl, rather than to compromise your Honor. The point to emphasize is that the Honor Code governs us in our relationship to everyone, and this includes girls."[52] The booklet does not, however, provide guidance when personal conscience clashes with established authority. And cadets and officers often display acute ethical insensitivity in precisely this area. It is not so much a question of immorality as it is of amorality; they are oblivious to certain kinds of moral tensions. In June 1970, for example, after three years at West Point, Cadet Cary Donham applied for discharge from the Army as a conscientious objector. The Department of the Army denied his request, provoking critical editorials from both the *New York Times* and the *Village Voice.*[53] "Anytime one of these guys appears," argued one West Pointer, "he becomes a little bullet for the critic who wants to eliminate this place. And the people down there at the Pentagon say, '$60,000 for a West Pointer who doesn't want to serve in the Army? Kindly explain to us what you are doing right.' "[54] From the perspective of a liberal journalist, such a statement may amount to a confession of moral bankruptcy. At West Point there was no cadet movement in support of Donham, but rather a strong predisposition among officers and cadets to see him as a crafty young man trying to escape his military commitment after three years of free education. Most officers were genuinely unable to imagine a choice of conscience over military service as anything other than a choice of self over duty. The Department of the Army rejected Donham's plea on the grounds that it demonstrated a "lack of depth of sincerity." [55]

A similar definition of honor operated for many years to make Academy officials impervious to the religious convictions of Jewish cadets. Until 1973, when the Supreme Court ruled that mandatory chapel was unconstitutional, all Jewish cadets were required to attend synagogue services on Sunday. In the minds of Academy officials, it was a simple case of personal conviction giving way to duty. "The Jews, of course, complained over the years that they were made to go to synagogue on Sunday when it was orthodox doctrine, as we all know, that the Sabbath is Saturday," argued one member of the faculty. "But you couldn't let the Jewish boys go to synagogue on Saturday. They'd be 'scot free' on Sunday and have all the Christian boys look at them and say, 'I'm going to join the Jewish chapel. Then I won't have to go to church on Sunday.' " [56] Similarly, when a representative from the dean's office questioned the propriety of Tom Wolfe's *The Electric Kool-Aid Acid Test*, which an instructor in the English Department had assigned for an elective course, neither of the top two officials in the department felt that a defense of the right to assign the book was a matter of honor. They agreed that it was an inappropriate choice for cadets, most of whom were within a year of going into the Regular Army where the "drug culture" Wolfe described is a severe troop problem for a junior officer. As for fundamental issues of academic freedom, apparently none of the authorities felt that the instructor had a right to assign any book he pleased. The resulting consensus prevented the kind of institutional trauma that would have ensued at most civilian colleges.[57]

Finally, the Academy's disenchantment with the possible court imposition of due process requirements on the deliberations of the cadet Honor Committee, while primarily rooted in the desire to maintain the Honor System in its current form, is exacerbated by an insensitivity to the moral assumptions underlying established traditions of American jurisprudence. Constitutional guarantees of due process are intended to protect individual rights, sometimes at the expense of conviction and at the cost of society. Most West Pointers, and most military men, see little sense in this system of priorities, because they regard individual rights as derivative of and dependent upon society. It is far better, they reason, to mistakenly punish a few innocent cadets than to allow a greater number of guilty cadets to remain in the Corps.[58]

Cadets are not taught to be skeptical of appeals to conscience or directly discouraged from developing a personal code of ethics. But, Academy claims to the contrary, the military atmosphere of the West Point culture puts a special premium on obedience to imposed standards of conduct at the cost of internalized ideals. Of course, the eventual goal of the Academy is to produce Army officers who have internalized the Academy's standards and who are, therefore, less likely to experience serious moral conflicts during their military careers. And virtually the entire West Point environment indirectly reinforces respect for the wisdom of established standards or, as one officer put it, "the presumption that it has all been taken care of by some pretty qualified people of high integrity and that, for the most part, their decision is as good a one as an individual could arrive at on his own." [59]

Most young men who come to the Academy have never before encountered a place so well-maintained, an organization so efficient, or adults so proficient at their jobs as he finds at West Point. "So the cadets begin to deduce," explains one officer, "that somewhere—the Supe's [superintendent's] house, the dean's house, somewhere—it has all been taken care of. They believe that somewhere there is some guy with a T-square who's got three or four guys to advise him and who's got all his shit together and he's squared away and they're squared away and the net result is steak on Wednesday night and a uniform that fits because some tailor had thirty seconds with you. It all comes out right. . . . There were forty-eight guys, forty-eight high school seniors in a completely disorganized mess and a month later they are marching on the Plain and the great American public is taking pictures and saying, 'Oh, look at that.' " This officer also suggested how confidence in the judgment of men in authority might have affected cadet reactions to the reports of the My Lai massacre and General Koster's alleged role in its cover-up:

> A good many cadets, I don't know how many, didn't believe they were getting the straight poop on it [My Lai], because the guys in charge would not let it happen. The people who take care of the right-fitting uniforms and all the other things simply wouldn't let it happen. Well, of course, some cadets realized that events can outrun even the best of men who have the best of intentions. . . . But the institution does tend to shoot you out of here with a great deal of confidence in official procedures and practices. But that is not the same thing as being insensitive to moral issues. It just means that it will require more evidence to convince them that the procedures can be wrong.[60]

And so the apparently exaggerated claims of West Point graduates like General Knowlton do have a certain legitimacy, if one is willing to recognize different shades of meaning in the use of the term "honor." West Point is "an inexhaustible reservoir of high-principled integrity" for the Army, in the sense that it annually produces officers who, unlike their peers in civilian colleges, retain considerable confidence in the wisdom of established authority and who are, therefore, more likely to insist on a rigorous enforcement of existent policies, even when enforcement is difficult, inconvenient, or personally unfulfilling. In those countless routine situations that comprise so much of military life and that call for mutual trust, unswerving devotion to high standards of performance and dedication to the successful completion of the mission, the West Pointer will usually outstrip the ROTC or OCS graduate. In those infrequent, but often crucial, situations that call for conscientious opposition to orders, the West Pointer may have greater trouble determining the parameters of his own moral position.[61]

AN ABSENCE OF HEROES

Some cadets insist that they represent a new generation of West Pointers who would be certain to assert their moral priorities when confronted with improper or illegal activities. An increasing number of cadets claim to have little respect for the judgment of superior officers and a more highly developed set of personal moral convictions. Cadets of this persuasion like to emphasize the differences between themselves and older members of the long gray line and to tell stories which dramatize the new cadet consciousness: "This general came up from the Pentagon to tell us about our career opportunities and said that we would have our combat chances, just like he had his war in Vietnam. Guys looked around at each other and said 'Who is this fool?' " [62]

Although few cadets regard their superior officers with a studied skepticism, they do make up an influential minority; and their opinions are sufficiently fashionable to put cadets who disagree on the defensive. "There's one good thing about this place," argued a first classman. "It's made me and my classmates get ourselves together, We've seen so much shit around here that we're not going to put up with when we get out there in the so-called 'real Army.' . . . A lot of us are going to say 'goddamn it, sir, you're wrong.' This is something, in a funny way, the institution has developed in us." [63] A recent graduate, who had just reported to his active duty unit, wrote of his disgust with the old Army traditions: "I am very, very, very tired of the petty details and the amoral bureautocracy [sic] with which the Army seems enthralled. Some of my classmates can experience disbelief, outrage, etc., but still temper it with the optimism that 'this won't happen again.' All I can muster is disgust, a certain sadness, some semblance of gallows humor and, often, despair." [64]

Most officers at West Point have taken notice of this new cadet attitude, which many claim is not at all unprecedented: "Yeah, well, we had a lot of classmates who were ready to go to the wall in order to maintain their integrity. And a number of them did go to the wall. And a number of them got burned. Suddenly, you see a classmate who is a captain attack what he regards as an injustice and you say to yourself, 'Hey, he's a dead man.' " [65]

The skepticism of the older graduates appears well founded. One cadet admitted that "candidly, those of us who want to change the system aren't truly convinced that we'll be able to survive it." [66] Whether or not this self-conscious minority of cadets is capable of retaining its rebellious spirit in the Army, the fact remains that such a spirit persists in the cadet subculture at West Point. Many officers attribute this development to the breakdown of parental authority in the family or, more generally, to "the permissiveness of modern American society." Others think that the war in Vietnam is mostly to blame, because it has cast a shadow over the legitimacy of all established authority, most particularly military authority. According to these explanations, West Point is the victim of the long-range and excessively liberal tendencies that swept through America in the 1960's. Spock, civil rights, protest movements against the Vietnam war, the abolition of grading systems in some colleges, rallies for indicted Black Panther revolutionaries, judicial concern for the rights of the accused in criminal trials, all are part of a national atmosphere in which West Point's insistence on obedience to duly constituted authority appears anachronistic. Most West Point officials regard this phenomenon as a challenge to the ideal of duty that West Point strives to inculcate and, therefore, a threat to their military conception of honor. And it is in the operation of the Honor System that the consequences of this individualistic, down-with-the-establishment mentality have become particularly visible.

It is natural for the Honor System to become the breeding ground for incipient cadet rebels, because much about the history and development of the Honor System makes it immune to the traditional forces that have shaped the other agencies and departments at West Point. Although many West Pointers insist that the Academy could not survive without the Honor System, it did so for over one hundred years. The Honor System in its present form is a virtual innovation when compared with the Thayer-inspired traditions; it has been an official part of West Point only since 1922. It is also the only one of the various systems at West Point that is not based on a conservative, pessimistic estimate of human nature: the Honor System assumes that each cadet can recognize right from wrong and is capable of action in accord with that recognition without coercion from superiors. In an institution that allows for little individual freedom and demands obedience to standards of conduct imposed from above, the Honor System is an anomaly. It is also the only cadet activity in which there are no distinctions of rank; a first classman and a plebe are equals. The Honor Committee is also the only major Academy agency that evolved as a grassroots organization from within the Corps of Cadets without the initial sanction of official authority. An ad hoc group of cadets known as the Vigilance Committee came into existence around 1897 and conducted covert honor trials for twenty-five years before General Douglas MacArthur, then superintendent, gave it "official status as the authoritative voice of the Corps . . . in administering the Honor Code." [67] Largely because of its unique origins, the operation of the Honor System is the only significant facet of life at the Academy that is under the control of cadets. "It's their system," General Feir insisted, "that's its great strength. If they perceive that it's run by Army officers, it's going to lose a great deal. Instead of being something they aspire to internally, it's going to be something to beat; another system, run by the green suiters; and something to beat." [68]

A minority of cadets already see the Honor System as "something to beat." By and large these are the same cadets who see themselves as rebels, the same cadets who refused to participate in the silencing of Pelosi, the same cadets whom West Point officials regard as an infection acquired from an American society temporarily infatuated with unfettered individualism. They are rebels with a very specific cause—the repudiation of institutional constraints on their freedom. Ironically, their mini-wars against the system are seldom waged in the name of personal conscience or conviction. What these cadets have in common is not a positive belief in the sanctity of individual ideals, but a negative attitude toward the symbols of authority at West Point. Liberal journalists who attempt to portray cadets like Pelosi and those who supported him as crusaders for a conscientiously inspired conception of freedom misunderstand the dynamics of the cadet subculture. These cadets are not Thoreauvian radicals committed to the pursuit of individual honor. They are Machiavellians committed to the pursuit of their own self-interest, and in this pursuit, not unlike many of their civilian peers whose anti-war protests were directly related to the possibility of their being drafted to fill Vietnam manpower needs.

One cannot learn very much about cadet attitudes toward honor by studying the publicized cheating scandals that periodically become matters of national concern.[69] There have been several massive cheating scandals at West Point since World War II, most noticeably in 1951 (90 cadets dismissed, 37 of them members of the football team), in 1966 (42 cadets dismissed), and 1973 (37 cadets tried, 21 dismissed). These irregular outbreaks of organized cheating are less a measure of prevalent cadet attitudes toward honor than of the pressurized Academy environment, the grade-oriented academic atmosphere, the multi-sectioned courses in which the same test is given to morning and afternoon classes, the willingness of Academy officials to maintain the unproctored and easily circumvented testing procedures. "The majority of our senior people are adamantly opposed to tightening up the procedures to make them cheat-proof," contended Colonel Saunders. "If we have to arrange everything so there's no test on the Honor System, then there's no point in having it at all." [70]

This uncharacteristically liberal attitude—imagine a tactical officer refusing to inspect cadet rooms because it would imply a lack of trust—has gone unnoticed in reports or these scandals; national attention has tended to focus on those features that provide a sensational contrast to the exaggerated moralistic rhetoric of some West Point officials. But if one begins with the assumption that the mythology surrounding honor at West Point is based on unrealistic expectations, then there is little reason to find the stories of organized cheating at the Academy so scandalous. It has happened in the past; it will happen in the future. Most of the offenders will be caught; many cadets who knew of the cheating rings but did not turn in the offenders will not be caught, even though they also violated the "toleration clause" of the Honor Code. Some Academy officers, in misguided efforts to "protect the reputation of West Point," will be less than candid with the press, so when the facts eventually become public knowledge the Academy will be susceptible to charges of a cover-up.[71] Some reporters will conclude that all cadets cheat regularly and that those caught in the scandal are unfortunate scapegoats, which is untrue. And spokesmen for the Academy will claim that all the cadets not implicated in the scandal are archetypes of integrity, which is also untrue. Meanwhile, the important questions about the day-by-day operation of the Honor System and the dominant cadet attitudes toward honor will go unasked and unanswered.

In the last ten years a large number of cadets have come to embrace a distinction that is crucial to an understanding of the emerging pattern of values in the cadet subculture. One second classman put it most graphically. "I believe in the Honor Code, but I think the Honor System is all fucked up." [72] Like Americans who endorse the political ideals of democracy but who are dismayed at the convoluted and corrupted state of American politics, cadets frequently express admiration for honor in theory (i.e. the Honor Code) and contempt for the ways in which it is implemented (i.e. the Honor System). In the vanguard of a growing movement within the Corps of Cadets are the self-conscious cadet rebels who believe that the Honor System has become a tool for "the green-suiters" to maintain their control. "Our honor is being used against us," is a typical lament, "and becoming a way to enforce regulations." [73]

The attempt to evade regulations has always been a part of life at the Academy. In the nineteenth century cadets regularly escaped from the post to drink beer in Benny Haven's tavern. More recent battles with the regulations have involved the discovery of ingenious hiding places for women in the barracks. There always was an element of gamesmanship in these unauthorized escapades, a tacit understanding between cadets and tactical officers that they were engaged in a battle of wits. Demerits were the acceptable form of punishment for a cadet who lost the contest.

In recent years this battle of wits has become more bitter and antagonistic. The change of mood dates back to the passage of the Service Academies Act of 1964, which authorized a dramatic increase in the size of the Corps of Cadets to bring it in line with enrollment at the other service academies.[74] The reorganization required to handle an almost doubled cadet population inevitably produced massive additions and refinements of the regulations. By 1971 the "blue book," entitled *Regulations: United States Corps of Cadets*, had ballooned to one hundred and eighty-three pages, with a sixty-four-page appendix and regular inserts and updates.[75] Few of the officers at West Point were pleased with the monstrous text and its hopelessly confusing distinctions. The commandant, General Feir, even called it "the easiest book to put down and never again pick up I ever saw . . . an absurd idea." [76] Cadets had also become increasingly irritated at the accretion of petty, "Mickey Mouse" regulations that, from their perspective, served no useful purpose. The result was not only an increase in the violation of regulations but also the creation of an atmosphere in which cadets who violated regulations frequently felt that they were doing nothing wrong. The absence of guilt and the parallel conviction that punishment was undeserved combined to sanction violations of the Honor Code (particularly lying) as a means to avoid getting caught. The principal purpose behind the abolition of the blue book and the adoption of a more simplified set of regulations in 1973 was to counter the burgeoning cadet cynicism toward "the system." The new book of regulations made no specific mention of honor, eliminated the chapter on the Honor System, and replaced it with a single paragraph which emphasized that "Cadets are expected to adhere to the professional ethics of commissioned officers in the United States Army." Despite the dramatic character of the regulation changes, the underlying cadet hostility toward officially sanctioned constraints, no matter how simply they are stated, continues to affect the operation of the Honor System.[77]

The moral problems continue to arise because there is still a gray area where regulations and honor overlap. For example, whenever a cadet is absent from his room he must mark his absence card. If he leaves his card unmarked, then steals away for a late-night rendezvous with his girl friend, he is likely to get caught, because a cadet or officer regularly inspects all rooms and is likely to notice the unmarked card. Until 1973, he would have been punished for a violation of Article 1003, section C, paragraph 3, as defined by Article 507, section C (i.e. he is not authorized to go off post during week nights). The new regulations make the definition of "limits" more comprehensible but still require cadets to use the absence card for reporting their whereabouts. The late night rendezvous is now a violation of paragraph 503, section C, and paragraph 504.[78] Punishment usually takes the form of demerits and loss of privileges. If the cadet marks his absence card "authorized beyond limits," however, he is less likely to get caught because the inspecting officer or cadet will assume he has obtained permission to be off post. But the act of improperly marking his absence card is not just a violation of regulations, it is also an honor violation, a lie. If caught, the cadet is subject to an honor trial and immediate dismissal upon conviction.[79]

Not all cadets, or even most cadets, choose to compromise their honor in order to escape the clutches of the tactical officers. Cadet David Cantlay captured the tone of the situation when he asserted that "today's cadets all too often see the honor code as no more than another attempt on the part of the enemy (officers) to limit their freedom: through the absence card, reports, et cetera, the honor code becomes in their minds an extension of regulations. And they observe it, if a little more seriously and routinely, in the same light as regulations. But the *spirit* is dying." [80] Meanwhile, another spirit is growing, a spirit of solidarity within the Corps of Cadets based on the common conviction that the integrity of the Honor System has been compromised by its connections with the infamous regulations.

There is little the cadets can do to change the regulations. But they can refuse to enforce violations of the Honor System committed in an attempt to evade regulations, because, as the *Honor Instruction* booklet puts it, "the Honor Code and System belong entirely to the Corps of Cadets." [81] Members of the Honor Committee have come under increasing pressure from their peers to prevent the conviction of cadets accused of honor violations that the corps regards as justifiable. "I had one particularly bad experience with plagiarism," said a former instructor in the English Department. "The cadet admitted that he knew what he had done, but he was not at all impressed with the wrongness of it. He *was* impressed by the fact that he was probably going to get away with it. And he did." [82] During honor trials the friends of accused cadets frequently stack the gallery and shout advice or even attempt to intimidate certain members of the Honor Committee. (Only one vote for the accused is required for a verdict of innocent.) As a result the Academy has been forced to install a heavy curtain between the gallery and the committee; it is drawn when the gallery becomes too vociferous. All votes are taken in the open, however, so that cadets know where each member of the committee stands. At the graduation ceremonies in 1972 the chairman of the Honor Committee, who had a reputation as a strict enforcer, was booed by many in the Corps as he came forward to receive his diploma. "I've seen it happen so many times," explained a member of the class of 1972. "If you think the rest of your classmates are going off on an unethical path, and you tell them, 'No!'—then, you are the one likely to get screwed. You're going to get reamed." "One of the biggest phrases going is 'cooperate and graduate,' " the cadet added, "It means don't hassle your classmates. Don't be a boat-rocker. If your principles are so high, if you're so different from the others, you're not going to be liked." [83]

Ironically, the cooperate and graduate syndrome is a lower-order manifestation of a sense of camaraderie which exists throughout the Army. Just as cadets band together against their military superiors at West Point, most soldiers harbor a sense of common loyalty and purpose which they do not share with civilians. In times of intense antimilitary sentiment, this common conviction becomes even more pronounced, since it bolsters military self-esteem and helps to shield career soldiers from public criticism. The alleged cover-ups of the My Lai and other Vietnam massacres and the less serious cover-ups of honor violations within the Corps of Cadets constitute dangerous applications of this sense of camaraderie. But the reflexive willingness to help a fellow cadet or officer also has certain benefits and attractions. At West Point the belief that "we are all in this together" creates a communal atmosphere. Officers who never met before exchange greetings on the sidewalks; cadets instinctively come to the aid of a classmate who is deficient in a math course; if one's car breaks down on post, there is no doubt that a passer-by will soon stop to lend a hand. Although the cover-up mentality and the West Point Protective Association both spring from this reflexive in-house loyalty, so do the conspicuous charitableness and self-sacrifice that many civilians identify with a bygone communal ideal.

The cadet version of guerrilla war against the authorities at West Point also has about it an aura of honor that is analogous to the sense of honor that existed in Vietnam among enlisted men who disapproved of the American involvement in the war and conspired to subvert the military efficiency of their units. It also borrows from the classic tradition of "higher law," which has provided an honorable rationale for civil disobedience in America from the time the patriots denounced George III in 1776 to the time the opponents of the Vietnam war refused induction.[84] Not that cadets identify with the young Americans who fled to Canada, or think about such analogies, or ponder the moral implications of their mini-rebellions. There is no coherent cadet moral philosophy, but rather an undercurrent of hostility toward superiors that has made the traditional equation of duty and honor more difficult. If it is true that West Point officers have a duty-oriented definition of honor that leaves little room for disagreements based on conscience, then those cadets who reject the equation of duty and honor seem to have nothing to offer as a substitute other than loyalty to their cadet peers. Those in search of the kind of moral hero who places his personal standards of integrity above either professional obligations, or allegiance to friends, or loyalty to authority should recognize that the Military Academy is barren ground.

And because cadet attitudes are primarily unconsidered reactions to the exigencies of their immediate situation, it is probable that their attitudes will change in undeterminable ways when they become officers who must compel others to obey regulations in the Army. The current generation of cadets is less the prototype for a new breed of Army officer than a group of ambivalent young men caught between the values of their civilian peers and the professional values of West Point. They are adolescents undergoing a socialization process which is designed to shape them into military men. Their small-scale stand against Academy authority permits them to retain a sense of union with civilian friends "on the outside" and helps to expiate whatever feelings of guilt they might harbor about their decision to attend a school for soldiers. In the process issues as dissimilar as the resignation of Koster and the silencing of Pelosi momentarily merge, moral distinctions are blurred and both Koster and Pelosi become the heirs to Patton, heroic warriors in the protracted and honorable war against the system.

Chapter Seven

★★★★★★★★★★★★★★★★★★★

WEST POINTERS AND THE COUNTRY

In the 1950's when Gar Davidson was Superintendent, he did a survey of the alumni. And I said that the most important thing that they ought to learn to do up there was to protect the individual who wants to be an individual and protect the maverick, contrary to what others would think of the Academy. . . . And another thing I said they ought to do was develop curiosity. Curiosity is a search for ideas, a search for knowledge. . . . But the Academy tends to stultify it and push it into a mold that might tend to deaden it, and that worries me.

Lieutenant General James M. Gavin (ret.) (1973)

I am not a great voter. I was raised in a military tradition. . . . Politics wasn't to be discussed by young officers in the dining hall. That was bad manners. I learned to be an observer in politics, not an advocate. I made value judgments and kept them to myself. But that's changing. I have strong views—I'm not a eunuch or a whore—but it's not an excessive burden to restrain them.

General Alexander M. Haig, Jr. (ret.) (1973)

★ ★ ★ WEST Point is a visible beneficiary of the unanimity with which the country pursues its national policies; and, if there is no unanimity, then . . ."; the major paused; but, rather than pursuing the troublesome idea further, he simply declared, "When there is no direction in the government and the nation doesn't know what it wants, this place can look pretty foolish." [1] West Pointers are not so much troubled by the changes in national policies as by the absence of forceful direction to whatever policies are in effect at a given time. Cadets are not encouraged to critique the assumptions and values which shape American policy-making. They are told that upon graduation: "Your total efforts as future Army officers will be guided by the needs to sustain the domestic and foreign policies of the United States." [2] Each cadet is instructed to refrain from making "any derogatory remarks about the President, Congress or his superior officers." He is told that he "will not submit a theme or deliver a speech containing material that is in bad taste." And "[i]f he is in doubt" about what constitutes bad taste, he is advised to "consult the instructor beforehand." [3] He is trained to perform as a "public servant" who does not question the wisdom or integrity of those in authority. And like much at West Point, this principle has the sanction of tradition. William Larned expressed it most graphically in 1902: "An order from a superior has the force of a cannon shot. To resist is not consistent with reason." [4]

The need for deference to authority seems perfectly reasonable to most West Pointers because they believe that the archetypal situation for which the Academy has prepared them is the combat order to lead other soldiers against a well-defended enemy position. Since World War II, however, the testing ground for career Army officers has increasingly been the corridors of the defense bureaucracy more than the battlefield. Somewhat surprisingly, the socialization process which emphasizes the preparation of effective combat leaders has produced successful administrators and bureaucrats. And in the 1970's General Alexander Haig provides a compelling example of the strengths and limitations many West Pointers bring to public service.

When General Haig was appointed White House Chief of Staff in the spring of 1973, comparisons were quickly drawn between President Nixon's decision to replace H. R. Haldeman with General Haig and President Eisenhower's decision to replace Sherman Adams with retired Army Major General Wilton B. Persons. As the *Congressional Quarterly* noted, "In each case, the military man was a trusted friend of the President and the appointment was aimed at helping restore public confidence in an executive office caught in a credibility crisis." [5] In scores of articles, Haig's status as a West Pointer was constantly invoked as tacit proof of whatever qualities of forthrightness, honesty, and integrity the author chose to assign him.[6] Even after his controversial actions in what he called "the fire storm" of the Archibald Cox dismissal and the Elliot Richardson resignation, columnists such as Tom Braden were cautioning readers not to come to hasty judgments about Haig's intemperate remarks and abrasive manner. "Haig has served his country as long as Richardson, and it may be argued, just as well," wrote Braden. "During the Cuban missile crisis, he worked with Robert Kennedy. In the White House, he worked with Henry Kissinger. He taught at West Point and commanded a battalion in Vietnam." [7] But others took a more practical view of Haig's value to the Nixon White House. Nick Thimmesch of the *Los Angeles Times* wrote:

> To President Nixon's way of thinking and operating, Gen. Haig is just the man he needs now. There is a fortress mentality at the White House. . . . The disciplined men who think of the President in terms of the Commander-in-Chief are the closest to Mr. Nixon.
>
> There is Haig, the West Pointer who became a four-star general. There is Haig's deputy, General John C. Bennett, U. S. Army, re-

> tired [USMA, '47]. There is Haig's aide, Maj. George Joulwan [USMA, '61], who talks pridefully of how he was able to rap with hippies and radicals and still keep his integrity as a military man. There is another West Pointer, Fred Buzhardt, recently a civilian official at the Pentagon, and now assistant White House counsel. And there is Ronald Ziegler, press secretary, who didn't have to graduate from West Point to attain the wooden obedience he shows the President.[8]

Many of the Army officers who have known Haig since his cadet days believe that dozens of West Pointers in his class, if given the opportunity, would have been equally successful. The chief ingredients in Haig's success—ceaseless hard work, superb staff skills, ability to ingratiate himself with key superiors, and a sixth sense for bureaucratic gamesmanship—characterize most of the hundreds of West Pointers now holding general officer rank.[9] The particulars of Haig's success, first with Henry Kissinger and then with Mr. Nixon, illuminate further the qualities shared by most successful West Pointers. A civilian who worked with Haig at the National Security Council summarized his successful maneuvering in the councils of American power:

> First, he is a man who can and does work fourteen hours a day, seven days a week without any apparent loss of enthusiasm for his work or in his commitment to it. Second, he has an instinctive political sense which causes him, in any situation, to indicate to the powers-that-be that he is their man. And he is extremely astute in his reading of people and conducts himself accordingly.
>
> His movement from Henry.'s Deputy to President Nixon's right hand man was due to his mastery of "the end run." He understood the importance of spending time alone with the President and in the process of doing this he became someone the President dealt with directly, rather than by going through Kissinger.[10]

Haig's success suggests a fact about West Pointers that is so obvious that it is often ignored: namely, that graduates of the Military

Academy advance to positions of responsibility and power in business and government as well as the Army not because of a sinister conspiracy, but because they possess skills valued by the nation's business and professional community and because they have been specifically trained to use those skills to meet the goals set for them.[11] Whether they are called company men or team players or mission-oriented managers, the result is a loyal subordinate who can usually be counted on to acclimate his personality and talents to the job at hand. West Pointers, in and out of the Army, also share with many successful Americans an ability to generate a passionate belief that what is good for IBM, or the Pentagon, or the President, is good for the country. And American involvement in the affairs of other nations has often been based on the presumptuous belief that what is good for America is good for the world. A blissful obliviousness underlies much of what passes for success in modern America. West Point has merely systematized a process for producing industrious professionals whose success has little connection with either a greater social good or an ethical imperative: lawyers prosper in an increasingly lawless country; doctors become richer as health care deteriorates; teachers enjoy a unique, if modest, prosperity as educational standards decline; and Army officers enjoy unprecedented financial and professional advancement as the result of a politically and financially disastrous war. Although at West Point the possibility that there might be an inverse relationship between professional military success and national well-being is unthinkable, events of recent years have caused some Academy officials to re-evaluate both their success-oriented ethic and their relationship to the public they are pledged to serve.

LOSING ON "THE FIELDS OF FRIENDLY STRIFE"

At West Point General Douglas MacArthur's reminder that "there is no substitute for victory" is more than just a pep rally platitude; it is a warning charged with implication.[12] When athletic teams or armies win, there is little need or inclination to investigate their morale or organization. When they do not win, their critics begin to ask probing questions. Such questions not only expose deficiencies that would have gone unnoticed after a victory but also force official spokesmen to justify practices which have gone unquestioned for decades and which, it turns out, may not withstand scrutiny.

The men who head the Military Academy are quick to recognize that the analogy between winning at football and winning at war derives its appropriateness from the decisive quality of both forms of violent conflict. The crucial connecting term is "winning." "Remember," said one graduate, "Vince Lombardi learned the importance of a winning attitude when he served under coach [Earl] Blaik right here." [13] In 1961, after a series of disappointing football seasons, West Point announced that it was signing the much-heralded Paul Dietzel as its new coach. Superintendent William Westmoreland explained that Dietzel was hired because "it is to the national interest, to the interest of the Army, and of the Academy that we, by our performance, create the image of a winner." And in 1974 Cadet Kerry K. Pierce asserted that "the average cadet is really interested in football. To cadets losing means a lot more, for some reason, than losing does in a civilian institution; perhaps because the football team is an outward expression of themselves. . . . Losing is just a tremendous crusher." [14]

By 1974, Dietzel had long since departed West Point for South Carolina where, ironically, General Westmoreland was campaigning for governor, an effort which many believed might satisfy the general's yearning for victory.[15] At Westmoreland's alma mater the football team, which he and Dietzel had sought to salvage, had experienced its worst season since 1890. Another MacArthur motto, on the arch of the cadet gymnasium, had ominous contemporary implications: "Upon the fields of friendly strife are sown the seeds that upon other fields, on other days, will bear the fruits of victory." [16] But there had been no Army football victories in 1973. A major rationale for defeat—"Teams like Tennessee and Penn State beat us up so bad that we're too weak to play well the next week"—was also undermined after Army lost by 45 points to "a California team which had been mortified by Alabama 66–0" the week before. "There is no question that it seriously affected everything," said Colonel Dick, "the morale of the student body, the morale of the faculty was seriously impaired." [17]

As this worst of all seasons unfolded, the superintendent not only moved to disassociate himself from the team's misfortunes, but he cast himself in the role of a prophet. In a statement to alumni, General Knowlton's first words were: "You will recall that in . . . March 1973 . . . , I mentioned the problems with this year's football season: 29 sweaters to fill, and one of the toughest schedules ever faced by an Army team." Although he acknowledged the "season has developed in an even more disappointing fashion than we had expected," he quickly added: "When I arrived in the spring of 1970, it was apparent the 1970 and 1973 schedules were more than we should ask cadets to face." As the defeats continued and the Army-Navy game approached, the generally unflappable superintendent made abrasive public comments about civilian "football factories." General Knowlton recalled, "I was at a civilian school recently and saw some of the football players there who apparently were let out by their keepers. Many of them pass classrooms every day but are blissfully unaware of the interior." [18]

Other Academy spokesman were no more charitable to other schools on their football players. Talking to an Atlanta reporter before an early October game with Georgia Tech, head coach Tom Cahill said:

> It's just the tenor of the times that football at the Service Academies is at a relatively low ebb now. The day will come when they'll be back up with the best of them. Times change, fortunes fluctuate, and the tenor of the times has a lot to do with it. It has been the most difficult ever during the days of the Vietnam war. Everyone wants to go to Heaven. Nobody wants to die. Everyone can tell you

how great this country is. But when the time comes to stand up and protect it, that's a different story.[19]

For the head coach to equate an unwillingness to play Army football with a lack of patriotism should not be surprising. Cahill was coaching in an environment where football losses had grave implications. But neither Knowlton nor Cahill could foresee the damaging publicity the Academy received in late November when the *New York Times* originated a story on West Point football entitled "Crippled by an Act of Congress." The *Times* reported, "An eleventh-hour reluctance to commit at least nine years of their young lives to the military turned a number of good football players away from Army in recent years." Since the late 1960's, the story noted, "West Point graduates have been required by an act of Congress to serve a minimum of five years in the Army after four undergraduate years at West Point." [20]

The five-year commitment to the Regular Army reminded potential cadets of the grim price the government could exact for four years of West Point. "I think the war changed things," admitted Colonel William Schuder, West Point's athletic director, but "there were other reasons—the lure of the pros, the bad publicity the service got, the Army being questioned by young people all over the country." Colonel Schuder seemed oblivious to the fact that these "other reasons" were inexorably related to the mandatory military commitment and Vietnam. But, whatever the reasons, Colonel Schuder understood the end result—"If it continues this way, Army will never be a national power." Interviews with five football players whom the Academy had unsuccessfully attempted to recruit revealed that the most serious problem was more troublesome than anyone from the superintendent to the athletic director dared admit. A general distaste for military service, more than specific concerns about Vietnam, had deterred young football recruits from attending West Point.[21]

"They say it's just a five-year commitment," explained Thomas

Parr, an outstanding quarterback at Colgate once pursued by Army football scouts. "But it's really nine years of military and martial life." Whether the source of discontent was Vietnam-inspired or a less definable animosity toward the martial virtues, West Point's winning image was clearly the victim. Cadets, officers, and alumni were visibly distressed. "We're losing," said Kingsley Fink, the team quarterback, "and cadets don't like losing." And Tom Cahill uttered words which ironically would soon serve as an epitaph for his Army coaching career. "When winning isn't important to the Army," Cahill said, "you're in trouble." While many regarded Cahill's comments as an oblique criticism of the congressionally imposed five-year obligation, he had nowhere to turn when a few weeks later Army lost the most one-sided Army-Navy football game in history, 51–0. Twelve days later Cahill was dismissed as head coach.[22]

Newspaper accounts noted that Cahill had been "only the second head coach dismissed under fire at the academy." The day of his dismissal Cahill said:

> I feel disappointed but it's not the end of the world. . . . When General Knowlton told me this afternoon, I said, "Is this because the football team hurts the image of the Army?" And General Knowlton said, "Yes." Then I said, "The problems with the football team are that it is suffering from the image of the Army." [23]

With Cahill's dismissal (technically his contract was not renewed) Army football recruiting was at a standstill. And the Academy sought a new head coach while attempting to develop easier schedules for future years. Schuder had announced during the season that moves were being made not only to schedule weaker teams but also to cancel tentatively arranged games with national powers. "Generally when these schedules were made there was a feeling here that Army could be No. 1 in the nation sometime. That is not the case now and it is not realistic." [24]

As West Point searched for a new coach during December and

January, General Abrams, unlike his predecessor General Westmoreland, made no public pronouncements about the importance of Army football to West Point's image as a winner. Nevertheless, West Pointers were not unaware of public rumblings on the right: "We seem to be getting tied in an awful lot of wars [i.e. Vietnam] lately," noted one observer. "But I guess that's easy to understand when our football teams at West Point are only trying to keep the score respectable." [25] When West Point announced at the end of January that its new coach would be Homer Smith, most Academy supporters were understandably bewildered. Not only had they never heard of Smith, but even those inclined to optimistic expectations were jolted when they learned from wire service reports that "Smith, who served five years as head coach at Davidson and then two years as head coach at the University of the Pacific, has a 32-38 won-lost record in his seven seasons as a head coach." He was, one officer acidly remarked, "a proven loser." That Smith was recommended by Princeton's athletic director as "one hell of a leader" was hardly comforting to graduates who dreamed of West Point's return as at least an occasional national football power.[26] And the persistence of the reasons for Army's uniquely dismal 1973 record certainly did not bode well for the future. "It's just like mixing a can of orange juice, you know," said one disenchanted senior officer. "If it says put three cans in and you put four or five cans in, then you just don't have as good a thing anymore." [27]

West Point's capacity for self-deception had seldom been as much in evidence as it was in the winter of 1974. Even Gordon S. White, Jr., of the *New York Times*, whom Academy officials had praised all season for his fair and sympathetic football reporting, wrote that West Point has "introduced a different approach to its football recruiting problem—the mandatory post-graduate five-year tour of military duty. The 'five-year opportunity' for young men. Thus Smith . . . can begin his most important and immediate task of recruiting high school football players by telling them what a great opportunity they have upon graduation from the military academy." When Homer Smith declared, "I can't wait to try my sales pitch, which I developed with talking to West Point people," some of the more cynical Vietnam veterans among the officer corps were reminded of George Romney in the grip of Vietnam "information specialists." Perhaps Gordon White summed up the situation most graphically when he observed that, although Academy spokesman Colonel Schuder "introduced the new approach to the old Army problem by giving it the name 'opportunity,' " "Smith—not Schuder—has to face the high school athlete and explain the 'opportunity' that is open to all West Point graduates." [28]

THE NEW CREED OF SELF-DISCIPLINE

The problem of what kind of opportunity is open to young Americans both while they are at West Point and after they leave is at the heart of almost any serious discussion of the institution and its past and future role in American life. For many Americans, and certainly the vast majority of West Pointers, the Academy offers an invaluable opportunity to master skills such as efficient budgeting of time, withstanding stress, fulfilling prescribed academic and Corps requirements. The refinement of these skills at West Point and after graduation is, in the view of most cadets and graduates, ultimately tested by how well one does in a competitive situation. West Pointers frequently point to graduates who have been successful outside of the military, in business and the professions. This American affirmation of West Point-honed skills is highly prized. But the most visible test is the competition on "the fields of friendly strife" or in a combat operation thousands of miles from West Point. And when the Army football team loses by astronomical scores to the University of California at Berkeley or to Navy, and combat troops withdraw from the Southeast Asian stalemate under the cover of Air Force bombing, then the Academy is susceptible to critics of diverse persuasions.[29]

Editorial writers may question the usefulness of traditional West

Pointer skills in dealing with complex problems of domestic and international relations in the last third of the twentieth century; but Academy graduates, particularly those at lieutenant general rank and above who make up the Army's leadership elite, were apprehensive about the survival of those traditional skills. They focused much of their criticism on the revision of the regulations governing cadet behavior which had been put into effect in 1973. Newspaper accounts had described the replacement of the cumbersome blue book of regulations with a sixty-four-page manual as a reform which "officials here explain . . . as part of its [the Academy's] continuing effort to modernize, and adapt to changes in society as a whole." [30] The words "reform," "modernize," and "adapt" were anathema to many older graduates, for these were buzz words, euphemisms for seductive civilian attitudes they usually categorized as "liberal." The very fact that the *New York Times*, *Newsweek*, and the television networks (all of which West Pointers tend to regard as avowedly liberal in sentiment) had applauded the change in regulations as well as the mid-September abolition of the "silence" was evidence that many older graduates found disconcerting.[31] The *Army Times* headline, "USMA Eases Life of Cadets," was even more troublesome. And an editorial in the *Wall Street Journal* not only used the wrong buzz words, but also suggested that West Point, like most American colleges, had given in to the whims of the younger generation: "In order to remain a viable force in 1970's America, it has little choice but to adjust to a society that has undergone considerable change during the turbulent past decade. . . . In this the academy somewhat parallels the position of most colleges and universities, which abandoned their in loco parentis role once it became clear students would no longer submit to such regulations and parents wouldn't force them to do so." [32] The *New York Times* quoted General Knowlton as saying that "We've been manning the bastions here, hanging tight to standards in a society that was saying there were no standards. Now we feel that the pressure is off, and the first step was to redo the 'blue book.' " Knowlton's words irritated old guard alumni, since his statement implied that the revision of the regulations was merely a prelude to future reforms.[33]

In the same statement in which he explained the reasons for the disappointing football season, Knowlton attempted to ease alumni anxiety about the change in regulations. He expressed surprise that "this became a headline story in many newspapers and was also covered on national TV." The traditional West Point emphasis on discipline had not, as these stories implied, become a thing of the past. "The new regulations were *not* designed to liberalize cadet life," he wrote. "They are *more*, rather than *less* demanding." [34] Inside the same issue of *Assembly* was an article, marked "approved by the Commandant of Cadets," which provided additional "authentic information." It opened with the assurance that "News media reports notwithstanding, the recent revision of cadet regulations was not intended to liberalize West Point, nor has it done so." The approved buzz word was not "liberal" but "self-discipline":

> Self-discipline is the all-important characteristic of a good Army officer, and therefore at West Point it is critically important. Self-discipline is a prerequisite for every value the Military Academy seeks to internalize in its graduates. It is essential if one is to have the right approach to duty and responsibility. It is a quality one must have if he is to have a correct perception of country. It plays a prior role in each of these because to have any one of them demands that a person be capable and willing to make tough choices . . . hard over easy; inconvenient over convenient; true over false; right over wrong. Each of these requires one to wrestle mentally with himself and ultimately to do what is right and what is expected even though not being watched or supervised . . . in other words, to be self-disciplined. Clearly West Point graduates must have this quality above all others. . . .[35]

Left unexplained was how a conservative, as opposed to a liberal view of cadet behavior would allow alumni to regard self-discipline as anything but a contradiction in terms. The rationale for having regulations for the Corps of Cadets was based on the conviction that cadets, like most young men, required external constraints in order to behave responsibly. Discipline, in the sense that West Pointers traditionally understood the word, was not something that could be self-imposed.

General Feir, the commandant, explained that tactical officers would still be present to correct cadets when they did not sufficiently discipline themselves, an explanation that seemed to render the term "self-discipline" either meaningless or misleading. The very imprecision of the official language was seen by some officers as an asset, because it allowed different constituencies, like the conservative alumni and the liberal press, to confirm their separate understandings. To others the language was not simply a public relations charade but rather an attempt to cover up a disquieting phenomenon. Not only had officials become defensive about their loser's image, but they also had become confused about what they were supposed to be doing to cadets. Captain Stephen Lifrak, a counseling officer at the Academy, claimed that West Point was confused about the values a soldier should possess because most Americans were confused about military virtues and vices after Vietnam: "What are the values we're supposed to inculcate here? I think they are changing. I don't know what they are, and I don't think West Point knows, and I don't think the Army knows. That is a danger because they end up inculcating something without knowing what it is. The reason it is dangerous is because they don't know what they're doing. That doesn't say they couldn't know, but very often this institution is involved in perpetuating what they would like everybody to see rather than trying to take a look at themselves in terms of reality. I don't think that self-analysis is very pervasive at this point in time." [36]

Although the Academy is quick to cite its endless series of self-study committees as evidence of official introspection, these committee reports are almost invariably regarded as *pro forma* exercises.[37] At the same time, there are many senior officials who are anxious, and even confused, about precisely what West Point academic and military training should consist of in the late 1970's and beyond. Not that Academy officials are visibly puzzled; temperamentally they are not men who display anything but the self-confident exterior they feel is expected of professional soldiers. And much of the inconsistency which, upon analysis, seems to characterize official rationales is actually a shrewdly calculated effort to appease the Academy's various audiences. The old graduates need reassurance that West Point is still committed to the principles of Sylvanus Thayer; potential cadets must be convinced that West Point is a first-rate academic institution; civilian officials in the Pentagon and Congress require proof that West Point graduates are sufficiently preferable to ROTC and OCS graduates to justify the cost of a West Pointer's training; the American public needs to believe that cadets are models of integrity who do not smoke pot, have live-in girlfriends, or cheat on exams, but who will also be inordinately efficient at destroying enemy soldiers. In the Academy's view, the inherently inconsistent character of these diverse demands requires a sophisticated public relations program proficient in verbal and statistical manipulations. With so many masters, they reason, a public servant cannot afford to be consistent.[38]

Moreover, the slogans and amorphous mottos that serve as statements of West Point's philosophy are not significantly less consistent in the 1970's than they have been throughout the Academy's history. Currently fadish terms like "self-discipline" are modern versions of older aphorisms like "Duty, Honor, Country." Just as most West Pointers do not regard the self as capable of discipline without exterior constraints, they have never resolved the tensions and contradictions between their obligation to obey orders, their obligation to follow personal ethical principles, and their obligation to serve the national interest. Similarly, Academic Board members have often talked of West Point's pedagogic goals in terms of "general education," but there is only modest evidence of any interest in or knowledge of educational philosophy. They simply use the phrase "general education" to oppose rigorous preparation in academic specialties because specialization would require fundamental curricular reform and complicate the planned placement of West Point graduates into occupational slots the Army anticipates filling. Even more obviously, twentieth-century West Point has never satisfied both the military and academic standards that the phrase "Military Academy" implies. But then official language and institutional labels have served primarily as verbal solutions to institutional problems which had no practical solutions. Until recently they have served such purposes effectively.

THE BIG FTX IN THE LAND OF THE LITTLE PEOPLE

Like most Americans, the officers on the staff and faculty at West Point are not eager to discuss the American involvement in the Vietnam war. Unlike most Americans, the vast majority of officers stationed at West Point have spent two or three years as soldiers in Southeast Asia. The rotunda of Thayer Hall contains two wooden plaques with the inscription "In proud memory of these graduates of the United States Military Academy who died in defense of freedom." Under the inscription is a list of over two hundred names and after each name is the date of death and the word "Vietnam." The two wooden plaques, the new tombstones in the West Point cemetery, the widows who gather for lunch at the Officers' Club, all serve as visible reminders that West Point has suffered more losses in Vietnam than any other American community of comparable size.[39] Another serious loss was invisible. "Since the 1960's, since our involvement in Vietnam," explained Lieutenant Colonel Thomas Blagg, "soldiering has not been looked upon as an honorable profession. Now there's certain enclaves, like certain parts of the South, where it is honorable. But basically everyone wants to know when you are going to get out. There's a tendency to apologize for being a soldier." Blagg believes that career officers are the most obvious targets for the anti-war sentiment generated by the sudden public awareness of what war involves:

> War is a pretty terrible thing. People who prosecute wars are, and have to be at least part of the time, pretty terrible people. It's a dreadful thing and always has been. When you think about it, and then when you see it all on television, you see children burning, you see homes burning, you see people with missing limbs, you realize war is a terrible thing. I don't think it's war that has changed much over the years, but public knowledge of it has changed. It's all on television. Americans liked to think of war in terms of two knights jousting on a horse with a lance. Some guy got knocked off and you picked him up. Now they know it's B 52 raids and napalm and artillery. I find myself apologizing for my role in the war, because everybody knows now, it's a terrible thing.[40]

According to Blagg's account, it was less the shifting rationales for American military involvement in Southeast Asia, or the fact that it was an unconventional war that did not allow for a clear winner or loser, but sudden public exposure to what war necessarily involves that provoked the public hostility toward soldiers. This account has certain advantages: it helps explain the hostility that many career officers have for reporters and journalists; it also diverts attention from the troublesome questions that Vietnam raised about the strategic wisdom, the organization, and the over-all competence of the American Army.

Few West Pointers would quarrel with Blagg's contention that the prestige of the professional Army officer has suffered grievously. "I heard that before the war, when you walked outside the gates of the Academy," said one cadet, "you were worshipped by everybody. Now guys avoid wearing their uniforms when they're on leave and when you go down to march in the Armed Forces parade crowds boo you." [41] Although most officers at West Point, like this cadet, concede that the Vietnam war has given the Army an "image problem" that may linger on for their entire active duty careers, they tend to discuss popular opinion as a product of journalistic distortions. Or they argue that Americans have traditionally reacted against soldiers and soldiering at the end of wars; the Vietnam war, they say, was merely another example of this ignoble American tradition. In fact, the most popular explanation for the inordinately long and elusive character of the war draws upon the conviction that civilians—elected or appointed officials and the general public—betrayed the Army in Vietnam. An Academy faculty member claimed that "The Army is being set up to take the rap for the failures in Vietnam which were the direct and inevitable result of civilian decisions and indecisions. In Vietnam, it was seldom the prerogative of the military man to define his mission. It was always imposed on him. The whole slant of the Vietnam experience has been vertical, from top to bottom. . . ." The officer then suggested how the ambiguity of the mission in Vietnam crippled the military effort:

> The Army was never given a specific and accomplishable mission in Vietnam because McNamara and Johnson and their people never resolved the problem of whether they wanted to risk war with China. So we end up out there in the boonies getting orders to win hearts and minds. And down there at battalion and company level the commander shakes his head, pats his guys on the ass and says, "Now go get 'em. And the first guy back gets the biggest banana." Then when the great American public gets fed up, it's the guys with uniforms on who have blood on their hands.[42]

Bound together by a sincere sense that they were betrayed and that civilians were disinclined to sympathize with their predicament in Vietnam, most West Pointers present a united front to outsiders. But the urge to close ranks around their own in the face of public criticism does not prevent them from unleashing, in private, scathing denunciations of certain military actions in Southeast Asia.

The junior faculty and most of the tactical officers at West Point were captains and majors in Vietnam. They were the officers ordered to "go get 'em," the men who received the nebulous mission statements sent down to battalion and company level by division commanders who were frequently far removed from the combat. Unlike most Army posts, West Point is populated almost entirely by senior company grade and junior field grade officers who saw the war from what they facetiously call "middle management positions." These officers benefitted enormously from Vietnam, because the war accelerated promotion rates and made available the command positions necessary for "career development." (A major with ten years of commissioned service earns over $1000 a year more than he would as a captain.) But their experience in Vietnam as company commanders, military advisers to South Vietnamese battalions, battalion commanders, or staff officers allowed them to perceive at first hand the crassness and stupidity of many American military policies. As one West Pointer saw it, "We were banging our heads against a cloud." [43]

West Point commentary on the Army's role in the war does not take the form of a sustained and systematic analysis of strategy or decision-making. Little of it goes on in the classroom with cadets, since the faculty are wary of disillusioning potential career officers. And cadets are not yet insiders who can be trusted to respond responsibly. The critical discussions go on in the Officers' Club, in departmental offices, or in officers' quarters after duty hours. Most are "war stories" drawn from the officers' personal experiences in what some call "the big FTX [Field Training Exercises] in the land of the little people."

The stories tend to be anecdotal variations on a "If you think that was bad, you should have been where I was" theme. The lore includes tales of the incompetence and corruption of the South Vietnamese Army, commanders who insisted that dead cattle belonged to the Vietcong and should be counted in the estimate of enemy casualties, hamlets declared secure which were ringed by cement markers on which the Vietcong had etched the elevation and deflection calculations necessary for a direct hit on all major buildings in the hamlet, generals who satisfied their thirst for battle by supervising fire-fights from the fourth tier of helicopters, 1500 feet above the battle, air-conditioned trailers which the Vietcong purposely did not sabotage for fear of killing the bungling American commander. If there is any common refrain, it is a sense that the senior officers in Vietnam who issued combat directives did not understand the war as well as junior officers who carried out the orders.[44]

"There's a difference between a body count and a list of your own casualities," explained one highly decorated major, "and there's a difference between all the goddamn numbers and holding a man in your arms when he dies. . . . Too many trailer park colonels never had the experience of the war except as an abstraction." In the same way that career soldiers at West Point believe that they were betrayed by civilians who never understood the war, many junior officers feel that they were victimized by senior officers who seldom understood the "real" war. "The guy in the command post who's not ridden on a chopper with recent casualties and hasn't seen the way the wash from the chopper causes the skin on the dead men to quiver like they were still alive, well, that guy, if he ever had that experience, wouldn't be able to 'war-game the problem' any more." A curious kind of double-vision runs through these junior officer ruminations. On the one hand these professional soldiers lament the fact that the American public was unable to sustain its support for American military actions in Vietnam. They regret that civilians lacked their particular sense of duty—the willingness to endorse the decisions of elected national leaders—that they believe characterized military behavior in the war. On the other hand, these junior officers question the wisdom and integrity of their own military superiors and civilian policy-makers. They express disrespect and distrust toward men who had authority over them. But for most of these professional soldiers the essence of military professionalism and the hallmark of a West Point graduate is obedience to duly constituted authority, even when it may not merit respect. They have less a sense or rage than of tragedy, a sense that they were and will be again the prisoners of self-serving superiors and absurd forces beyond their or anyone else's control.[45]

INTRUSIONS

The majority of senior Academy officials, especially the permanent members of the Academic Board, never served in Vietnam. Academic Board members remained at West Point, worrying about the impact of the war on cadet commitment to a military career, on the faculty "input" flowing through the "pipeline," and on the public image of the Academy. The Vietnam war coincided with, and in the minds of some Academic Board members was indirectly responsible for, a series of civilian intrusions into the operation of West Point which they observed with increased annoyance. And each intrusion produced changes that eroded the control Academy officials were accustomed to exercising over its internal affairs. What made the revision of the cadet regulations so ominous, in fact, was that it seemed responsive to an ongoing pattern of outside civilian pressures stemming from the mounting public opposition to American involvement in Southeast Asia and an increasing civilian apprehension about military men.[46]

Predictably, the admissions process was one of the areas most sensitive to public opinion. Contrary to reports published in several newspapers, the Academy experienced a gradual increase in applications throughout the 1960's. In 1970 more young men (i.e. 6003) received nominations to West Point than any other previous year in its history. The director of admissions, Colonel Manley Rogers, admitted that he was surprised: "When you pair this up with the national sentiment [toward the military], it is a kind of miracle." Between 1970 and 1974, however, the absolute number of applications went down, a decrease that Colonel Rogers attributed to "television coverage of the Army, the Vietnam war. It couldn't help but have an adverse effect on a youngster's interest in West Point." Despite the absolute increase in applications in the 1960's, Colonel Rogers believes that the publicity associated with the Vietnam war significantly reduced the Academy's drawing power. "Had it not been for Vietnam," said Rogers, "I think we would be at the level of 10,000 nominations a year instead of the high in 1970 of about 6,000." Moreover, the academic quality of all cadets admitted from 1966 to 1973, as measured by the college board scores and class rank, had decreased significantly. An increase in applications and nominations (i.e. 6095) in 1974 gave rise to hopes that public sentiment was shifting back to pre-Vietnam patterns.[47]

Officers are inclined to speak only in generalities about admissions difficulties and a host of other Academy troubles. The underlying causes for these troubles, they argue, arise from American civilian culture rather than from within the United States Army. Those few officers who willingly and publicly discuss the Army's problems do so cautiously. But, even when speaking judiciously, officers like West Pointer William L. Hauser in his *America's Army in Crisis* make remarks with ominous implications. "The United States Army is undergoing the most trying period in its long history," Colonel Hauser contends. And the problem is not, as some Academic Board members prefer to believe, that civilians have simply misunderstood the Army and its most sacred institution, West Point. The 1970's is the "most trying period" for West Point and the Army because "the Army's ills . . . constitute a manifold crisis":

> It is a crisis of confidence, born of an "unwon" war, of charges of mismanagement and incompetence attendant on that war, of increasing manifestations of public anti-militarism and of doubts about the role of ground forces. . . . It is also a crisis of conscience, stemming from charges of war crimes and official coverups, service club and post exchange kickbacks and embezzlement, larceny by the Army's top police official, and allegations of self-serving careerism in the professional officer corps. Finally, it is a crisis of adaptation, as

> the traditionally hierarchical and disciplined armed service attempts to come to terms with . . . a revolution in American styles, manners, and morals.[48]

Despite the implications of such comments, many staff and faculty members quickly argue, "Well, after all, this is West Point, not the 'Army.' " But to an increasing number of Americans, West Point is no longer immune from their skepticism, if not hostility, and this skepticism grows out of a disenchantment with "the Army's ills." However, most of the major officials at the Academy convey the ambience of islanders removed from the problems of the mainland. They ask, "How can we carry out our training mission if we have to worry about all that crap on the outside. They'll [cadets] have to deal with the real world soon enough." For many officials the Academy's insularity is a crucial natural barrier which has historically shielded West Point from many civilian and military tribulations. The increased intrusions of recent years are viewed as unwelcomed irritants from a more troubled world that must not be allowed to infect the local population.[49]

The most visible contemporary intrusion began in the late 1960's when pressure from the Congress to implement the spirit of the civil rights legislation of the early and mid-1960's began to take effect. In 1968 only nine blacks were admitted as cadets. From 1969 to 1974 the Academy admitted an average of fifty blacks into each plebe class. Although Colonel Rogers would like to have admitted more than twice that number of blacks in order that "this Academy represent the country ethnically as the Congress intended that it represent the country geographically," even the modest increase in the number of blacks into the Corps of Cadets produced serious problems. The more structured character of the West Point curriculum made the addition of racially oriented courses that blacks requested more difficult than at civilian colleges. Since there had been very few blacks at West Point prior to 1969 (more blacks were enrolled as cadets in 1972 than had graduated from the Academy since 1802), some of the traditions and regulations struck the blacks as discriminatory.[50] For example, blacks argued that the haircut regulation did not take the different texture and shape of black hair into account. "The head envisioned by the person who wrote the regulation was not a black head," said one black cadet. "What the authorities had in mind was a blond, blue-eyed Spartan." [51]

In 1970 the blacks began to complain that there were few black girls at the dances or "hops" arranged by the authorities at West Point. After some white cadets expressed their resentment that blacks were dancing with white girls, Academy officials granted the blacks permission to schedule a dance of their own. During this time the black cadets flooded a pre-existent cadet organization, the Behavioral Science Club, and turned it into the vehicle for other black reform efforts. The Behavioral Science Club became West Point's version of the Black Student Alliance and successfully opposed the construction of a monument to the Confederacy on Academy grounds (a suggestion made by President Nixon), staged a rock concert for the benefit of the Sickle Cell Anemia Foundation, and issued a militant manifesto which listed the grievances of West Point's blacks in the form of the grievances against George III set forth in the Declaration of Independence. By 1974 the black protest movement had died down, in part because the Academy officials had granted many of the black requests and had conducted a number of racial seminars designed to increase communication between the blacks and the whites on the post. But the Academy's willingness to modify traditional policies to accommodate uniquely black habits or preferences disturbed those West Pointers who insisted that "there can be only one mold here and everyone has to fit himself into it or leave." By the mid-1970's it was becoming more difficult to think of the Corps of Cadets as a monolithic and uniform whole. Blacks constituted a separate and distinct faction that claimed to have interests and needs different from the remainder of the corps. From the perspective of a modern-day disciple of Sylvanus Thayer, this was subversive.[52]

Another series of challenges which threatened the disciplinary goals of the Thayer System came from the federal courts. In 1972 three cadets who had been dismissed from the Academy for "deficiencies in their military conduct" hired a lawyer affiliated with the American Civil Liberties Union who secured an injunction against the Academy, arguing that the procedures employed to dismiss the cadets violated their legal right to due process. The Academy appealed, but the appeal was denied. The three cadets were reinstated at West Point and the long-standing disciplinary system of the Academy was subjected to legal scrutiny. For six weeks the members of the Academic Board met in a series of marathon sessions in which they attempted, in the words of one of the members, to "crank due process into the system." This meant that they were trying to insert provisions guaranteeing the individual rights of each cadet into a disciplinary system that for over a century and a half had operated on the assumption that individuals must surrender certain rights upon entering West Point in order to facilitate their indoctrination as soldiers. Although the Academic Board followed the directive of the courts, some senior officers considered the court ruling inappropriate, for it imposed liberal, civilian standards on a military institution that must remain martial, they thought, if it was to produce disciplined Army officers; and the courts were assuming jurisdiction over Academy procedures which West Point officials had come to regard as their exclusive preserve.[53]

At the same time that the disciplinary system of the Academy was being debated in the courtroom and within the Academic Board, another case was being adjudicated in the federal courts. Ever since the superintendency of Sylvanus Thayer, cadets had been required by regulation to attend weekly church services. Colonel Sumner Willard offered a candid explanation of the Academy's position on required religious ceremonies: "I personally feel that mandatory chapel is not a bad thing. It was never raised as an issue throughout most of the Academy's history until we came into the present era of permissiveness. . . . It was not 'religion by the numbers' or making people go to church on a 'goddamn it' basis. It was construed historically as being part of man's moral formation, part of the formation of his character." [54] In January 1973, however, the courts ruled that none of the service academies could require attendance at church, for to do so violated the cadets' constitutional right to religious freedom provided by the First Amendment. Chaplain James Ford estimated that about 50 per cent of the Catholics and 30 per cent of the Protestants were in attendance at chapel on January 14, 1973, the first Sunday after the court ruling went into effect. "The numbers have gone down significantly," he admitted. "But then, where do you go from a hundred per cent?" [55]

The elimination of compulsory chapel evoked many of the same issues raised by the court rulings on the disciplinary system the previous autumn. The challenges to procedures governing honor trials the following spring also reasserted the contention that the Military Academy could not claim that its unique military mission made it immune to the protections accorded American citizens under the Constitution. In the minds of some West Pointers it was reminiscent of the scenario in Vietnam: the professional soldiers had been given a mission, then deprived of the means to carry out the mission. "The courts don't understand what's going on here," one tenured professor asserted. "No court could understand even with the best of good will. . . . They've opened up a kind of Pandora's box by stripping us of the means to inculcate our values into the cadets." [56] And throughout the Academy there was much speculation that the chapel decision had implications which went even deeper. According to Chaplain Ford, mandatory chapel had ensured that each cadet would recognize that there was an absolute religious sanction for a soldier's actions. "These men had to go out of here knowing they would be involved in the taking of life," he explained. They needed what Ford called "an ethical taproot" or a "transcendental, not just a relative ethic." [57] Chapel helped to provide men who must fight wars with a belief in the absolute rightness of their cause. A West Point veteran of the Korean and Vietnam wars recalled that "my business was in leading men in a combat situation with other men and the other men were pretty darn dedicated to destroying you. There's only one way to do that, you know. You've got to be convinced that what you're doing is right, or, you just can't do it." From this perspective the elimination of mandatory chapel was not just another case of judicial intrusion into a matter historically recognized as the prerogative of a necessarily illiberal institution, but a tampering with the spiritual certification most soldiers necessarily crave.[58]

WHAT DOES THE FUTURE HOLD?

Although the Academy has managed to preserve its insularity throughout most of American history, its isolation from American life has never been complete. West Point has always sought approval from those whose sons are "the annual input of manpower" on which the institution operates. It has also attempted to cultivate a wide base of public support, because the presence of a large number of civilian supporters has been psychologically important to West Pointers, who genuinely conceive of themselves as rendering service to the country. West Pointers in the United States Army still think of themselves as men who are duty-bound to follow civilian dictates and who are ultimately dependent, psychologically and financially, on the support of their fellow countrymen. But the need to sustain both forms of support coexists with the desire to retain control over how the support is used.

The reforms forced upon the Academy in the late 1960's and early 1970's not only altered the racial, legal, and religious practices which officials regarded as sacrosanct traditions, but also constituted a series of challenges to the Academy's belief in its right to control its own affairs. In the eyes of many West Pointers, who were not accustomed to having their rhetoric analyzed and their inconsistencies examined, civilian intrusions are regarded with hostility. The officials at West Point, especially the members of the Academic Board, view the remainder of the decade as a time for withdrawal, consolidation, and retrenchment. One junior faculty member put it more cynically: "It's time for the low-profilers again. Those guys just want to be left the hell alone. The world has been tinkering with their parade and they don't like it." [59]

In the spring of 1974 General Knowlton was preparing to leave the superintendency after his four-and-a-half-year tour. His replacement, Major General Sidney B. Berry, was a West Point graduate (class of 1948) with a reputation for stern discipline and a sterling combat record.[60] Academy officials were pointing, on one hand, to liberalizing changes effected during Knowlton's reign, and, on the other hand, suggesting that the selection of Berry indicated that hallowed military traditions remained in force. As for scheduled future changes (and there are always contingency plans which can be invoked to demonstrate that the Academy is "keeping up with the times"), officials pointed to a possible 10 per cent cut in the amount of a cadet's scheduled time, continuing refinement of the new cadet regulations, modifications in expenditures due to an ongoing Government Accounting Office study, and perhaps even the elimination of the requirement that plebes sit erect on the front edges of their chairs during meals.[61] The latter plan prompted one officer to observe, "Now that they can get enough to eat, they'll probably be thinking of sex all the time. When I was a plebe, all I could think about was chocolate chip cookies." But the isolation of plebes from the rest of the Corps will remain, because "they still can't talk to upperclassmen unless they [plebes] are spoken to first. Not that it really matters; they don't want to talk to anybody but each other anyway." [62]

Nor is West Point eager to "talk to" outsiders. The plebes' programmed remoteness from upperclass cadets mirrors the Academy's remoteness from the American public. In both instances West Pointers prefer to initiate whatever communication occurs and to control the extent of the exchanges. Insulation from public scrutiny will allow the Academy to retain its military mission—"to instruct and train the Corps of Cadets so that each graduate will have the qualities and attributes essential to his progressive and continued development throughout his career as an officer of the Regular Army"; it will also allow the Academy to avoid redefining what these "qualities and attributes" should be in the last quarter of the twentieth century. Nor will there be widespread discussion of the Thayer System's continued appropriateness as a method for inculcating these qualities, even though Academy graduates are likely to occupy sensitive positions in which they will shape as well as implement national policies. Despite the interminable in-fighting that will persist among the conflicting vested interests inside the Academy, the generally unfailing reflex will be to present a united front to all outsiders, whether they be visiting Congressmen or tourists from Muncie.

Despite the recent federal and private "intrusions," the withdrawal behind the stone walls of the fortress on the Hudson will allow the basic facts of Academy life to remain intact: Beast Barracks and the Fourth Class System will separate those unwilling to conform and socialize those who stay; the inbred faculty will give their primary allegiance to military as opposed to academic concerns; the four-year cadet experience will prepare men to operate under stress in order to meet prescribed goals assigned by higher authorities. Admiral Thomas H. Moorer observes this pattern of events with enthusiasm: "One can't fail to look at these graduates," he said in June of 1973, "and not only get a thrill over what they represent, but more than that, a feeling of confidence for the future." [63] General James M. Gavin, an Academy graduate and self-confessed maverick, is less sanguine. In the 1950's he advised Superintendent Gar Davidson that "the most important thing" the Academy could do "was to protect the individual . . . and protect the maverick." And he also urged West Point to "develop curiosity" which is "a search for ideas, a search for knowledge." But he admitted, "I don't think the idea ever sunk in," and he continues to worry that "the Academy tends to stultify curiosity and put it into a mold that might tend to deaden it." [64]

Moorer's optimism and Gavin's anxiety grow out of differing visions of what Americans of the future will expect and demand of their soldiers. If they want energetic combat leaders with organizational and administrative skills, West Point is likely to satisfy their desires. If Americans require soldier-statesmen equipped to examine the assumptions underlying our domestic and foreign policies, West Point is less likely to serve national interests. Regardless of what American civilians want, the Academy is likely to make the contention that it stands ready to fill all national needs.

Notes

Chapter One

1. Quoted in Thomas J. Fleming, *West Point: The Men and Times of the United States Military Academy* (New York, 1969), 19. See Stephen E. Ambrose, *Duty, Honor, Country: A History of West Point* (Baltimore, 1966), 1–37, for the best account of Williams' superintendency.

2. Carl Cramer's "The Heritage of the Hudson," which serves as a foreword to John K. Howat's *The Hudson River and Its Painters* (New York, 1972, 19–24), evokes the nostalgic charm of this area as do the handsome reproductions of nineteenth-century work of West Point and the surrounding countryside by American painters Crospey, Durand, Kensett, and Weir, the English artist William H. Bartlett, and the French designer Pierre Charles L'Enfant.

3. Interview with the Reverend James D. Ford, March 1973. The Academy maintains a Visitors Information Center from April 15 to November 15 where "personnel are on duty to help visitors plan a self-conducted tour and to answer questions. A West Point movie is shown here." Academy officials estimate that "approximately two and one-half million persons visit the Academy each year." Data obtained from USMA, Information Office, November 1973.

4. From a four-page pamphlet distributed at West Point in 1973 describing the Cadet Chapel, the Old Cadet Chapel where "[f]unerals and Jewish Services are held," the Post Chapel which is "a family chapel for the faculty and post personnel other than cadets," and the Catholic Chapel.

5. George S. Pappas, *The Cadet Chapel: United States Military Academy*, 3rd ed. (West Point, 1965), 33.

6. USMA, *Bugle Notes, 1973* (West Point, 1973), 81–96, 127–28; Senior Chapter, Daughters, United States Army, West Point, *The West Point Guide Book* (West Point, 1973); USMA, *Fourth Class Knowledge* (West Point, 1962), 7, and *Visitors Information Pamphlet* (West Point, n.d.). Willis is quoted in Howat, *The Hudson River*, 151.

Since 1908 *Bugle Notes* has been an official publication of the Corps of Cadets. It is prepared by a cadet staff under the supervision of West Point officers and is primarily "used as a vehicle of enlightenment for each entering fourth class" but it "also provides a handy pocket reference for both the cadet and the graduate." See *Bugle Notes, 1973, 234.*

7. *Bugle Notes, 1973,* 55.

8. USMA, *The Fourth Class System* (West Point, 1972), 11–12, and USMA, *The New Cadet: Information For The Parents of The Class of 1977* (West Point, 1973), 11.

9. Mahan Hall, which first opened to classes in 1972, is the Academy's newest academic building. A nine-story structure with five floors below and four floors above the level of the Plain, it is visible proof of the Academy's determination to preserve its traditional atmosphere. During its early construction in the late 1960's, workmen on the project speculated about when the structure, perched precariously on the banks of the Hudson, would topple into the river. In USMA, *Report of the Board of Visitors* (West Point, 1970), there is an acknowledgment that "the completion of this building has suffered a delay of approximately one year because of engineering difficulties encountered in foundation work caused by geological anomalies not revealed in test borings. As a result, the Army has found it necessary to submit . . . a deficiency funding request for this facility in the amount of $2,581,000. Alternatives to seeking deficiency funding were thoroughly explored, but were rejected because they . . . would have resulted in a facility incapable of performing its mission." (11) In USMA, *Report of the Board of Visitors* (West Point, 1971), there is a notation that a "$2.6 million deficiency for the Academic Building was approved by Congress in December 1970" (Annex 1-1).

West Point, United States Military Academy: 1973–74 Catalog (West Point, 1973), describes the Board of Visitors as a group "appointed under the provisions of an Act of Congress approved 29 June 1948. This act specified that a Board of Visitors shall visit the Military Academy each year and inquire into the state of morale and discipline, curriculum, instruction, physical equipment, fiscal affairs, academic methods, and other matters relating to the institution which the Board may decide to consider and submit a written report to the President of the United States giving its views and recommendations . . ." (168).

10. *Bugle Notes, 1973*, 124. A USMA pamphlet, *The West Point Expansion Program* (West Point, n.d., 1) which was publically circulated at the Academy in 1970 stated:

> Legislation was approved by President Johnson on 3 March 1964 to expand the USMA Corps of Cadets from a strength of 2529 to 4417 cadets. . . . The increase in Cadet strength began almost immediately following authorizing legislation. Actual strengths of entering classes from 1964 through 1967 averaged 1050 new cadets, increasing the size of the Corps by about 200 cadets each year. Subsequent incoming classes are programmed to average approximately 1360 new cadets, continuing the incremenal increase and bringing the Corps to its authorized strength of 4417 by July 1972.

A 1970's attrition rate of almost 35 per cent has kept the Corps far below its authorized strength:

USMA CADET ATTRITION CLASSES OF 1968 THROUGH 1977

Class	*No. Entered*	*No. Graduated*	*Per Cent Lost*	*Class*	*No. Entered*	*No. Enrolled (April 19, 1974)*	*Per Cent Lost*
1968	989	706	28.6	1974	1373	846	38.4
1969	1132	800	29.4	1975	1339	870	35.1

Class	*No. Entered*	*No. Graduated*	*Per Cent Lost*	*Class*	*No. Entered*	*No. Enrolled (April 19, 1974)*	*Per Cent Lost*
1970	1017	749	26.4	1976	1378	955	30.8
1971	1054	729	30.9	1977	1376	1110	19.3
1972	1244	822	34.0				
1973	1438	944	35.1				

In a statement to authors on April 19, 1974, Lieutenant Colonel Thomas P. Garigan of the USMA Public Affairs Office (formerly Information Office) noted "that the Class of '77 is running nearly four percentage points less in attrition than was the Class of '76 on this date a year ago (23.4% to 19.6%)." The Corps has approached its authorized strength "almost every July, when the new class enters . . . 6 July 1971 (4,258), 20 July 1972 (4,227), and 9 July 1973 (4,162). . . . Our strength figure, when the new class enters this July [1974], will be near 4300."

Above calculations based on Office of Institutional Research's *Trends in Admission Variables Through the Class of 1976* (West Point, January 1973), 30; Michael J. Krisman, ed., *Register of Graduates and Former Cadets of the United States Military Academy* (West Point, 1973); and statement to authors by Lieutenant Colonel Thomas P. Garigan, April 19, 1974.

11. Interview with West Point officer, January 1973.

12. Samuel P. Huntington, *The Soldier and the State: The Theory and Politics of Civil-Military Relations* (New York, 1957), 464–65.

13. Philip Rieff, " 'Fellow Teachers,' " *Salmagundi*, XX (Summer-Fall 1972), 15.

14. Transcript of Bob Hope's remarks supplied by Lieutenant Colonel Patrick H. Dionne, Information Officer, USMA, June 1973.

15. Lieutenant General William A. Knowlton, letter to "Fellow Graduates and Friends of the Military Academy," *Assembly*, XXX (Fall 1971), inside front cover.

16. John P. Marquand, *Melville Goodwin, USA* (Boston, 1951), 252.

17. John P. Lovell, "The Cadet Phase of the Professional Socialization of the West Pointer: Description, Analysis, and Theoretical Refinement," unpublished Ph.D. dissertation (University of Wisconsin, 1962), 99–124.

18. U. S. Grant to C. W. Ford, May 3, 1871, U.S. Grant Papers, Library of Congress. Citation courtesy of Professor William McFeely, January 1974. Professor McFeely is preparing a biography of Grant.

19. Dwight D. Eisenhower, *At Ease: Stories I Tell to Friends* (New York, 1967), 4.

20. "*Assembly* Visits General Eisenhower," *Assembly*, XXVII (Spring 1968), 4.

21. Martin Blumenson, ed., *The Patton Papers*, 1885–1940 (Boston, 1972), 155, 198.

22. Maxwell D. Taylor, *Swords and Plowshares* (New York, 1972), 121.

23. Lovell, "Cadet Phase of Socialization" (1962), 38.

24. Quoted in *Look*, October 6, 1970, 36.

25. "Founders Day 1971," *Assembly*, XXX (Spring 1971), 17.

26. Huntington, *The Soldier and the State*, 466.

27. Ernest B. Furgurson, *Westmoreland: The Inevitable General* (Boston, 1968), 290.

28. Abbot Boone, "To Get Ahead Requires Hard Work . . . but a little luck helps," *Assembly*, XXVIII (Spring 1969), 49. Due to his status as the oldest graduate in attendance, Boone (class of 1907) had given three previous speeches at West Point Founders Day dinners. Many West Point officers welcome the provocative rhetoric of an elderly graduate like Boone; however, concern for their image as apolitical professionals usually inhibits critical generalizing about American society as a whole. But West Point officers welcome extravagant remarks from others even though the rhetoric can border on the hysterical. For instance, in the November 5, 1973 *Civilian Personnel Bulletin* Joseph V. Sparmo, West Point's Civilian Personnel Officer, addressed these remarks to "Employees of West Point":

> Have you been touched by the magic of West Point, as I have? Has it occurred to you that you work for the most magnificent Institution this country has ever known? Can you sense the presence of history that oozes from the buildings where you work and from the grounds where you walk? It will do you well to reflect upon this occasionally during your daily routine.
>
> When you look into the fresh, young faces of the Cadets do you see Grant, Lee, Pershing, Goethals, Patton, MacArthur or Eisenhower? They are there you know. Believe me when I tell you, *they are there!* As an employee of West Point you are entitled to take comfort in the knowledge that you are a part of America's greatness. Take advantage of this to ease your mind. Share the joy of it with your co-workers, your friends and your family. It's available only to you who work here . . . .
>
> The huddled masses yearning to breathe free indeed came to America. They came for freedom and liberty. This freedom and liberty has been protected and insured for you in large measure by the leadership of those who have passed through West Point.
>
> You who mop the floors, clean the latrines, pick up the trash, serve the tables, operate the machines, man the typewriters, all of you who work here; stand tall and proud. You work at West Point!

Within the confines of West Point, such remarks (which were also translated into Spanish for the scores of Puerto Ricans who hold menial jobs on post) are viewed by many as perhaps overzealous, but not inappropriate in their basic emphasis.

29. Lee Ewing, "Col. Anthony Herbert: The Unmaking of an Accuser," *Columbia Journalism Review* (Sept.–Oct. 1973), 8–14, offers a systematic account of the publicity Herbert attracted and of his fateful appearance on CBS-TV's *60 Minutes* in February 1973.

30. Anthony B. Herbert's Foreword to K. Bruce Galloway and Robert Bowie Johnson, Jr., *West Point: America's Power Fraternity* (New York, 1973), 16.

31. Anthony B. Herbert, with James T. Wooten, *Soldier* (New York, 1973), 73–74. Colonel John D. Foldberg was the tactical officer in charge of the Ranger

class Herbert describes. Foldberg disputes Herbert's version of what happened, claiming that "Tony tells a good story—it just didn't happen the way he described it." Foldberg recalls that Herbert was not stationed at the Ranger School when the incident occurred, that Herbert misspelled his name, incorrectly identified Foldberg as a former Army All-American fullback (he was an All-American end), that the Ranger class was composed of both ROTC and West Point graduates, that only five West Pointers participated in the mini-mutiny. Furthermore, Foldberg claims, no one threw rifles into the swamp. The five officers refused to perform a "confidence exercise, the log walk and rope drop over the Yellow River." Interview with Colonel John D. Foldberg, August 1973. Professor John P. Lovell, USMA '55, was in this 1955 Ranger class and corroborated Colonel Foldberg's account in a telephone interview, March 1974.

32. Bruce Galloway and Robert B. Johnson, Jr., "Playboy Interview: Anthony Herbert," *Playboy* (July 1972), 61. For an argument supporting the advantages of a band-of-brothers feeling among West Pointers and "the team spirit of the professional Army," see Matthew B. Ridgway's *Soldier* (New York, 1956), 27–28.

33. Ewing, "Col. Anthony Herbert," 12–14; Peter Braestrup, "A Soldier's Tale," *Book World*, in *Washington Post*, February 18, 1973, and Barry Lando, "The Herbert Affair" *Atlantic* (May 1973).

34. Galloway and Johnson, "Playboy Interview: Anthony Herbert," 61.

35. Lee Ewing, "Why One 'Soldier' Won't Fade Away," *Family* in *Army Times*, July 4, 1973, 18. Despite the fact that *Soldier* was a best seller at the time of Ewing's comments, Herbert's credibility has subsequently eroded. He was in the news again in 1974 "when a Cranbury, N. J. gas station operator refused to sell gasoline to Colonel Herbert" and Herbert "allegedly stated he was an Army Criminal Investigation Division agent working for the Internal Revenue Service. . . . The F.B.I. said that Colonel Herbert denied the station operator's charges, and that Federal officials in New Jersey decided not to press a possible charge of impersonating a Federal official. . . ." *New York Times*, February 22, 1974, 35.

36. See the advertisement for King's book entitled "Is corruption killing the U.S. Army?" in *New York Review of Books*, June 15, 1972, 29. Although few reviewers shared Seymour Hersh's absolute conviction about the merits of King's book, it was generally well received in the press. Among most Army officers, King's generally undistinguished career compromised his credibility.

37. Edward L. King, *The Death of the Army: A Pre-Mortem* (New York, 1972), 115–26, and Ward Just, *Military Men* (New York, 1970), 16. Just's skillfully written, but highly impressionistic, chapter on West Point ("The Academy", 15–52) so agitated Academy officials that officers were assigned to scrutinize Just's text and locate every error of fact in what is a generally perceptive discussion. After compiling a list of errors (e.g. incorrect biographical data on officers and incomplete statistical information on various aspects of Academy life), the Academy unsuccessfully attempted to find a public forum for a response to Just. They almost succeeded when Professor John Seelye of the University of Connecticut used some of the material the Academy had prepared for critical essay on the "New Journalism" with Just's work as the

primary focus; however, Seelye's essay, which was reportedly scheduled for publication in *The New Republic*, was not printed because of a last minute editorial decision.

The irreconcilable differences in methodology between Ward Just's impressionistic *Military Men* and most West Pointers' preoccupation with "getting the facts right" is suggested by Just's comment on "facts." He said, "The die was cast for me in 1969 when I went to the [*Washington*] *Post* editorial page. I found I had no more respect for facts after my Vietnam experience [as correspondent]. Here I was trying to make sense of facts on the edit[orial] page, and I was thinking that facts don't lead you very far, facts don't lead you to the truth, they just lead to more facts." Quoted from Michael Kernan's interview with Ward Just in *Washington Post*, July 20, 1973, B1, B8.

38. King, 119. Major Josiah Bunting served in the departments of Social Sciences and History from 1969 until his resignation from the Army in 1972. His novel *The Lionheads* (New York, 1972) based on his service with the Ninth Infantry Division in Vietnam under Major General Julian J. Ewell, USMA '39, was generously praised by Ward Just, Harrison Salisbury, and William Styron. See the *New York Times Book Review*, June 11, 1972, 10. For critiques of *The Lionheads*, see reviews by Charles Black, the *Columbus* (Ga.) *Enquirer*, April 24, 1972, 7, and Robert H. Moore in *The New Republic*, August 19 and 26, 1972, 22–23, and *Book World*, in *Washington Post*, September 16, 1972, C4.

Bunting's resignation from the Army was the subject of national attention. See Seymour M. Hersh, "33 Teachers at West Point Leave Army in 18 Months," *New York Times*, June 25, 1972, 1, 42; Lucian K. Truscott, IV, "Major Bunting's Farewell Address," *Saturday Review*, July 29, 1972, 7–8, 12; and Thomas Moore, "A man of letters marches out of West Point" in "Parting Shots" section of *Life*, July 28, 1972. *Harper's* announced in its October 1972 issue a forthcoming article giving "Josiah Bunting's insider's view of why West Point turns smart plebes into stupid generals" (119), but the article never appeared. Bunting's public presence continued to be an annoyance to the Academy when Lee Ewing's feature story on Bunting, "Army Dropout," *Family*, in *Army Times*, January 3, 1973, 4–5, 10, produced a controversy within the superintendent's staff over whether or not Ewing's story was a satiric attack on Bunting or "more of Bunting putting us in a bad light." Interviews with West Point officers, October 1972 and January 1973.

After his 1972 resignation from the Army, Bunting became professor of military history at the Naval War College, Newport, Rhode Island until his selection as the president of Briarcliff College in New York State in the summer of 1973.

39. Galloway and Johnson, *West Point*, 22. Significant portions of Galloway and Johnson's discussion of the curriculum and faculty in their third chapter, "Take Seats!" are drawn from conversations with us at USMA in June 1971, material we supplied, and subsequent conversations with RHM in August 1972 and February 1973. In the winter of 1973, Mr. Johnson provided copies of the advance, uncorrected proofs for this book which presented in the Introduction their conclusion "that the Academy should be abolished, for it rests at the heart of the separation of

the American Army from the American people." When Mr. Johnson indicated his intention of acknowledging our assistance in the published text, he respected our request not to do so. In the specific context of the Galloway and Johnson Acknowledgments, such a citation would have suggested a tacit approval of polemical intentions and conclusions which we do not support.

40. *Ibid.*, 388.

41. This listing of West Pointers in positions of national prominence and power won plaudits from many reviewers of Galloway and Johnson's book. We are not aware of a review which discussed the irony that what many civilian readers regarded as an exposé is based to an extraordinary extent on the Academy's own alumni publications. There are over seventy primary citations to *Assembly* and of the thirty-two issues of *Assembly* published from 1964 to 1971 the authors used quotations or other substantive material from twenty-eight issues. Among the more interesting reviews of the book are those by Arthur Cooper in *Newsweek*, June 11, 1973, 108; James A. Donovan in *Chicago Tribune*, June 17, 1973, Sec. 7, 1–2; Franklin R. Silbey in *Book World* in *Washington Post*, July 17, 1973, B2; and Gore Vidal in *New York Review of Books*, October 18, 1973, 21–22, 24, 26–28.

42. Galloway and Johnson, *West Point*, 18, 21. In addition to this book, Robert Johnson has published other work on the Academy and the Army. He is most compelling in drawing on his personal experience to demonstrate how the regimentation of Army life and Vietnam combat became intolerable for him. See Johnson's "The Tainted Image of West Point," *The Progressive*, XXXV (February 1971), 13–18; "Testimony from the War's Trigger End," *Washington Monthly* (August 1971), 22–35, and "The Army, from the Hudson to Mekong" [review of books by King and Bunting cited above], *Baltimore Sun*, October 22, 1972, D7.

43. *Ibid.*, 279.

44. Interview with Colonel Lee D. Olvey, June 1973.

45. General Knowlton's comments about "a hostile outside world" and the American "environment" were made in alumni speeches he gave in March 1972 and his charges against the "erratic fraction of one percent" of West Pointers were made in alumni speeches in March 1973. Copies of the basic texts General Knowlton used in an annual series of Founders Day speeches in March (1971–73) and in his annual fall term address to West Point officers from 1970 to 1973 were provided by General Knowlton in February and March 1974.

The unnamed individuals General Knowlton believed to be responsible for "this latest wave" of "unwelcome publicity" and "antimilitary propaganda" and against whom he makes his allegations were apparently Robert Bowie Johnson, Jr., Josiah Bunting, and Lucian K. Truscott, IV, a 1969 graduate and writer for *The Village Voice.* Knowlton's hostility to these men is better understood in light of: Galloway and Johnson's suggestion of Knowlton's involvement with "war crimes" during his service "as the 'hustling Director of the Revolutionary Development Support Directorate, Pacification Chief' in Vietnam" (*West Point*, 375–76); Bunting's portrayal of the personality of the villainous Major General George S. Lemming in *The Lionheads*, in part a reflection of Bunting's view of General Knowlton; Truscott's articles in *The*

Village Voice and elsewhere (see his *Saturday Review* article on Bunting cited above), which have been critical of West Point since Knowlton assumed the superintendency. In an August 1973 speech to West Point officers, General Knowlton observed, "The period since I arrived in March 1970 has been a very sporty one. And yet I think West Point has survived this period in relatively good shape when one considers the forces with which we have to contend."

46. Interview with West Point officer, June 1972.

47. Interview with Cecilia O'Keefe, January 1973.

48. Interview with West Point cadet, May 1972. *Regulations for the United States Corps of Cadets* (West Point, 1973) states in paragraph 214: "A cadet quoted in the various news media concerning official matters is likely to be perceived by the audience as officially representing the United States Corps of Cadets and the United States Military Academy. Since cadets normally will have neither the authority nor the full knowledge required for such representation, they will not grant interviews concerning official matters to members of the news media without the specific approval of Headquarters, USCC, or the Information Officer, USMA. The [last-named] individual is specifically designated and authorized by the Superintendent to represent the United States Military Academy to the news media, and to act as a liaison agent between the Academy and media representatives." *Cadets who did not have "the specific approval" cited above have not been identified by name nor have we identified West Point officers whom we interviewed unless they had the appropriate approval to grant interviews. We are especially grateful to our former students in the Corps of Cadets and the officers on the West Point faculty and staff for consenting to interviews which were not officially sanctioned by the Academy.*

49. Interview with West Point cadet, June 1972.

50. Interview with West Point cadet, March 1973.

51. The Office of Institutional Research [OIR] in "carrying out . . . [its] mission . . . conducts research and studies on candidates, cadets, and graduates; provides professional consulting services to other USMA agencies engaged in institutional research; and maintains USMA central information files on candidates, cadets, and graduates." In fiscal year 1973 this agency completed twenty-seven reports on matters ranging from "Characteristics of the Class of 1976" to "A Research Note on the Civilian Occupations of USMA Graduates." See OIR's *Summary of Institutional Research at the U.S. Military Academy for Fiscal Year 1973* (West Point, 1973), 2, 36.

Unless otherwise noted, all of the OIR studies we cite were provided at our request by Colonel Gerald W. Medsger, director of OIR, with the understanding that these studies were "non-sensitive reports which already had been cleared for release outside the Academy or which I [Colonel Medsger] could release on my own authority under the provisions of USMA Regulation 70-1." This statement is from Colonel Medsger's "Memorandum for the Record," March 23, 1973.

52. OIR, *Characteristics of the Class of 1976* (West Point, 1972), 1, 8, 19, 29. See also OIR's *A Comparison of New Cadets at USMA with Entering Freshmen at Other Colleges, Class of 1976* (West Point, 1973), 1, 5, 6. In a May 1973 interview Colonel Gerald W. Medsger spoke of the precarious role of his office in a school where peo-

ple "are very jealous of their own prerogatives" and of the "natural human tendency not to be over enthusiastic about somebody looking at you and coming up with findings or conclusions that you don't necessarily agree with." He noted, "There are those who believe in this kind of research and who want to see it take place and who support it and there are those who don't believe [in it] and don't want to see it take place. . . . I've been very fortunate. The two superintendents [Samuel W. Koster and Knowlton] that I've had, and most of the commandants, have been interested. They have supported this [office]. I'm keeping my fingers crossed that if I'm here when the next group comes along that I'll be as fortunate.

53. *A Comparison of New Cadets* (1973), 16, 17, 19, 21.

54. *Barron's Profiles of American Colleges: The United States Military Academy* (Woodbury, N.Y., 1974), 1–2, 8–9; OIR's *Summary of Institutional Research, 1971* (West Point, 1971), 6, 35. See Chapter Four, note 52, for a discussion of the costs for one cadet.

In a May 1973 interview, Colonel Gerald W. Medsger commented on why substantial numbers of West Pointers were resigning after completing their five-year commitment:

> From what I saw, both on the basis of our survey data and some personal interviews, they looked around and they saw what colonels were doing and generals were doing, the environment of the Army, and said, "I don't want to spend 20 years of my life working hard to get up to that position and do that." I would say that was the single biggest thing. They just said "Hey, I don't want to be a colonel or a general! If that's what it entails, if that's what they do and how they're treated, it's all so pointless. Just too much work and too much time for too little. And I feel that I can do more for myself and perhaps more for my country outside in some other profession."

Aside from this new factor, Colonel Medsger contended that "the general reasons are still the same" as in the 1960's—" 'I can do better on the outside. My wife doesn't like the Army' and so on. It is surprising that there has not been a more dramatic change in the reasons."

55. Interview with West Point officer, January 1973.

56. OIR, *Civilian Careers of USMA Graduates* (West Point, 1972), 9.

57. Interview with West Point officers, January 1973.

58. Interview with West Point cadet, March 1973.

59. Interview with Cadet Philip R. Linder, March 1973.

60. Interviews with recent West Point graduate, June 1972, and West Point cadet, January 1973.

61. February 1973 letter from recent West Point graduate to authors.

62. January 1973 letter from recent West Point graduate to authors.

63. Interview with former cadet Donald D. Cantlay, November 1972.

64. Interview with West Point cadet, May 1972.

Chapter Two

1. Interview with West Point officers, January 1973.

2. The Pelosi case is discussed in Chapter Six. Thirty-six per cent of the graduates of the class of 1915 "became general officers. . . . The class produced two Generals of the Army [Bradley and Eisenhower], two Generals [Joseph T. McNarney, who commanded the Air Force in Europe and James A. Van Fleet who commanded the 8th Army in Korea], seven Lieutenant Generals, 24 Major Generals, and 24 Brigadier Generals." See *Pointer View*, May 4, 1973, 1. *Pointer View* is "an authorized unofficial publication, published weekly under the supervision of the Information Office, USMA" (2).

3. Interview with Colonel William F. Luebbert, Director of the Instruction Support Division, June 1973. Colonel Luebbert enjoys the unusual privilege of knowing that the array of machinery and manpower at his disposal gives him what is probably the outstanding program of its kind in the country. In addition to commanding the Academic Computer Center, Colonel Luebbert's responsibilities also include the Instructional Technology Center facilities consisting of "a new RCA color studio and control room with studio cameras, professional video tape recorders, slide and motion picture equipment, and special effects generators. Working closely with faculty, the Center produces 16mm educational films, single-concept, super 8mm films, and multi-image and multimedia instructional programs. A closed-circuit color distribution system carries the instructional programs to over 440 classrooms and to the Library. Large screen television is available in auditoriums and lecture halls, and candid videotapes of classroom and physical skills situations are recorded on portable equipment." See *West Point: 1973–74 Catalog*, 107–8.

4. The best of the standard histories is Ambrose, *Duty, Honor, Country*, which addresses many of the important military and educational issues that shaped the historical evolution of the Academy. Fleming's *West Point*, written for the general reader with the support of funds from the *Reader's Digest*, is anecdotal rather than analytical; and Colonel R. Ernest DuPuy's *Men of West Point* (New York, 1952) is a eulogy. A book by the Academy's former librarian, Sidney Forman, *West Point* (New York, 1950), is more scholarly than the books by Fleming and DuPuy, but we found it less complete than Ambrose's work. No single history of West Point covers the subject in the depth it deserves. We have relied on all the above histories, but have found four unpublished doctoral dissertations the most helpful guides through the Academy's complex past. These unpublished dissertations are: Edgar Denton, III, "The Formative Years of the United States Military Academy" (Syracuse University, 1964); James L. Morrison, "The United States Military Academy, 1833–1866: Years of Progress and Turmoil" (Columbia University, 1970); Walter Scott Dillard, "The United States Military Academy, 1865–1900: The Uncertain Years" (Washington University, 1972); and Roger H. Nye, "The United States Military Academy in an Era of Educational Reform, 1900–1925" (Columbia University, 1969). Dillard and Nye are West Point graduates of the classes of 1961 and 1946 respectively.

5. Account given in Fleming, *West Point*, 30. Fleming notes that he was "the first

historian of West Point to make use of the collected and annotated edition of the papers of Sylvanus Thayer, which the West Point Library prepared in 1964–65" (381). This edition was part of a campaign to elevate Thayer's status as an American educator; see note 6 below.

6. Letter from George Ticknor to his wife, June 17, 1826, quoted in Fleming, 64. R. Ernest DuPuy's *Sylvanus Thayer: The Father of Technology in the United States* (West Point, 1958) is the only biographical work on Thayer. It was published by the Academy's Association of Graduates during their campaign to win Thayer's election to the Hall of Fame for Great Americans located on the University Heights campus of New York University. Thayer was eventually chosen by the College of Electors on October 28, 1965, and joined West Point graduates Grant, Lee, Jackson, and Sherman as well as ex-cadets Edgar Allan Poe and James Abbott McNeill Whistler as one of the ninety-three American men and women members. See R. Ernest DuPuy, "Sylvanus Thayer: Man of Destiny," *Assembly*, XXIV (Winter 1966), 3–5, 26, and "Bulletin Board" notice in same issue of General W. D. Crittenberger's receipt of "the Superintendent's plaque . . . for his diligent and successful efforts on behalf of Thayer" (19–20). General Crittenberger, USMA '13, headed the committee which lobbied for Thayer's election, a campaign which some graduates regarded as an embarrassing attempt to enhance the Academy's status as a historically important "educational" institution.

7. The best account of the implementation of the Thayer System during the nineteenth century is Morrison, "USMA, 1833–1866," 37–41, 177–99.

8. Quoted in Fleming, *West Point*, 130.

9. USMA, *A Study of the Programs of the United States Military Academy* (West Point, December 15, 1972), iii–xi.

10. Interview with West Point department head, May 1973.

11. Interview with West Point graduate and former instructor, August 1972.

12. When most West Point department heads speak of change, what they have in mind is how the Academy has changed from their day as cadets, not how it has changed in relation to American colleges. A modification in an institutional ritual, which some West Pointers would view as substantial, would appear to most outsiders as inconsequential. For instance, on the matter of recitations in mathematics classes, the department head observed:

> I don't think we're as formal in the rigidity of the students standing at the board as we used to be. We feel the students can do a little bit better in a relaxed area. Starting about 5 or 6 years ago, I guess it's about 10 years ago now, we relaxed the emphasis of the cadet talking to the instructor saying, "Sir, I was required to prove. . . ." And now they say, "Gentlemen, I was required to prove. . . ." They are not talking to the instructor, they are talking to their classmates. We are trying to develop more give and take between the cadets themselves to encourage them to follow what the man is saying.

Interview with Colonel John Somers Buist Dick, May 1973.

13. In most required courses at West Point each instructor teaches four sections

of 15 cadets the same material. Between 16 and 20 instructors are usually needed to teach a course which cadets must take in a prescribed academic year. In many civilian colleges one or two instructors frequently teach required courses in large lecture classes of 500 or 1000 students. For more on faculty teaching duties, see below, Chapter Five.

14. For discussions of other institutions, see Lawrence A. Cremin, *American Education: The Colonial Experience, 1607–1783* (New York, 1970), which surveys early American curricula and pedagogy.

15. Frederick Rudolph, *The American College and University: A History* (New York, 1962), 287–306; also Samuel Eliot Morison, *Three Centuries of Harvard, 1636–1936* (Cambridge, Mass., 1936), 324–26, 358–61, 389–90.

16. Russell F. Weigley, *History of the United States Army* (New York, 1967), 325.

17. See Dillard, "USMA, 1865–1900," Chapter Three, and Nye, "USMA, 1900–1925," 102–38.

18. Quoted in Dillard, "USMA, 1865–1900," Chapter Four.

19. See Dillard, "USMA, 1865–1900," Chapters Three and Four.

20. Nye, "USMA, 1900–1925," 139–83.

21. Quoted in *ibid.*, 233–34, 305.

22. Rudolph, *The American College*, 3–22, surveys the role of Latin in colonial colleges; see also Joseph J. Ellis, *The New England Mind in Transition: Samuel Johnson of Connecticut, 1696–1772* (New Haven, 1973), 15–33, for a discussion of languages at early Yale and 218–43 for early Columbia.

23. Samuel Tillman, quoted in Nye, "USMA, 1900–1925," 305.

24. Edward L. Thorndike, *Educational Psychology* (New York, 1903), and his *The Psychology of Algebra* (New York, 1923). Thorndike's work suggested that mental skills were transferable only to activities closely related to the activities in which the skills were acquired.

25. Nye, "USMA, 1900–1925," 18, 139–83.

26. Quoted in *ibid.*, 16–17.

27. *Ibid.*, 194–95.

28. *Ibid.*, 19, 184–222. During the first decade of the twentieth century a number of prominent civilian educators were members of the Board of Visitors, a committee entrusted with an annual examination of the Academy's operation. In 1902, Charles Eliot was so dismayed at the collapse of educational standards that he wrote the superintendent that West Point was "incapable of remedy within itself" because "the selection of its young teachers invariably from its own graduates, and generally for a short term of service, has inevitably tended to the perpetuation of its own methods, uninfluenced by the great changes in educational methods which have been gradually evolving during the past eighty years" (226). Shortly thereafter the Academy removed prominent educators and critics like Eliot from the Board of Visitors.

29. Interview with Colonel Gilbert W. Kirby, May 1973.

30. Interview with Colonel Edward A. Saunders, March 1973.

31. Interview with West Point officer, August 1973.

32. The Academy has found support from civilian leaders for such principles

throughout its history. In 1972 the group known informally as the Kappel Board said near the end of its "Summary Report"—"The fundamental purpose of the United States Military Academy is to provide officers who are capable of fulfilling the requirements of the Army. Accordingly, the curriculum must be a function of those requirements." *A Study of the Programs of USMA* (1972), x.

33. Interviews with Colonel Gilbert W. Kirby, May 1973, and Lieutenant Colonel James B. Hall, March 1973. Most West Pointers view the Academy as "a winner." They believe that their alma mater has contributed more than any other public agency or institution to American military successes. Few West Pointers seem aware that only a true believer could accept such a notion as a self-evident proposition, or for that matter overlook the Academy's thousands of average or undistinguished graduates as well as the involvement of its most "professionally successful" graduates in military stalemates in Korea and Southeast Asia. The economist Mancur Olson, who was an Air Force Academy faculty member in the 1960's, offers an instructive discussion of the difficulties of measuring "the true output of a public agency" or of "the contribution to output of any particular employee, procedure, or . . . input" in his "Public Services on the Assembly Line," *Evaluation*, 1, No. 2 (1973), 37–41.

34. Morten Jay Luvaas, "A Visiting Professor's Impressions of USMA," *Assembly*, XXXII (June 1973), 18–19, 38–39. Professor Luvaas is a military historian on the Allegheny College faculty and was in Duke University graduate school with the USMA department head, Colonel Thomas E. Griess. In December 1972 Major Donald W. Williamson reported in the department's newsletter, *Perspective*, that "the original decision" had been "not to select a Visiting Professor for next year ['73–'74]" because "the void year was planned . . . as a year for program evaluation, but Colonel Griess is considering now accelerating the entire process" (2). Professor Luvaas contributed a report on his first months to the same issue of *Perspective*, in which he noted that "my contact with cadets thus far has been limited to a number of guest lectures, a few cadets pursuing independent studies. . . ." He characterized his contact with the faculty as "close, spontaneous and stimulating," but commented that he was "perplexed by the system of grading here. . . . I hope that in teaching my elective next semester I can feel free to use examinations not only to measure knowledge but also as a fertile teaching device." And in contrasting West Point with Allegheny, he noted with relief that "those who look down upon the field from the more lofty heights do not hiss 'murderer' as one walks by" (Incl. 1, 1–2).

Both Professor Luvaas and Academy officials seemed well pleased with his West Point stay and in the fall of 1973 Professor Frank E. Vandiver "former professor and chairman of the Dept. of History at Rice University and currently on a leave of absence as Provost" became the Academy's second visiting professor of history. Interviews with West Point officers August 1973; for Vandiver see *Assembly*, XXXII (March 1974), 24–25.

35. *Constitution and By-Laws of the Association of Graduates of the United States Military Academy* (as amended at annual meeting, June 1, 1973), Article I, Par. 1. Docu-

ment supplied by Colonel Robert J. Lamb (ret.), executive vice-president, Association of Graduates [AOG], August 1973.

36. According to AOG, *Constitution and By-Laws* (1973), these events, activities, and publications are governed by Article V which states: "Political, or any other discussion foreign to the purposes of the Association as set forth in this Constitution, or any proceedings of such a tendency, are declared inimical to the purposes of this organization and are prohibited." For an impassioned attack on such claims, see Galloway and Johnson's "The Apolitical Politicians" chapter, 234–95.

The Association does its primary work through USMA class organizations and West Point Societies. The latter are the 74 alumni groups (as of August 1973) in 32 states, the District of Columbia, England, Philippine Islands, Puerto Rico, Thailand, and Venezuela. Interview with Colonel Robert J. Lamb, August 1973; AOG memorandum of August 13, 1973, supplied by Colonel Lamb; and Michael J. Krisman, ed., *Register of Graduates and Former Cadets of the United States Military Academy* (West Point, 1973), 15–17.

37. Cadets "now at the Academy, and those former cadets who were members of the classes not yet graduated" are not listed. *Register of Graduates* (1973), 35. In the Foreword to this edition, Michael Krisman notes, "This . . . is the 28th annual revision"; but, "this edition omits the classes all of whose members are dead (through the Class of 1894)." Perhaps the most extraordinary practice reflected in this publication is the fact that thousands of graduates up-date their own biographies every year which makes "this continuing record of achievements available to many readers" (3).

38. *Register of Graduates* (1973), 106 and 90. One of the many curiosities of West Point history is that although the Academy has graduated scores of distinguished military leaders, its most distinguished alumnus in American cultural life has been Edgar Allan Poe, who lasted less than eight months. Among the regulations that must have troubled Poe when he entered in the summer of 1830 was one which read, "No Cadet shall keep in his room any novel, poem, or other book, not relating to his studies, without permission from the Superintendent." Poe's stay at West Point was terminated in early 1831 when a general court-martial found that, among other offenses, he "neglected to report for parades and roll calls thirteen times between 7 and 27 January and failed to attend church and class two times after having been ordered to do so." J. Thomas Russell, *Edgar Allan Poe: The Army Years* (West Point, 1972), 15–19.

In his *High Priest* Timothy Leary gave an ambiguous account of his resignation from West Point after having been "silenced" by his fellow cadets for an alleged honor infraction. Leary wrote: "August 18, 1941 . . . the Honor Committee of the Cadet Corps agrees to accept the verdict of the Court Martial. Not guilty. . . . That afternoon I packed my gear in a jeep and drove to the railroad station down by the Hudson under the granite fortress cliffs." See the College Notes Text, Inc. edition of *High Priest* (New York, 1970), 282–83.

39. Statement entitled "Original Criteria for Thayer Award" supplied by Colonel Robert J. Lamb in August 1973 and *Register of Graduates* (1973), 14.

40. Transcript of William Franklin Graham's speech of May 4, 1972, provided by Lieutenant Colonel Patrick H. Dionne, Information Officer, USMA, June 1973. General Omar N. Bradley's remarks of May 9, 1973, based on verified transcript prepared by the authors.

The 1974 Thayer Award went to 79-year-old retired career diplomat Ambassador Robert D. Murphy, former chairman of Corning International Corporation and director of Corning Glass Works, who is presently chairman of the Commission on the Organization of the Government for Conduct of Foreign Policy. In accepting the award, Ambassador Murphy sounded "a cautious note concerning détente with Russia" and warned that "relaxation of America's security efforts 'would be an act of abysmal folly.' " See *Pointer View*, April 19, 1974, 1 and May 10, 1974, 1.

41. See USMA, Department of Law, *An Extract of the Sections of the United States Code that Directly Pertain to the United States Military Academy and Faculty* (West Point, September 1, 1972) and *West Point, 1973–74 Catalog*, 8, 20–21, 92. There are actually thirteen departments at West Point. The Department of Military Hygiene gives occasional instruction to all four classes but offers no formal semester courses. The department is headed by a U.S. Army physician who is usually assigned to the Academy for a three-year tour. As a non-tenured member of the Academic Board and commanding officer of the West Point hospital, his advice is usually restricted to medical matters rather than curricular policies. Interview with Colonel Lloyd B. McCabe, USMA Surgeon, May 1973.

42. *Register of Graduates* (1973), 512, 522.

43. Interviews with West Point and Pentagon officers, June and July 1973.

44. Interview with Brigadier General John R. Jannarone, March 1973.

45. *Ibid.*

46. Quoted in Lovell, "Cadet Phase of Socialization" (1962), 46. See John W. Masland and Lawrence I. Radway's *Soldiers and Scholars: Military and National Policy* (Princeton, 1957), 169–271, for an examination of the undergraduate education in the 1950's at West Point, Annapolis, the Air Force Academy, and in ROTC programs. Since West Point has always accepted substantive changes in educational policy and practice slowly, much of this book remains illuminating for the 1970's.

47. *Ibid.*, 46–47, and *Superintendent's Curriculum Study, USMA: Report of the Evaluation Committee* (West Point, November 18, 1958), A-1 to A-3.

48. Findings summarized in *Superintendent's Curriculum Study* (1958), 3, and Appendix A.

49. Interview with Colonel Sumner Willard, May 1973.

50. Preface, *Superintendent's Curriculum Study* (1958), i–ii.

51. From the four-page document, "Summary of the Report of the Evaluation Committee." This summary was much more widely circulated at West Point and elsewhere than the actual *Superintendent's Curriculum Study* (1958).

52. Interview with Brigadier General Elvin R. Heiberg (ret.), former head of Department of Mechanics, September 1973. General Heiberg served on the West Point faculty from 1949 until his retirement in 1968.

Conflict between the Academic Board and the superintendent is an inevitable bureaucratic fact of institutional life at West Point. For example, Academy publications celebrate Douglas MacArthur's superintendency for modernizing West Point, but they fail to mention that his reforms were generally resisted by the Academic Board and alumni and that his successor, Brigadier General Fred W. Sladen, attempted, as D. Clayton James has noted, "to abolish nearly all of the reforms his predecessor had introduced" (289). Although the superintendents who followed Sladen "generally concurred in MacArthur's reforms" (293), the battle lines which characterized MacArthur's reign have remained remarkably intact and a reform-minded superintendent in the 1970's would experience *déjà vu* by reading James' assessment of MacArthur's superintendency:

> MacArthur realized that he had failed in the area which most needed reform, namely, the curriculum. The conservatives at the academy and in the Regular Army admitted that some changes in training in weapons and tactics were in order after the experiences of the World War, but they rejected MacArthur's theory of the new type of officer which the academy should produce to lead the citizen-soldiers of the future. They saw the West Pointer as a technical specialist: MacArthur conceived of him as a versatile leader of men, knowledgeable in civilian ways and affairs and obtaining the obedience and loyalty of his troops through understanding and respect, not through fear and strict regimentation. As MacArthur endeavored to create his ideal officer through the broadening of the cadets' knowledge of the social sciences, making them more aware of rights and responsibilities and increasing their contacts with the civilian world, the old guard viewed his moves as threats to the essential order, discipline, and specialized function of West Point. To many alumni especially, who were alarmed over the radicalism allegedly rampant in the nation, less exposure of the cadets to the outside world, rather than more, seemed in order (282–283).

For a detailed discussion of MacArthur's superintendency, see James' *The Years of MacArthur*, vol. 1 [1880–1941] (Boston, 1970), 259–94.

53. Interview with Brigadier General John R. Jannarone, March 1973. Although General Davidson was not successful in bringing about the reforms he sought, the period since 1957 has witnessed a multitude of curriculum adjustments which officials present to appropriate civilian audiences as conclusive evidence of West Point's being "modern in concept." The *Report of the Board of Visitors* (West Point, April 28, 1973, 6) spoke glowingly of "a continuing series of examinations of the curriculum since 1957" and then proceeded to list them:

> (1) Superintendent's Curriculum Study (1957) introduced elective program, provided program of course validation; Academic Board studies (1963 and 1964) examined and rejected establishment of majors, reduced core curriculum, authorized four electives and four areas of elective concentration; Board of independent consultants (1965) reviewed entire curriculum, again rejected majors; several Academic Board studies (1968) further reduced core curriculum, increased electives to eight; Institutional Self-Evaluation for

Middle States Accreditation Association (1969); Academic Board study (1969) decided against cooperative degree programs, established interdisciplinary management field (elective); Academic Board study (1970) reviewed foreign language programs, reaffirmed stand against majors; Academic Board study (1971) examined total cadet academic load and credit hours and established guidance on preparation hours required of cadets; Academic Board study (1971) examined total sequencing of courses in four-year curriculum; Academic Board study (1971) examined organization for behavioral science instruction; Academic Board study (1971) examined means of achieving more flexibility in academic calendar; Curriculum Review Board Study (1972).

54. *Ibid.* A pamphlet distributed to cadets by Academy officials in 1973–74 gave this explanation of the West Point credit hour breakdown:

> *Credit Hour*—The unit used to measure and record academic work. One credit hour at USMA represents at least 45 hours of instruction and associated preparation time per semester. This is equivalent to the typical semester credit hour in civilian undergraduate institutions.

TYPICAL DISTRIBUTION OF CREDIT HOURS

Component	*Credit Hours*
Core Curriculum	
(19 Math-Science-Engrg Crses—62.5)	121
(21 Soc Sci-Hum Crses 58.5)	
*Electives (8 Crses @ 2.5)	20
Military Science	7
Physical Education	7
	155

> Credit hours or weights assigned to each course for each class are determined annually by the Academic Board.
>
> * Total elective credits may vary depending on specific elective courses selected. . . .

See USMA, *18 Questions Cadets Frequently Ask About the USMA Academic Program* (West Point, n.d.), 12.

55. Interview with former West Point instructor, March 1973.

56. Lieutenant General William A. Knowlton, "Founders Day Speech," March 15–19, 1973 and "Founders Day 1973," *Assembly*, XXXII (June 1973), 6. Except in the cases of academic validation, the required course of study for every West Point cadet is given below:

CORE ACADEMIC PROGRAM

	First Term	*Second Term*
Fourth Class (Freshman) Year		
*Mathematics	MA 107	MA 108
*English	EN 101	EN 102

CORE ACADEMIC PROGRAM (*continued*)

		First Term		*Second Term*
+*Foreign Language		L- 101		L- 102
*Environment		EV 101		EV 102
*Engineering Fundamentals		EF 101		EF 102
Third Class (Sophomore) Year				
*Mathematics		MA 205		**MA 206
Physics		PH 201		PH 202
(One sequence to be selected)	or	PH 201		PH 204
*Chemistry		CH 201		CH 202
+*Foreign Language		L- 201		L- 202
English		EN 201		—
*Psychology		—		PL 202
History		HI 201		HI 202
(One sequence to be selected)	or	HI 203		HI 204
Second Class (Junior) Year				
Electrical Engineering		EE 301		EE 304
*Mechanics		ME 301		**ME 302
*Mechanics		ME 303		—
Physics		—		PH 303
		—	or	PH 305
Law		LW 301		LW 302
*Social Sciences		SS 301		SS 302
		Elective		Elective
First Class (Senior) Year				
Engineering		*CE 401		*CE 402
(One sequence to be selected)	or	CE 453		CE 454
	or	*OE 401		*OE 402
	or	EE 401		EE 402
	or	GE 401		GE 402
Leadership		PL 401		—
English		—		EN 402
*Social Sciences		SS 401		SS 407
*History		HI 401		HI 402
		Elective		Elective
		Elective		Elective

* Advanced versions of these courses are offered to qualified individuals by the department concerned.

** Those cadets enrolled in the Humanities and National Security and Public Affairs areas may substitute electives for these courses.

+ The Department of Foreign Languages offers programs in Chinese, French, German, Portuguese, Russian, and Spanish.

See *West Point: 1973–74 Catalog*, 24, and USMA, Office of the Dean, *Academic Program, AY 1973–74* (West Point, 1 March 1973), II-1 to 3 and III-1.

57. Interview with Colonel Gilbert W. Kirby, May 1973.
58. Interview with Academic Board member, May 1973.

59. Interview with Colonel John Somers Buist Dick, May 1973.

60. Interview with Colonel Elliott C. Cutler, Jr., March 1973. Among his Academic Board colleagues, Colonel Cutler is perhaps the most widely respected department head. One of the most important West Point documents of the early 1970's was a five-page memorandum of July 10, 1972, which Colonel Cutler circulated to his instructors. Colonel Cutler discussed academic requirements and "why the USMA curriculum appears to contain such a heavy emphasis on mathematics, science, and engineering [MSE]." He pointed out that the "proper standard of measurement . . . is the need of the Army" and the Army has wanted cadets educated "for a general military career, without specification or restriction of branch choice or career pattern."

Although he discussed two alternatives to this historic educational emphasis ("preparing each cadet to enter a *particular* branch" or allowing cadets to choose "between an MSE-based track and a non-MSE-based track"), Colonel Cutler emphatically concluded:

> . . . As long as the current mission of preparing all cadets for an unspecialized Army career remains in effect, a substantial MSE component must be maintained in the core curriculum. None of the 36 boards and committees that have reviewed our curriculum, or parts of it, since the Second World War have come to any contrary conclusion. This does not mean that the curriculum is, or should be, static. On the contrary there has been a distinct shift over the years away from engineering, which has decreased from 11 courses to 6, in favor of the NSPA [National Security and Public Affairs] component, which has increased from 8 to 13 courses. In the last 10 years the total number of MSE courses has decreased from 25 to 19, while the total number of NSPA and Humanities courses has remained constant at 21. But the premise on which this shift has been based is that MSE component remaining should be adequate to meet the minimum MSE needs of the general unspecialized Army career pattern for which cadets are being prepared.
>
> The shift in core-curriculum emphasis has been evolutionary rather than revolutionary, a factor that may account for its static appearance in the perception of some cadets. The advantages of the evolutionary mode of change in placing a stable educational objective before the cadet should not be underrated. Nothing is more discouraging to students than sudden oscillations in the goals set before them and the accompanying uncertainty as to what they are expected to accomplish.

61. Interview with Colonel Edward A. Saunders, March 1973.

62. Interview with Colonel Lee D. Olvey, June 1973.

63. Interview with Brigadier General John R. Jannarone, March 1973.

64. *Ibid.* Despite General Jannarone's contentions, the superintendent of the Air Force Academy, Lieutenant General A. P. Clark, continued to emphasize the individual. "Choosing a career suitable to your particular aptitudes and interests is not an easy decision," noted General Clark. "The Air Force Academy has evolved a unique academic program which provides each cadet with a broad education and

offers the individual a specialty related to an Air Force career field." There is a certain irony to this emphasis since General Clark, as well as the commandant of cadets, and two of the other four principal officers in the USAF Academy administration are West Point graduates. *The United States Air Force Academy Catalog, 1973–1974* (USAF Academy, Col., 1973), 2–3.

65. See James P. Sterba's front-page story, "Dropouts Plague The Air Academy," *New York Times*, June 3, 1973, 1, 47. The Air Force Academy's attrition rate for the class of 1972 was slightly over 40 per cent. In December 1973, the USAF Board of Visitors recommended a full study of its candidate selection procedures and stressed that "every effort [should] be made to select only those candidates whose personal objectives are consistent with the academy's objective of graduating career Air Force officers." Quoted in the *Washington Post*, December 27, 1973, A12.

One senior West Point official, in comparing the two academies in a May 1973 interview said: "The superintendent of the Air Force Academy [General Clark] wants to be *first*. 'Whatever it is, *I'm* going to be *first!*' He wants to be the first to take women, wants to be first to do this or that. I'm not criticizing whether his programs are good or bad, but there is this difference in attitude. Here, our approach is almost opposite. If it *has to* happen, it'll happen. Let's not rush it."

66. *West Point: The United States Military Academy: 1972–1973 Catalog* (West Point, 1972), 3. Although a similar statement also appears in the 1971–72 catalog, the 1973–74 catalog suggests General Knowlton's opportunism and shrewdness in marketing West Point during a national recession. The emphasis of previous years is somewhat muted and a new paragraph is interjected: "A key factor in your decision for higher education may very well be your concern about the means by which you finance your education. In that regard you should know that every young man selected for admission to West Point receives a full scholarship. In addition, he receives a salary from which he pays for his books and uniforms" (*West Point: 1973–74 Catalog*, 3).

67. Interview with Colonel Manley E. Rogers, March 1973 and Kenneth Keniston, "The Agony of the Counter-Culture," Commencement Address, Notre Dame University, May 23, 1971. Speech provided by Notre Dame Department of Information Services, September 1971.

68. Interview with Colonel Manley E. Rogers, March 1973.

69. *Ibid.*

70. *Ibid.*

Chapter Three

1. Professor Daniel P. Moynihan's address is published as "An Address to the Entering Class at Harvard College, 1972," in *Commentary*, LIV (December 1972), 55–60.

2. *Ibid.*, 55, 59.

3. *Ibid.*, 59–60. For fall 1973 discussions of Harvard's freshmen and institutional changes, see Howard Whitman, "How To Go to Harvard Without Passing 'the Boards,' " *New York Times*, September 23, 1973, Sec. 10, 1, 16, 17, and Stephen

Isaacs, "What's Happened to Harvard?" *Washington Post*, November 25, 1973, C1 C4, C5.

4. This sense of having a common bond with peers at prestigious eastern schools is a pattern which many West Pointers believe has passed. In the view of one second-generation West Pointer, it reflected West Point's former drawing power at eastern prep schools. "If you had taken a poll some years ago of where people from Groton or Exeter went to college, you would have found that they went to prestigious eastern universities and always a couple went to West Point or Annapolis," the officer noted. And this was important because "thirty years later when all these guys would get together for state occasions, the guys from West Point and Annapolis would have prep school classmates, graduates of eastern colleges, in high civilian positions and that counted for a lot." The current superintendent, Lieutenant General William A. Knowlton, is a 1938 graduate of the St. Mark's School in Southborough, Massachusetts, and one of a diminishing number of West Pointers with elite eastern prep school backgrounds.

5. Interview with Colonel Frederick A. Smith, Jr., May 1973.

6. *Ibid.* This view of West Point uniqueness, even in relation to other service academies which also have their versions of "a fourth class system," finds expression when some West Pointers discuss almost any aspect of Academy life. For a discussion of a cadet's first year at Annapolis, see David Edwin Lebby's unpublished dissertation, "Professional Socialization of the Naval Officer: The Effect of Plebe Year at the U.S. Naval Academy" (University of Pennsylvania, 1970), especially 62-103. Lebby's findings suggest West Point's fourth-class system is not unique. He reported, "Within a few short weeks of their arrival in Annapolis each new plebe class demonstrates visible evidence of the outward transformation they are undergoing. By late summer they are no longer individual civilians but members of a coordinated military unit who have already acquired a surprising amount of military bearing" (93).

7. Lieutenant General William A. Knowlton, "To The Parents of The Class of 1977," in USMA, *The New Cadet: Information For The Parents of The Class of 1977* (West Point, 1973), inside front cover.

8. *The New Cadet* (1973), 9.

9. In a May 1973 statement which accompanied *The New Cadet* booklet and other materials sent to parents, Lieutenant General Knowlton said, "When your son enters West Point . . . , he will become a member of the United States Corps of Cadets, one of the most respected groups of young men in the world." General Knowlton then discussed the "rigorous transition process to cadet life" while at the same time he invoked the image of "the campus" of West Point in an apparent attempt to reassure parents that West Point did represent a college experience. And he closed his letter with a greeting and an admonition: "Finally, I would like to welcome your family to the long tradition that is West Point and to emphasize that only through working together with you, the parents, can we best assist your son. I hope that we may count on your support." Information supplied by Headquarters, New Cadet Barracks, August 1973.

10. Information taken from sheet entitled "2 July 1973 Orientation Program Itinerary," supplied by Headquarters, New Cadet Barracks, August 1973.

11. United States Corps of Cadets [USCC], Department of Tactics, *Administration and Logistic Plan: New Cadet Barracks, 1973* [*A & L Plan: NCB* (1973)] (West Point, 1973), 1.

12. *A & L Plan* (1973), H-3-1.

13. A detailed account of this processing is given in "Appendix 3 (Station Responsibilities) to Annex H (Reception and Processing of New Cadets)" in *A & L Plan* (1973), H-3-1 to 4. Months of planning and hours of preliminary meetings go into preparing for "R Day" [Reception and Processing Day]. Intensive rehersals begin on "R Day-8," eight days before the candidates for entrance arrive. See *A & L Plan* (1973), H-2-1 and H-2-2.

The majority view of West Pointers is that this initial processing is the first step in a four-year experience of what, according to Douglas MacArthur, "might be euphemistically called democracy-in-action." This decivilianizing is seen as crucial because it "has ever been a source of pride to those interested in West Point that the democracy of the Corps assured every individual cadet a standing won by his character and personality, irrespective of his social or financial position outside the walls of the institution. Every member of the student body throughout his four-year course wears the same clothes, eats the same food, passes through the same course of study, rises and retires at the same hours, receives the same pay, and starts always without handicap in the same competition." See MacArthur's *Reminiscences* (New York, 1964), 80.

14. *A & L Plan* (1973), H-3-2.

15. See "Appendix 7 (Processing Resignees or Rejectees on R-Day) to Annex H . . ." of *A & L Plan* (1973), H-7-1.

16. *A & L Plan* (1973), H-3-3, and H-5-1.

17. *A & L Plan* (1973) states in I-8-1 that the squad leader is "*THE MOST IMPORTANT MEMBER OF THE DETAIL*" and the squad leader is advised to begin preparing for his duties in the preceding spring:

> 1. Preparation.
>
> a. Spring:
>
> (1) The most important thing the squad leader can do during this period is to get himself in the proper frame of mind for NCB. You are the one daily close contact that the new cadet has with West Point. You are the living example of what each new cadet is striving for, and as such you must present the highest standards of appearance, discipline, conduct, professionalism and impartiality.
>
> (2) Start learning subjects you must teach, e.g., squad drill, manual w/M14 rifle, assembly and disassembly of M16 rifle.

18. Interview with Colonel Hugh G. Robinson, Jr., August 1973.

19. Interview with Cadet Andrew Joseph Green, August 1973.

20. Interviews with Cadet Gary Stephen Coleman, August 1973; *ibid.;* Captain

Stephen T. Lifrak, August 1973. The active participation in Beast Barracks training of officers like Captain Lifrak reflects the Academy's increasing use of professional counselors. This counseling staff of the Office of Military Psychology and Leadership publishes documents such as *Guidelines for Counseling* (West Point, n.d., 1-28) which is "to be used as a reference and a guide by officers and members of the Cadet Chain of Command" (i). In an introductory statement, "General Approach to Counseling at USMA," the pamphlet notes, "The counselor is interested in changing *feelings*, *thinking*, and *behavior*" and it advises:

> As counselors we must keep in mind that we are attempting to help the young man to adjust to and grow within the environment of the U.S. Military Academy; it is not our purpose to change the environment of the Academy to suit the individual. We may possibly manipulate minor factors within the environment as an attempt to help, but we must not lose sight of the Academy's mission. It should be our earnest belief and hope that we can both satisfy the demands of the Academy and meet the needs of the individual. The young man is here to be shaped and molded; we can help him in this process to achieve that which he might not otherwise achieve—his full potential.

21. Interview with Cadet Andrew Joseph Green, August 1973.

22. Interview with Colonel Hugh G. Robinson, Jr., August 1973.

23. Interview with Cadet Michael Richard Clifford, August 1973. One group of rising first class cadets conducts the first half of NCB training and another group conducts the second half. See *A & L Plan* (1973), K-1, K-2.

24. Interviews with West Point officer, August 1973. Some of the cadet hostility toward tactical officers in the 1970's was explained by Colonel Gerald W. Medsger during a May 1973 interview:

> I suspect one of the reasons the tactical officers are singled out as the bad guys is that they're the guys who give cadets the quill and won't let them go on leave. They do all these nasty things to them. But the disappointment is expressed in the feeling "Well, if this is the best the Army has got to offer, I don't want to be like that guy." How much of it is due to the fact that there maybe something wrong with the officers and how much of it is just the cadet misunderstanding, or not realizing, that that's what the tac's supposed to be doing, I don't know. . . .
>
> Cadets have never gone around saying, "My tactical officer is a great guy, I really love him." You just didn't do that. But at the same time I would never have written down a statement going to the superintendent or something saying, "My tactical officer is a liar and a cheat and a no good bum and shouldn't be in the Army. I'm discouraged from an Army career because of his attitude, and all the rest of them seem to be the same." I never would have done that. And not just because I was afraid of doing it, but I didn't feel that way.

25. Interviews with Brigadier General Philip R. Feir, March and August 1973;

Lieutenant Colonel Hugh G. Robinson, Jr., June 1973; West Point officers and cadets, May, June, and August 1973.

26. Colonel Robinson's description of his first meeting with President Johnson is characteristic of the sense of himself he brings to his work. When asked in an August 1973 interview if the public announcement of his selection was a memorable day for him, he replied:

> O God was it. It scared me to death. When he announced it (you see, I was the first black ever to be appointed as military aide to the President), there must have been 100 cameras and 200 newsmen all assembled outside his living room down at the ranch for this news conference. . . . I was there when he got back from church, which was Sunday morning. And he walked in from church and the first thing he said was, "Hi, Major. I'm Lyndon Johnson." He just walked up to me and said, "Hi, Major. I'm Lyndon Johnson." I felt like saying, "No shit."
>
> And we chatted for a little bit and he said, "One of the reasons that I wanted you to be my aide was because you're black. But you weren't selected because you're black, it just so happened that is the way it worked out." You can take that with a grain of salt, at least I did. . . . He also said, "The other thing is, I wanted junior aides. I want people who will work for me and not turn around and tell somebody else to do something that I told him to do. And that is the way it was when I had a general."

27. Interview with Colonel Frank J. Kobes, August 1973. *A & L Plan* (1973) sets forth the mission of commanding officer, NCB, and his staff: "Plan, conduct, and evaluate Fourth Class Summer Training, to include Instructor Training Week for the details in coordination with the Directors of OMI [Office of Military Instruction], OPE [Office of Physical Education] and MP&L [Office of Military Psychology and Leadership] "(1). The men listed in these offices in *West Point: 1973–74 Catalog* are predominantly West Point graduates, and all but 6 of the first 21 officers listed in "Organization of NCB Staff and Commanders" for 1973 were graduates. Data obtained from USMA, Department of Tactics, June 1973.

28. Interview with West Point officers, January 1973. For a response to the indoctrination of plebes in the context of other American initiation rites, see "On Initiation Rites and Power: Ralph Ellison Speaks at West Point," ed. Robert H. Moore, *Contemporary Literature*, XV (Spring 1974), 165–186.

29. Interview with Army officer, March 1973. A study of a national cross-section of college students by Daniel Yankelovich, Inc., in the early 1970's discovered "a massive revulsion against the idea of violence" as well as many other findings which suggested West Point's remoteness from other American colleges and universities. See especially "The College Scene, 1968–1971," in *The Changing Values on Campus* (New York, 1972), 1-88.

30. Every year the USMA Admissions Office distributes scores of *gratis* copies of Colonel Red Reeder's *Heroes and Leaders of West Point* (New York, 1970) to organizations and individuals. In his Introduction (11-12), Colonel Reeder pays tribute to

Vince Lombardi, who coached at West Point in the 1950's, for his encouragement to "write a book about heroes of West Point' "; and Colonel Reeder contends, "The most important aspect of West Point's immense value to the nation is the leadership its graduates have given when the country's life was at stake."

31. Interview with West Point officer, March 1973.

32. Interview with West Point officers, January 1973. One of the more candid defenses of the service academies indoctrination and training of new cadets came from Rear Admiral James B. Stockdale who was a POW in Vietnam from 1965 to 1973. "I came out of prison being very happy about the merits of plebe year at the Naval Academy," Admiral Stockdale said. "I hope we do not ever dilute those things. You have to practice being hazed. You have to learn to take a bunch of junk and accept it with a sense of humor." See Admiral Stockdale's "Experiences as a POW in Vietnam," *Naval War College Review* (January-February 1974), 2-6.

33. *Bugle Notes, 1973*, 121.

34. *The New Cadet* (1973), 6. This schedule is taken from the parents' booklet which does not reflect the West Point and Army time system of 2400 hours.

35. *Ibid.*, 6.

36. USCC, Department of Tactics, *Operations and Training Plan: New Cadet Barracks, 1973* [*O & T Plan* (1973)] (West Point, 1973), II-B A-1-1 and II-B A-1 T-A-1 to 4.

37. *O & T Plan* (1973), II-B A-1 T-B-1 to 15.

38. Interview with Colonel Hugh G. Robinson, August 1973. West Point's belief in the importance of physical training in developing "mental toughness" and self-confidence is well illustrated by Colonel Frank J. Kobes' defense of boxing's place in the curriculum. Colonel Kobes, Director of the Office of Physical Education, said:

> My quick answer to most people as to why we have boxing is that we are training fighters. That's our purpose, to train a young man to be a leader on the field of combat, which is a very physical thing. And you don't learn to fight out of a book. There's only one way to learn to fight and that's to fight. And that's where you learn to communicate. I tell the plebes this when I talk to them. When you give a guy a punch on the nose, that is basic communication. There's no question in the other guy's mind what the hell you're trying to tell him. The same is true in football. When you make a hard block or a hard tackle, that is basic communication; you don't have to say a damn word. He understands what your purpose is. And you learn to get up and to fight back. You learn not to quit, to keep on going. And this is the purpose of boxing, to teach a guy to fight, to handle himself, a little bit about self-defense and attack.

Interview with Colonel Kobes, August 1973. The officer scheduled to succeed Colonel Kobes when he retires is Lieutenant Colonel James L. Anderson, who said in a February 1974 interview that he was completing a Ph. D. dissertation at Indiana University on the role of boxing in the USMA physical education program.

39. *O & T Plan* (1973), II-A-4.

40. Interview with Colonel Hugh G. Robinson, Jr., August 1973. Colonel Red Reeder's description of his first day at West Point in 1919 vividly demonstrates how a concern for "carrying out orders" has long dominated the new cadet's indoctrination. Reeder remembers his tactical officer asking:

> "Didn't I tell you about twelve minutes ago to work on your room?"
> "Yes, sir."
> "Then why aren't you doing it?"
> "Sir, I was getting ready to. I thought—"
> "The answer is, 'No excuse, sir.' "
> "Yes, sir. No excuse, sir."
> "That's better." The officer smiled pleasantly and I felt relieved. Then he said quietly, "I am reporting you for failure to carry out instructions. I'm sure you are the first one in your class to be awarded six demerits."
> That shook me up and I felt shakier studying the puzzling room-arrangement card. The last thing my father told me when I left home was, "Carry out the orders." I had been at West Point two hours and had already been reported for going against them. "*Awarded*," the Tac had said, as if I had won a prize.

See Reeder's autobiography, *Army Brat: Life Story of a West Pointer* (New York, 1967), 83.

41. "Professional socialization" is defined in John P. Lovell's "The Professional Socialization of the West Point Cadet," in *The New Military: Changing Patterns of Organization*, edited by Morris Janowitz (New York, 1964), 154, and his discussion of West Point as a "total institution" is in his "Cadet Phase of Socialization" (1962), 1-22.

42. Interview with Captain Harold A. Jenkins, August 1973.

43. Interview with West Point officers, January 1973.

44. Interview with four West Point plebes, February 1974.

45. Interview with Colonel Hugh G. Robinson, Jr., August 1973.

46. *Ibid.*

47. *The Long Gray Line* was released in 1955 and featured Tyrone Power (as Marty Maher, a popular athletic trainer in the early decades of this century), Maureen O'Hara, and Ward Bond. Unlike the "Easy Out" procedures depicted in the movie, resignation involves a complex series of interviews and administrative procedures outlined in "Annex F (Resignations)" of the *A & L Plan* for the 1973 NCB: "All interviews conducted by the cadet Chain of Command will be documented on USMA Form 2-210," and the interviewing process normally begins with the cadet's squad leader, followed by his platoon leader, and his company commander. This process alone may take three days, but "If the New Cadet still persists in his desire to resign, the company commander will proceed" to process the paperwork to the company tactical officer. Another round of interviews then begins, which may stretch over four or five days and involve interviews with the Tac, and MP & L consultant, the cadet's parents or guardian, officers from various Academy agencies, the Executive Officer and the Commander of NCB. Throughout this processing the cadet

"will not miss scheduled training and will be expected to meet required standards of performance."

48. Interview with Colonel Hugh G. Robinson, Jr., August 1973. In providing "guidance" to the cadet chain of command, Annex F of the *A & L Plan* (1973) states: "The fact that a squad leader is confronted with one or two new cadets who desire to resign is not necessarily a reflection on his leadership and job performance." But, as the cadets are well aware, it is hardly a plus for his performance as a detail member. "At each echelon in the Chain of Command . . . do your best to both gain the facts . . . and present a balanced view of West Point," the *A & L Plan* advises. "Makes a particular effort to determine if the real reason for resignation can be alleviated in the West Point environment. If the cadet is not dissuaded in his desire to resign in a reasonably short time, move him up the chain."

49. Interview with Colonel Hugh G. Robinson, Jr., August 1973. In a May 1973 interview Colonel Gerald W. Medsger cited two major causes for resignations from West Point in any given class over a four-year period:

> I think the experiences we're having is parallel to that in most other colleges and universities, particularly in professional types of schools. The major reason a person leaves is really career goals. . . . Somewhere along the line he decided that "I'm really not interested in the Army as a career. I want to do something else. I may want to be a doctor, lawyer." That's probably the biggest single reason that people leave. The next one is what is known in our business as "student environment discordance." A guy just doesn't like this college. [He says,] "It's too conservative," "It's too liberal," "It doesn't match my personality."

Both reasons fall in the category of what the Academy calls "motivational losses," and Colonel Medsger acknowledged that "there's no question, at least in our accounting procedures, that the motivational losses have been climbing over the past ten years, whereas the academic losses have been dropping."

50. Lovell, "Cadet Phase of Socialization" (1962), 5–7. In addition to this "integration into the 'system,' " Lovell cites two other "functions" of the eleven-month plebe experience which begins with Beast Barracks. "It is a 'testing' or 'weeding out' process, a tribal 'rite de passage' " (7); and a "third function of plebe year is to teach obedience" (8).

51. Interview with Major Francis E. Conrad, August 1973.

52. Interview with West Point officer, January 1973.

Chapter Four

1. *The New Cadet* (1973), 5.

2. Lovell, "Cadet Phase of Socialization," (1962), 172–77.

3. February 1973 letter from former West Point cadet to authors.

4. Interview with West Point officer, March 1973.

5. Interview with West Point officer, January 1973. The predominant view of Academy faculty and staff about cadet "gripes" is reflected in these remarks by Colonel George Walton (ret.):

> I recall when my son was at the Academy he would bring home over a holiday a number of his friends whose families were overseas. Daily the entire breakfast time would be spent in gripes at the rigors of life in the Corps. I would stand this for several days then blow my top, pointing out that no one was forcing them to remain at the Academy, that when at the end of the holiday the car returned to West Point there was not one of them who need be in it if that was not his desire. Needless to say, they all returned and almost all of them are still in the Army and have reached that stage of life when they have begun to look back on their school days—including the Point—with nostalgia. All of us today take a little too seriously the immature although often well-founded gripes of youth.

See Walton's *The Tarnished Shield: A Report on Today's Army* (New York, 1973), 160–61.

6. Interview with four West Point officers, March 1973.

7. Interview with West Point officer, January 1973.

8. Interview with Mount Holyoke student, February 1973.

9. Interview with West Point officer, June 1972.

10. Others who finished last in their class include George Edward Pickett (1842) who "was made immortal by Pickett's Charge at Gettysburg during the Civil War, where he and his troops were repeatedly repulsed by the Union Forces"; Medal of Honor winner Powhatan Clark (1884) "who rescued a fellow soldier under heavy fire during the Mexican War"; and Ting Chia Chen (1909) "who rose to be a Major General in the Chinese Army" in the early 1930's. Data supplied in "Press Kit" by USMA, Information Office, for June 6, 1973, graduation ceremonies.

11. The Academy's class ranking system is the General Order of Merit. It takes into account not only academic performance but military and physical aptitude as well. Approximately the top 5 per cent of a class are designated "Distinguished Cadets" and are authorized to wear gold stars on their collars. As of December 1973, West Pointers had won 53 Rhodes scholarships, making West Point the fourth highest producer of Rhodes scholars among American schools. Data supplied in "Press Kit" by USMA, Information Office, for June 6, 1973, graduation ceremonies. West Point's fifty-third Rhodes scholar, Cadet Kerry K. Pierce, was announced in the *New York Times*, December 17, 1973.

The Academy's large number of Rhodes scholars is frequently cited in Academy publications as proof of West Point's continuing academic excellence; however, Rhodes scholars are selected from eight geographical districts and the Academy's national representation gives it a considerable advantage over most other schools. West Point also actively counsels cadets, who compete from various districts, for the Rhodes competition.

12. Interview with West Point cadet, May 1972.

13. Interview with West Point cadet, March 1973.

14. Interview with West Point graduate on active duty, May 1972.

15. Cadet Donald D. Cantlay to Brigadier General John R. Jannarone, September 28, 1971.

16. *A Study of the Programs of USMA* (1972), 97–99, lists tables which suggest that cadets who entered West Point in 1968 are generally comparable in class rank and college board scores with their peers at the Naval Academy, the Air Force Academy, Vanderbilt, Tulane, Georgia Tech and state universities such as Michigan, Virginia, and Penn. State. The mean college board scores of entering freshmen at Middlebury (650 V, 650 M), Oberlin (650 V, 650 M), and Stanford (640+ V, 640+ M) are considerably higher than the score for entering plebes at West Point (563 V, 635 M). *Barron's Profiles of American Colleges* (1972), 69–70, 542–43, 605–6, 801.

17. OIR, *A Comparison of New Cadets at USMA with Entering Freshmen at Other Colleges*, 1–6; OIR, *Trends in Admission Variables Through the Class of 1976* (West Point, 1973), 11–12; Lovell, "Cadet Phase of Socialization" (1962), 91–93.

18. *Barron's Profiles of American Colleges: United States Military Academy* (Woodbury, N.Y., 1973), 1, 2, and 12. Each year West Point sends thousands of these profiles (which retail for $1.50) *gratis* to prospective applicants. From 1969 to 1974 the profile was revised each year. Such frequent revisions are uncommon in the Barron's Profiles In-Depth series and are apparently the result of yearly West Point bulk purchases which also gives the Academy considerable editorial influence over the contents of the profile.

19. Briefing by Office of the Dean, USMA, March 1973.

20. *West Point, 1973–74 Catalog*, 7.

21. *Washington Post*, May 21, 1972. In recent years, studies by USMA's Office of Institutional Research have demonstrated that the overwhelming reason given by young men for coming to West Point has been that it "has a good academic reputation." Interview with OIR director, Colonel Gerald W. Medsger, May 1973. In the summer of 1972, 87.9 per cent of the new cadets surveyed indicated the Academy's academic reputation was "a very important [reason] in selecting this college." See OIR's *A Comparison of New Cadets Class of 1976*, 15.

22. Interview with Brigadier General John R. Jannarone, March 1973. Colonel Charles H. Schilling, head of the Department of Engineering, is a particularly vocal critic of cadets who want to decrease the prescriptive nature of the curriculum. And his reasons are also those of most Academic Board members:

> I am one that believes that the only reason we have a United States Military Academy is to prepare people to enter this profession. And if we have a major, this is our major—*the military profession*. I don't like majors. I don't like specialized programs. I am a very, very firm believer in the generalized education and I think all you need to do is look at the results of the Academy and its graduates, both those who have stayed in the service and those who have gotten out. This gives you all the evidence you need that this general education approach is the right approach.

Interview with Colonel Schilling, May 1973.

23. Interview with West Point officer, January 1973.

24. Interview with Colonel Edward A. Saunders, March 1973. Although Acad-

emy publications frequently emphasize the availability of civil schooling upon graduation, graduates are strongly encouraged to forgo such schooling until they have fulfilled their five-year commitment; and then, if they pursue civil schooling at Army expense, they incur further military obligation. About 80 per cent of Academy graduates who remain on active duty eventually attend graduate school. Even those few cadets who enter medical school upon graduation (under a new program allowing "no more than 1 per cent of the class" to go) are, according to the Chemistry Department head, Colonel Donald G. MacWilliams, being "divisionary" because "we are principally here to provide people for the combat arms and anybody who goes to medical school cuts down on our ability to place people in combat arms. And there is the feeling that those people who go into medicine should be people who are physically disqualified from going into the combat arms or combat support arms. Going into medicine is not essential and therefore it is divisionary." Interview with Colonel MacWilliams, May 1973.

25. Interview with West Point officer, June 1972.

26. Interview with Brigadier General Philip R. Feir, March 1973.

27. Interview with West Point officer, January 1973. Although more cadets go into Infantry than any other branch of service, they become infantrymen because most of them have few other, or no other, options. The February 8, 1974, *Pointer View* noted, "Cadets chose [branches] in order of their General Order of Merit ranking with 47 of the first 131 First Classmen selecting the Corps of Engineers . . . the quota for that branch was quickly filled." Quotas for the class of 1974 were then filled for Military Police with a quota of 19, Military Intelligence (38), Signal Corps (55), Armor (112), Field Artillery (167); and, after the 738th ranking cadet had chosen, all quotas were filled except for the Infantry and the over one hundred cadets remaining were "ranked" into Infantry to fulfill its quota of 262. *Pointer View* noted in its front-page story that "This was the last West Point class to be allowed commissions in other services. Twenty-six chose Air Force, six chose the Marines and four chose Navy." The paper also reported, "Eight cadets will be commissioned and will attend Medical School immediately following graduation."

28. Interview with Brigadier General Philip R. Feir, March 1973.

29. This "typical day" is based on interviews with and letters from seven cadets during 1973–74. Each cadet class has somewhat different responsibilities and class schedules, but we selected a "firstie" day because it contains more "free time" and a more liberal set of academic courses. Although a first classman has more cadet responsibilities than a "yearling" or a "cow," he also endures less harassment. Since our contention is that cadet schedules preclude extended study, we wanted to present the most lax portion of a cadet's career, thereby developing our discussion at the point where the evidence was weakest. A day in the life of a fourth classman, for example, is more crowded. See also OIR's *Cadet Time Survey: Academic Year, 1966–1967* (West Point, 1967).

30. Interview with West Point officer, October 1972.

31. Interview with former West Point instructor, June 1973.

32. Interview with West Point officer, June 1972.

33. Interview with Cadet Philip R. Linder, March 1973.
34. Cantlay to Jannerone, September 28, 1971.
35. Interview with West Point graduate, June 1972.
36. Interview with Lieutenant Colonel Thomas E. Blagg, March 1973.
37. Interview with West Point officers, January 1973.
38. *Ibid.*
39. Interview with Second Lieutenant Richard M. Saunders, June 1973.
40. *West Point, 1973–74 Catalog*, 80–82.
41. This description of a class in plebe math is based on interviews with Colonel John S. B. Dick, May 1973, and his Deputy, Colonel Jack M. Pollin, August 1973; interviews with and letters from West Point cadets in May 1972 and January 1973; and on a memorandum written by Colonel Dick and supplied by him entitled "Precepts For Mathematics Instructors," August 31, 1972, 1–5. The unique nature of many directives issued by West Point department heads is well illustrated by the concluding paragraph, precept eight:

> 8. *Maintain an Atmosphere of Sophistication.* Specifically:
>
> a. Set a tone of friendliness and relaxation, combined with alertness and close attention.
>
> b. Encourage humor when, and only when, it is: (1) spontaneous; (2) pertinent to the subject of discussion; (3) in good taste.
>
> c. Allow no levity.
>
> d. Refrain from sarcasm or irritation.
>
> e. Be kind and sympathetic in dealing with intellectual difficulties.
>
> f. Be businesslike in matters of professional responsibility.

42. Charles P. Nicholas, "Mathematics and the Making of Leaders," *Assembly*, XXVI (Spring 1967), 14. This article is headed by a picture of Colonel Nicholas standing before a bookcase of mathematics texts contemplating an object in his right hand; the descriptive notation reads, "Colonel Nicholas examines a plastic model of the human brain" (13).
43. Interview with Colonel John S. B. Dick, May 1973.
44. Interview with Lieutenant Colonel James B. Hall, March 1973.
45. Colonel Nicholas, "Preparing the Weapon of Decision," XXVIII, *Assembly* (Winter 1959), 18.
46. Interviews with Colonel Lee D. Olvey, June 1973, and Colonel Charles H. Schilling, May 1973. Colonel Schilling is especially anxious to demonstrate the relevance of "the engineering approach" because "there are a goodly number of cadets here who, if they were not required to do so, would *not take* engineering. And since they are required to take it, I feel they are entitled to have some presentation as to why they *have to* take it." Colonel Schilling explained the rationale he offers and the cadet reaction:

> We are teaching engineering and, to me, engineering is dealing with the scientific facts involved, which at least at our level is *design*. Design is a specification of exactly how a task is to be accomplished. In my choice of words, this relates directly to the mission of a military officer. An operational order is, in fact, a *design* that tells you exactly how to accomplish that purpose. The purpose here [of an operational order] is to capture a hill; the purpose here [of an engineering design] is to hold up a load 300 feet above the ground. So I try to make this [example] be my chain of relevance. . . . Now, even after I make my presentation, they still don't accept it. But I tell them at that point, OK, this is where the old experience of the teacher and the young man who is unwilling to accept that statement of experience come head to head, and the young man is going to one day learn that that experience is *true*. So I just accept that as a fact of student-teacher relationship.

47. Interview with West Point officer, January 1973.

48. Interview with Second Lieutenant Richard M. Saunders, June 1973.

49. Interview with West Point officer, March 1973.

50. Interview with West Point officer, January 1973. John A. Knubel's recollections of his 1960's midshipman days at Annapolis provide instructive parallels to aspects of cadet life which we have discussed in this chapter. Knubel, a Rhodes scholar and Federal Energy Agency administrator, recalled in a March 1974 interview:

> One of the things I most remember about classes at the Naval Academy was that the classroom was, physically, a break. Most of the time we were so exhausted that a third of the class would be asleep if they didn't stand up. [Cadets at various academies are allowed to stand up in class rather than fall asleep in their seats.] Another thing I remember is that the framework for a problem was always given as well as all the elements of the answer. All you really had to do was to learn the formula that applied to the problem at hand. The key phrase was "plug the formula." The framework was already set up and all you had to do was plug it [the formula] in.

51. USMA, Office of the Dean, *Academic Program, 1973–1974* (West Point, March 1, 1973), II-1 and 2.

52. In 1973 Lieutenant General Bernard W. Rogers told the House Defense Appropriations Subcommittee that each cadet costs the Army $59,366 for four years at West Point. The Army also spends $5022 for the young graduate to attend the officer branch basic course. *Army Times,* October 24, 1973. Many Academy observers feel that when all the costs of maintaining and operating the physical plant, summer training for cadets, and paying for the salaries and benefits of officers, enlisted men, and staff are figured in, the costs are double that figure. *Newsweek* contended in its January 21, 1974, issue that "the average cost of putting a student through" West Point or one of the other service academics "is about $70,000 (some critics say the figure is more like $140,000)" (98).

A three-way breakdown of total funding supplied to West Point by Department of the Army in fiscal year 1973 is given below:

USMA DOLLAR RESOURCES
FY 1973

USMA FUNDING PROGRAM	
Military Personnel, Army Appropriation	$44,558,696
Operation and Maintenance, Army Appropriation	39,622,000
Family Housing Management Account	2,351,000
Reimbursements	6,732,000
Total	$93,263,696
USMA OPERATIONAL EXPENSES	
Military Pay and Allowances	$28,663,000
Civilian Pay and Allowances	29,123,000
Cadet Pay and Allowances	15,895,696
Travel and Per Diem	1,995,000
Supplies and Equipment	17,587,000
Total	$93,263,696
USMA OPERATIONAL EXPENSES BY FUNCTIONAL CATEGORY	
Logistic Activities	$31,828,000
Academic Areas	14,195,000
Tactics Department	9,010,000
Hospital	4,704,000
Stewart Field	3,706,000
Other Post Activities	13,925,000
Total	$77,368,000
(Excludes Cadet Pay and Allowances)	$15,895,696

See USMA, *The Annual Report of the Superintendent, 1 July 1972–30 June 1973* (West Point, 1973), 100. According to these figures, which do not include all possible items, one cadet's four-year experience at West Point could cost the American taxpayer in excess of $100,000. Definitive estimates are difficult, given the malleable character of the data and the elusive reasoning employed by Academy officials.

53. Interview with West Point cadet, March 1973.
54. Interview with West Point cadet, June 1972.
55. Interview with Second Lieutenant Richard M. Saunders, June 1973.
56. Interview with Cadet Philip R. Linder, March 1973.
57. Interview with West Point officers, January 1973.
58. Interview with West Point officer, March 1973.
59. Interview with West Point officer, June 1972.
60. Cantlay to Jannarone, September 28, 1971.
61. Janowitz, *The Professional Solider* (1971), 21–75.

62. February 1973 letter from former cadet to authors and interview with West Point officer, January 1973. See also Adam Yarmolinsky's *The Military Establishment*, abr. ed. (New York, 1973).

Chapter Five

1. From 1968 to 1974 officer reassignments were made for participating in wife-swapping rings and Peeping Tom activities. Homosexuality appears to be uncommon; Colonel Lloyd B. McCabe, a physician who heads the USMA Hospital and the Department of Military Hygiene, said in a May 1973 interview that he was not aware of any instances of homosexuality at West Point. It was his professional opinion that the extensive supervision the cadets receive as well as the rotation of roommates in a dormitory environment decreased the probability of homosexual activity involving cadets. For an examination of official policies toward homosexuality by the various branches of the military from 1940 into the 1970's and male homosexuals in the armed forces, see Colin J. Williams and Martin S. Weinberg, *Homosexuals and the Military: A Study of Less Than Honorable Discharge* (New York, 1971).
2. Interview with Colonel Elliott C. Cutler, Jr., March 1973.
3. Interview with department heads, March 1973 and May 1973. A variation on this theme are stories about cadets who had very weak academic records at West Point but who have done outstanding work in civilian professional schools. In a May 1973 interview, Colonel John S. B. Dick spoke about a cadet near the bottom of his class who "decided he wanted to go into medicine. He's now the third man in the medical class . . . at the University of Louisville. So either he's a late bloomer or he had a good basic across the board foundation [at West Point]. And now that he's studying what he feels is his calling, he's getting down to brass tacks and shining."
4. Figures based on charts, "Personnel Data-Professors USMA" (September 1973), 3 pages and "Personnel Data-Permanent Associate Professors, USMA" (September 1973), 3 pages supplied by USMA, Dean's Office, February 1974.
5. Figures compiled from the *Bob Jones University Bulletin: Catalog Issue, 1973–74* (Greenville, S.C., 1973), 234–43, reveal that 83 per cent of their faculty are alumni. Page 2 of the catalog reads:

> *Important*
>
> It is understood that attendance at Bob Jones University is a privilege and not a right, which privilege may be forfeited by any student who does not conform to the standards and regulations of the institution, and that the University may request the withdrawal of any student at any time, who, in the opinion of the University, does not fit into the spirit of the institution, regardless of whether or not he conforms to the specific rules and regulations of the University.

West Point: 1973–74 Catalog contains a similar message in its discussion of "Cadet Life":

> The Leadership Evaluation System functions in accord with the basic responsibility of the Academy to produce officer leaders for the Armed Forces. The system assists in the maximum development of the leadership capabilities of each cadet and insures that graduates meet the standards required by the Army. The procedures of the system provide for evaluation of the leadership performance and potential of each cadet, counseling and guidance in those areas in which any weakness is detected, and separation of any cadet who proves incapable of achieving the required standard of leadership.
>
> The evaluation of cadet leadership is accomplished primarily through a program of ratings by officers and cadets. A relative standing for each cadet is established by mathematically combining the ratings of the Tactical Officer and cadets.

Bob Jones University's commitment to institutional socialization, like West Point's, is further demonstrated by its catalog statement of student regulations: "All students, under twenty-five years of age, except those residing with their parents or close relatives in the local community are expected to live in the University dormitories. . . . Freshmen and sophomore dormitory students under 21 years of age will not be permitted to bring an automobile to the campus unless they have had at least two full years of active duty in the armed forces" (34).

6. When David Christ, director of admissions, Bob Jones University, was asked in early 1974 to compare his school of 5,000 men and women students with West Point, he replied that while he was "not specifically aware of many of the policies and practices . . . at West Point, I am sure there will be a number of similarities between their institution and ours. . . . Our approach here is that the best way to teach discipline is to have the student place himself voluntarily under a program which enforces discipline as he applies the spirtual lessons we attempt to teach." Statement to authors from Mr. David Christ, February 11, 1974.

7. Interviews with Colonel John S. B. Dick, May 1973; Colonel Gilbert W. Kirby, March 1973; and Colonel Elliott C. Cutler, Jr., March 1973.

8. Interview with Colonel John S. B. Dick, May 1973.

9. *Ibid.* When we asked General Knowlton in the spring of 1974 about future plans for bringing OBV's on the faculty and the related question of nongraduates on the faculty, he replied:

> I think your question on OBV's is a strawman in that you do not address the real issue. Since the tour at West Point is a three year tour, we try to avoid two year officers unless they are needed to fill a gap which may exist in wartime because the expansion calls regular officers away from West Point. I did use a couple of OBV's in the Tactics Department in the summer training when they were young officers who had returned from Vietnam with six months left to serve in the Army. We have a summer training requirement for lots of officers working with [firing] ranges or such things.
>
> Before sending an officer off to graduate school, to be followed by a tour here as an instructor, we try to select regular officers so that the return on the in-

vestment in education will be a continuing one in subsequent tours in the Army. From the time that I was Executive Officer in the Department of Social Sciences, and before, we have tried to bring the mix of officers at West Point up to as high as one-third of our instructors being graduates of other institutions. This has been difficult to do, partly because the regular Army officer from another college tends to hide his intellectual interests during the first few years of service and prove that he is a good soldier. By the time that he surfaces as being interested in this sort of thing, it is often too late to adjust his career pattern without hurting him. That five year chunk out of a young officer's life must come at a carefully selected point if it is to help him rather than hurt him. In every unit in which I have been stationed, I have always addressed the officers and urged graduates of other institutions to write to West Point in the field of their interest and ask how to go about becoming an instructor.

Statement to authors May 22, 1974.

10. Interview with Colonel Lee D. Olvey, August 1973. All but a few officers on the Law Department instructional staff were OBV's in the early 1970's because "Public Law 488 [passed in 1952] . . . in effect, denied the use of appropriated funds for the legal education of military persons." Although Law Department Head Colonel Frederick C. Lough was insistent in a May 1973 interview that his OBV officers were not a major irritant to the Academy's administration (particularly in their energetic counseling of cadets who ran afoul of the honor and conduct systems), the evidence suggested otherwise. In addition to complaints about "Lough's lawyers" expressed to us in 1973–74 interviews, there is this revealing summary of General Knowlton's presentation to the 1972 Board of Visitors:

> Most of the present instructors in USMA's Law Department, although they have been adequately trained in the technical-legal sense, are young officers of the Reserve Components with scant, if any, practical military experience. Some of them are excellent instructors; but, personally inexperienced in the practical problems of the Army, they sometimes are inclined to become overly concerned with technicalities, and occasionally fail to understand the broader aspects of discipline and good order in the Army and the role that the military justice system, of necessity, plays in maintaining an effective defense establishment responsive to the national need. The Superintendent convincingly argued that the effectiveness of the cadets' education, as well as the best interests of the Army in which they will hold responsible positions, will be most effectively assured by exposing them in their law classes here to the teaching of Regular Officers not only competently trained in legal matters, but possessed as well of a resonable amount of practical command and staff experience in the active Army. The Superintendent solicited the understanding of the Board in this matter, and sought its support in recommending deletion of those features of the Defense Appropriations Act which act to inhibit the acquisition of legally trained, practically experienced, Regular Officers for the Academy's law faculty.

See *Report of the Board of Visitors* (1972), 10.

11. *Ibid.* Colonel Olvey is one of the few department heads who maintains an active professional, as opposed to administrative, relationship with civilian academics. Each fall since the 1940's his department has hosted a Student Conference on United States Affairs (SCUSA) which in 1972 involved "160 students representing one hundred colleges and universities" who "participated in the four-day program of lectures, seminars, and round-table discussions which concentrated on the topic, 'Emerging Roles in a Transitional International Environment' " (*The Annual Report of the Superintendent, 1972–73*, 31). Each summer the Social Sciences Department also sponsors a three-day Senior Conference which draws scholars and government leaders together for discussion; the 1973 topic was "The American Army and Changing National Priorities" (USMA, *Senior Conference Program, 21–23 June 1973*).

Colonel Jack L. Capps, the Deputy Head of the Department of English, is another exception to the predominant West Point pattern of limited communication with civilian academics. Colonel Capps has served since 1970 as the chairman of a project preparing a concordance to the works of William Faulkner. Random House, Inc. and the Universities of Maryland and South Carolina are also associated with this project as are a distinguished group of Faulkner scholars. RHM has been the Executive Secretary of this project since its inception. See James B. Meriwether's "William Faulkner" in *Sixteen Modern American Authors: A Survey of Research and Criticism*, ed. Jackson R. Bryer (New York, 1973), 260, and *The Faulkner Concordance Newsletter*, Nos. 1–3 (1972–74).

12. Interview with Lieutenant Colonel Thomas E. Blagg, March 1973.

13. *Ibid.* In *West Point: 1973–74 Catalog* five pages (102–6) are devoted to listing the name, professional title, school or organization, and topic of recent Academy lecturers. The *Dean's Standing Operating Procedures* (DSOP) requires five pages to cover "procedures and policies governing the Lecture Program." Few visitors understand that their impending visit was "staffed" weeks before their arrival and fewer still can resist the pleasantries which are accorded them by their congenial hosts. Even Kurt Vonnegut, Jr., who described West Point as "a military academy which turned young men into homicidal maniacs for use in war" [*Breakfast of Champions* (New York, 1973), 153], conceded in a May 1974 conversation that he found himself charmed by the affable officers he met during visits there in the early 1970's. What West Point frequently hopes to gain from an official visit by an outsider, especially if he is an academician, is a potential friend on the outside, particularly one who can help smooth the way for West Pointers in his university's graduate school. See DSOP of 15 August 1972 for "ITEM V. LECTURE PROGRAM," 1–4 and Appendix I as well as the DSOP amendment of 1 February 1973. Documents supplied by Dean's Office, February 1974.

14. Interview with West Point officer, January 1973.

15. Interviews with cadets, January 1973 and March 1973. Such cadet sentiments also reflect the views of most Academy officers toward Annapolis, and to a lesser extent, the Air Force Academy. Officers in the combat arms emphasize that West Point is training young Americans to do something that the Navy and Air Force do not require. "I was a rifle company commander in the Korean War, and a battalion

commander in Korea and then a brigade commander in Viet Nam," said Colonel Richard L. Gruenther, director of the Office of Military Instruction, "and I've just seen enough of war to tell you that producing men who can lead other men in combat—ground combat—is a vital thing to our country. That's different than training men to run a battleship or a destroyer . . . or flying an airplane. You've got to be able to produce men who will be able to lead guys in a ground attack on another unit, one usually trained in my time under the Communist system. And I'll tell you, if we gave out Medals of Honor every time a man gave his life in combat, then we'd give a hell of a lot of them to the enemy. That's right! I've seen just too many guys on the wire to underestimate that." Interview with Colonel Gruenther, March 1973.

16. USMA, *Department of English Handbook: 1970–1971* (West Point, n.d.), 2, 23–26.

17. Interview with West Point officer, January 1973.

18. Interview with West Point officers, January 1973.

19. The U.S. Air Force Academy has a similar turnover every year but the U.S. Naval Academy with its 40 per cent civilian faculty does not.

20. Morris Janowitz has noted, "Since Pearl Harbor . . . [t]he system of continual rotation has come to be a main ingredient of family and community life" for the professional soldier. Janowitz also observed that by the late 1960's the military services were operating "with a computerized personnel system which makes possible worldwide and frequent changes of station." For the potential West Point instructor this meant that many more Army agencies and superior officers had the opportunity of requesting his services. See Janowitz's instructive summary discussion on military communities and social change in the 1971 Prologue to his *The Professional Solider*, xxxv–xl.

21. Interviews with Colonel Elliott C. Cutler, Jr., March 1973, and West Point officers, August 1973. Other variations in instructor selection, especially the extraordinary time and energy it consumes, were exemplified in a May 1973 interview with Colonel Charles H. Schilling:

> I think that, of all of my jobs, the picking of instructors is the most important one. And I probably spend as much time doing that as I do on any other single aspect of the department. I do it all myself, nobody else in the department does it. I maintain contact with my old instructors who are now out in the field. If they see a young officer that looks like a good sharp officer, they will write me and say, "Keep Joe Schultz on your list; and, when he gets the proper age, you should go for him." So I get good feedback from them, and I maintain good contact with them after they have left so I can get this benefit from them.

22. Interviews with Colonel Gilbert W. Kirby, March 1973. Some department heads are beginning to experience unaccustomed difficulty in getting graduates to come back to their departments. Colonel Donald G. MacWilliams, head of the Chemistry Department, observed in a May 1973 interview:

> With the advent of fields of concentration, it really boils down to the fact that we can't expect any West Pointer back unless they have taken chemistry electives. . . . So we are essentially limited to those people who have chosen our electives. . . . [And since few *choose* chemistry,] we just can't compete. There is no more open market. It used to be that we would sit down and match out for the top people. They had multiple interests and they were just as qualified in engineering as they were in chemistry. . . . They still have the same basic chemistry today and they can still go and get an MA in chemistry in two years as they always have, but they just don't want to.

23. An official West Point account of this development is given in the "History of Curriculum Development" chapter of *A Study of the Programs USMA* (1972), which notes, "In 1969 the Department of Ordnance and the engineering half of the Department of Military Art and Engineering were merged into a single Department of Engineering. At the same time, the History of the Military Art courses were placed in a new Department of History. In the following year, 1970, the courses in the History of Europe and America were transferred from the Department of Social Sciences to the Department of History" (13–14). While teachers of European and American history were not eager to leave the prestigious confines of the Social Sciences Department to join with fellow officers in what many considered to be the non-field of Military Art, they were far more reluctant to join in those in the most peripheral of all West Point academic areas—the humanities.

At the Naval Academy courses "in the fields of American, European, non-Western, naval, and military history" are taught in the History Department which is a part of the Division of English and History. See *Annapolis, The United States Naval Academy: Catalog 1973–1974* (Annapolis, 1973), 126–31. The Department of History at the Air Force Academy is in the Division of Humanities with the Department of English, Foreign Languages, and Philosophy and Fine Arts. See *United States Air Force Academy: Catalog 1973–74* (USAF Academy, 1973), 19–21, 108–10.

24. Interview with Colonel Lee D. Olvey, August 1973, and West Point officers, August 1973. Class rank is not an absolute prerequisite in returning to West Point as an instructor since its importance depends on the department an officer aspires to join. For instance, in Social Sciences, of the 23 graduates holding professorial rank (full, associate, or assistant), 3 graduated first in their respective classes, 2 graduated second, 1 graduated third. Over all, a total of 13 graduated in the 95th percentile, 6 others were well within the 85th percentile, and 3 of the remaining 4 finished in the 75th percentile. In English, *only one* of the 17 graduates holding professorial rank finished within the 85th percentile, 4 others were in the 80th percentile. *All but one* other officer were in the bottom 3/5 of their respective classes. West Point class rank figures for the faculties of the departments of Earth, Space and Graphic Sciences and Foreign Languages are similar to those of the English Department.

In an environment as highly competitive as West Point, such an imbalance between Academy backgrounds has a very debilitating effect on the morale and self-esteem of officers in departments like English because in the words of one officer, "We know, they know, we've got a lot of goats. Now our guys may be terrific officers and most of 'em are, but they're no great shakes as scholars. And when they get in the firstie course [Readings In Philosophy] and try to handle Plato and Lucretius without *ever* having had an honest to God philosophy course, it's MURDER—for them, for the cadets, and for Lucretius." Interview with West Point officer, October 1972. Professorial staff compilations based on officers listed in *West Point: 1973–74 Catalog* and their class ranks in *Register of Graduates* (1973).

25. Interview with Colonel Gilbert W. Kirby, March 1973.

26. Interviews with Lieutenant Colonel James B. Hall and West Point officers, March 1973.

27. Interview with Colonel John S. B. Dick, May 1973. The *Army Times* in its December 12, 1973, issue published a chart which showed what "current annual 'salaries' would be" if everyone "in the service received cash allowances for their housing and subsistence." A captain with six to eight years of commissioned service makes $17,409, with eight to ten years $18,174. A major with eight to ten years of commissioned service makes $19,245, with ten to twelve $20,138. The *Times* noted "these are the Regular Military Compensation rates which, as defined in law, comprise basic pay, BAQ, subsistence and the tax advantage gained from the two untaxed allowances. The tax advantage is calculated on an assumed 'average' family, but would actually vary for each service member depending on his specific tax circumstances." *Not calculated* into these sums are many other substantial benefits such as PX and commissary privileges and medical benefits.

28. Interview with West Point officer, January 1973. Although the elaborately prearranged communities such as the one Colonel Dick described at Rensselaer are increasingly the exception rather than the rule, the vast majority of prospective instructors participate in programs where other officers are, or have recently been, in residence. They frequently "have made book" on the school (i.e. have facts and opinions on courses and professors) and can assist their fellow officers in locating the relevant attack arrows.

29. Interviews with West Point officers, June and August 1973, and Colonel Frederick A. Smith, May 1973. West Pointers in the mid-1970's attend graduate school under various restrictions. These include a late 1973 directive to "officers attending civilian college at Army expense . . . to 'dress up' . . . their appearance" and to *not* let " 'their hair grow longer than allowed by Army regulation' " (*Army Times*, November 28, 1973, 28). Under pressure from House Armed Services Chairman F. Edward Hebert, no university which abolished ROTC during America's Vietnam involvement "is to be eligible for federally funded enrollment of military officers for advanced or graduate training." As Robert D. Heinl, Jr., pointed out in an *Army Times* article, "Hebert Collects Ivy League 'War Debt' " (April 24, 1974, 13), the House passed in 1972 "a legal prohibition against sending officer-students to schools that had kicked out ROTC;" but, actions by the Senate Armed Services Committee prevented it from becoming law. "Since then, Hebert has arm-twisted the Defense Department" into policies "identical with those his amendment would have made mandatory." Heinl suggested that Hebert's actions have not run into more widespread resistance because in 1973 Senator William Proxmire "released

studies showing that nearly half the officers [from all services] who get postgraduate training and degrees at government expense never employ their expensive, advanced skills in subsequent assignments." See also Lee Ewing's "DOD 'Miscounts' Training Budget," *Army Times*, March 13, 1974, 25.

30. Interview with West Point officer, June 1973.

31. Interview with former West Point instructor, October 1973.

32. Interview with Academic Board member, May 1973.

33. Interview with West Point officer, January 1973.

34. Interview with Major Francis E. Conrad, August 1973.

35. Interview with Brigadier General Philip R. Feir, January 1973. Feir's reputation as a man "not to be messed with" was well established during his tour as an instructor according to officers who were cadets then. "When he taught 'Juice' [Electricity], we called him FEAR. When you dozed off on him, you'd wake up dodging erasers and chalk. And if you didn't wake up quick enough, he'd be helping you out of the room." Interview with West Point officers, March 1973.

36. Interview with Colonel Richard L. Gruenther, March 1973.

37. Interviews with former West Point instructor, September 1973, and West Point officer, March 1973.

38. Interview with former West Point instructor, August 1972. This emphasis on mechanics is not an aberration of the English Department, rather it is an inevitable response to Academy academics. In the American military generally, and at West Point in particular, observing the details of institutionalized form and decorum are prerequisites to an individual's survival. Thus, when "guidance for the submission of written work at the United States Military Academy" is set forth in *The Style Manual*, which is prepared by the Department of English, it is predictable that the English Department would be the leading enforcer of those standards. And those standards specify everything from correct diction (expressions which are "informal or slang are unacceptable in cadet papers") to the correct paper and margins ("Use notebook or typewriter paper of standard size, 8 x 10½ or 8½ x 11. Write on one side of paper only. . . . Insure one and a half inches on the left margin, one inch on all others.") See Department of English, *The Style Manual: Standards for Written Work* (West Point, July 1973). By simply ignoring the specific "standards" cited above, a cadet theme could be graded as "deficient" (i.e., failing).

39. Interviews with West Point officers, January 1973 and June 1973. The courses involving cadets who are in their last two years are not as carefully supervised as courses involving plebes and yearlings. Colonel Charles H. Schilling commented in a May 1973 interview on engineering courses for the former group:

> Now, we do visit [the classroom]; but I must say that fortunately here I have been able to develop an attitude where the instructors don't resent this, and we are not impinging upon academic freedom. What I tell them . . . is mainly to achieve the objective and the rest is theirs. When we go in and visit, if we see something from experience which we know may be bad, and I talk to them, they know that it is a suggestion. . . . And they all know that

> if I get to the point where I want something done I'll tell them, "Do it!" And I'll be honest and blunt with them.

40. Interview with Colonel John S. B. Dick, May 1973.

41. Interviews with West Point officer, August 1972, and former West Point instructor, October 1973.

42. Interview with West Point officer, June 1972.

43. Interviews with West Point officers, June 1972, and Seymour M. Hersh, "33 Teachers at West Point Leave Army in 18 Months," *New York Times*, June 25, 1972, 1, 42.

44. Interview with former West Point instructor, July 1972.

45. Interview with West Point officer, January 1973. One source of junior faculty confusion is the frequently incongruous character of departmental directives. For instance, in 1973–74 Colonel Thomas E. Griess sent his officers a five-page statement entitled "The Teaching of History at the United States Military Academy." Colonel Griess commented on educational objectives ("Any university, including all of our military academies, must have as objectives the personal and social growth of their students; otherwise the public is cheated of the fruits of its endowment.") and on the benefits of studying history ("Thus while an appreciation of the past should lead to the ruthless and utter destruction of childish optimism and naïve faith in the perfectibility of man, it should not produce despair."). But, most revealingly, he made the attempt to reconcile departmental dogma with academic freedom:

> *Considerations in Teaching.* The philosophical meaning which an individual attaches to a study of the past is a private matter—as personal as one's views on religion—and I would no more ask that an instructor in this department subscribe to a particular philosophy of history than I would demand that he embrace a certain faith. On the other hand, it is necessary that I summarize for you my views on how our history courses should be oriented, why they should be oriented in that way, and what contributions our offerings in history should make to the education of cadets. . . . This summary constitutes a philosophy of teaching history rather than a philosophy of history as such.

Immediately after summarizing his philosophy of teaching, Colonel Griess wrote: "As a member of the department, you will be responsible for insuring that the lines of approach I have delineated are followed in the classroom."

46. Interview with former West Point instructor, August 1973. Retired Army Colonel James L. Morrison, associate professor of history at York College and author of the dissertation "USMA, 1833–1866," drew on his experiences as a West Point faculty member during the 1960's and early 1970's to offer this critique of the Academy faculty:

> At USMA Ph.D.'s, educated at public expense, are not employed as scholars or teachers, but as administrators. The excuse that their departmen-

> tal and institutional duties necessitate this is just that, an excuse, a transparent "cop out." They administer and politic because they prefer that to teaching and writing, not because they have to do it. Thus, the system is wasteful of public funds and, worse, does nothing to upgrade the quality of instruction.
>
> Similarly, the vast majority of the actual teachers are semi-pro's at best. Most take the job because of future career opportunities, not because they are dedicated teachers. Admittedly, most try hard, and some do quite well in the classroom, but because of their lack of education and the failure of the tenured staff to guide them, the stuff they put out is probably more on the level of a junior college than a state college. At the same time USMA operates on a budget with a faculty-student ratio which would compare favorably to Harvard. . . . Where else can a full-time faculty member get away with three preparations a week plus having his tests and lesson notes written for him?

Statement to authors, February 1974.

47. Interview with former West Point instructor, November 1973.

48. Interviews with West Point officers, January 1973, March 1973, and June 1973. Professor Sam C. Sarkesian offered a somewhat different view of what he called "the dilemma of the professional officer as to intellectual orientation or professionalism:"

> One will find that by the time the officer reaches his second or third year at the Point as an instructor, he falls into one of three categories: one who is convinced that graduate education is a reinforcement of his career orientation; one who is convinced that graduate education opened his eyes and implicitly has made a decision to retire or go on an intellectual track within the Army, i.e., research, teaching, etc.; or one who simply views graduate education as another assignment to do as well as one can for a good efficiency report. There may be a few who are truly in a dilemma—but these are a distinct minority.

Statement to authors, April 1974. For a further development of Professor Sarkesian's views see his *The World of the Professional Army Officer in a Changing Society*, to be published in Chicago by Nelson-Hall in late 1974.

Chapter Six

1. The frequently inflated rhetoric of the Academy is offered in USCC, *The Cadet Honor Code and System* (West Point, n.d.) and *Bugle Notes, 1973*, pp. 98–119. Equally inflated, but on the other side, is Arthur Heise's *The Brass Factories* (Washington, D.C., 1969), which concentrates on the periodic honor scandals at West Point and the Air Force Academy. A detailed discussion of the complicated operation of the Honor System is given in USCC, *The New Cadet Barracks Honor Instruction Booklet* (West Point, 1972). *The Cadet Honor Code and System* was circulated in response to

Honor System inquiries on the part of congressmen and others during 1973. Telephone interview with USMA Information Officer representative, July 1973.

It should be noted that the second half of the *Bugle Notes* discussion reproduces the words of General Douglas MacArthur, including his 1962 Thayer Award speech in which he presented his explication of "Duty-Honor-Country." Academy officials seem oblivious to the irony of invoking in this context a soldier who was relieved of his command for what Dean Acheson has described as "willful insubordination and incredibly bad judgment." See Acheson's *Present at the Creation: My Years in the State Department* (New York, 1969) for his account of MacArthur's "schizophrenic" behavior (463–77) and the circumstances involved in "relieving the General of all his commands and removing him from the Far East" (521–28).

2. Scott's monologue is based on a speech Patton actually delivered to his troops that is quoted in part in Edgar F. Puryear, Jr., *Nineteen Stars* (Orange, Va., 1971), 245.

3. Two officers challenged this contention, citing Patton's son, George S. Patton, III, a 1946 graduate, who had recently been promoted to brigadier general and who allegedly achieved notoriety as a colonel in Vietnam by telling journalists "I like to see the arms and legs fly." A fellow West Pointer, Dr. Gordon S. Livingston, who served in 1968–69 as regimental surgeon to then Colonel Patton's Eleventh Armored Cavalry Regiment ("Blackhorse") in Vietnam remembers a Patton who "told his staff that 'the present ratio of 90 percent killing to 10 percent pacification is just about right' " and who sent out Christmas cards in 1968 "featuring a color photograph of dismembered enemy bodies and bearing the greeting, 'Peace on Earth, Colonel and Mrs. George S. Patton.' " The younger Patton is to many a modern-day version of his father and his style has not impeded his career. He was promoted to major general in 1973. For discussions of George S. Patton, III, see George S. Livingston, M.D., "Healing in Vietnam," in *Crimes of War*, edited by Richard A. Falk, Gabriel Kolko, and Robert Jay Lifton (New York, 1971), 430–440.

4. The officer probably appropriated the story from Janowitz, *The Professional Soldier* (1971), 25.

5. Interview with West Point officer, March 1973. At a press conference prior to receiving the Thayer Award at West Point on May 9, 1973, General Omar Bradley expressed a view of Patton that undercuts his crusader image:

> General Patton was a very complex character in many ways. He took considerable handling. But when you got all through with it and added it up, he ends up being a damn good soldier. He was 6 years my senior. I served under him in Africa and Sicily, and he [gave me good service] when he served under me, and he never questioned it. I think that is a mark of a soldier. He could change the status as a senior officer to a junior officer and never question it. I've had many people tell me that they've heard him talk about everybody from the President down but that they never heard him say anything against me. So he was a very loyal subordinate.

Remarks from verified transcript of interview prepared by the authors.

6. Thomas F. Fleming, "West Point Cadets Now Say, 'Why, Sir?' " *New York Times Magazine,* July 5, 1970, discusses the cases of Steinke and Font as well as Captain David B. Bean, class of 1967, who was released from active duty as a conscientious objector.

7. *New York Times,* October 16, 1969, 1, 16.

8. Interview with West Point cadet, May 1972.

9. The last sentence of General Koster's remarks is not reproduced in West Point's account of this incident in "General Koster Leaves USMA," *Assembly,* XXIX (Spring 1970), 34–35, 52. Koster is hailed in the unsigned article as a man who "[w]ithout a doubt will be remembered not only as one of the most popular Superintendents in the Academy's history, but also as one who concentrated on skillfully guiding the Academy's progress through a critical period." Ironically, Koster's popularity was a result more of his role as a martyr after his resignation than of any strong support he previously had among officers or cadets. Koster's replacement, General William A. Knowlton, did not mention Koster by name in his superintendent's letter in the Spring 1970 issue of *Assembly* but referred obliquely to "the sadness of the events that led to the change." He further reported, "Throughout this difficult period, the attitude of the Corps has been one of getting on with its work."

10. *New York Times,* March 18, 1970, 36.

11. Fleming, "West Point Cadets Now Say, 'Why, Sir?'," 42. For a perceptive discussion of Koster at West Point, see Ward Just's *Military Men* (New York, 1970), 20–32.

12. Interview with West Point cadet, January 1973.

13. Interview with West Point cadet, March 1973.

14. Interview with West Point cadet, May 1972.

15. February 1973 letter to authors from 1972 graduate on active duty.

16. *Army Time*'s account (December 12, 1973) of Koster's futile appeal was carried on its second page in bold black lettering with the general's photograph. The story noted that in addition to his demotion Koster had appealed as "unfair and unjust" being "stripped of his Meritorious Service Medal [sic., Distinguished Service Cross] and publically censured." The paper also reported in a related story that the findings of The Peers Commission on the My Lai killings which produced Koster's professional difficulties "may never be made public" because of a December U.S. Court of Appeals ruling that the Peers report was "exempt from the Freedom of Information Act" and "not subject to public perusal."

While many West Pointers resented the prominence given to General Koster's final professional misfortune, few expected a Nixon administration embroiled in scandals to reconsider General Koster's case and thus to refocus attention on the question of field grade and general officer involvement in My Lai as well as on the President's politically expedient responses to Lieutenant Calley. There was also the feeling that Koster was pressing his luck by appealing actions which were far less harsh than he might have expected. For an account of the Army's apparent reluctance to punish Koster, see Seymour M. Hersh's *Cover-up: The Army's Secret Investigation of the Massacre at My Lai 4* (New York, 1973), especially 254–68 and 294–97.

17. Interview with West Point officer, January 1973.

18. Interview with West Point cadet, May 1972.

19. Interview with West Point officer, June 1972.

20. Mary McCarthy, *Medina* (New York, 1972), 72. Similar sentiments are also reflected in the West Pointers on Policy and Command Responsibility section of The Citizens Commission of Inquiry, eds., *The Dellums Committee Hearings on War Crimes in Vietnam* (New York, 1972), 5–80.

21. Linda Greenhouse, "Silent Agony Ends for Cadet at Point," *New York Times*, June 7, 1973. Ms. Greenhouse's detailed account of Pelosi's silencing began on the first page with a photograph of Pelosi and was continued with another photograph for over half an inside page. This almost unprecedented prominence given to a West Point story and its distribution by the *Times* News Service constituted the first major national exposure received by Pelosi. Many West Pointers were understandably stunned by this media bombshell the day after graduation, especially since a brief account of the graduation ceremonies and Admiral Thomas H. Moorer's address appeared on page 51. Ironically, the major "story" of that day may well have been that Admiral Moorer, as chairman of the Joint Chiefs of Staff, neither mentioned Richard Nixon's name nor referred to any of his accomplishments. But in discussing "the outlook for you young men starting your military careers in this changing world," he invoked throughout "the late President Franklin D. Roosevelt."

22. *The Cadet Honor Code and System*, 3–4.

23. Interviews with West Point officers involved in the case, July 1973.

24. Interviews with cadet Honor Committee members, March 1973.

25. Greenhouse, *New York Times*, June 7, 1973.

26. *Washington Post* editorial "Where Is the Honor?" reprinted in *Newsday*, June 14, 1973; section on "Headliners" in *New York Times*, June 10, 1973; *Newsweek*, June 18, 1973; *Commonweal*, June 29, 1973.

27. *Army Times*, July 11, 1973. Diverse responses to the editorial appeared in the July 25, 1973 issue.

28. Linda Greenhouse, "Neighbors Fete West Pointer Shunned by Classmates," *New York Times*, July 13, 1973.

29. The cadets' case was reported in the *New York Times* issues of May 27, June 6, June 8, June 16, 1973. On June 15, Judge Whitman Knapp dismissed the case on the grounds that the cadets had not demonstrated that their constitutional right to due process was denied by the board of officers which reviewed cadet Honor Committee decisions. The cadets appealed the verdict.

30. Interviews with West Point cadets and officers, June 1973.

31. There is a "Pelosi Fact Sheet" at the Academy to which we were denied access but which we were able to obtain through unofficial channels. Apparently, the Academy officials are reluctant to release the facts about Pelosi's trial to the press because they have been advised by the Department of Army that the Pelosi case is likely to become a factor in federal court litigation of other honor cases and publication of the facts might affect the verdict in those other cases. According to the "Pelosi Fact Sheet" one cadet testified that he observed Pelosi cheating on a quiz

on September 13, 1971. He alerted the instructor, Captain Martin J. Michlik, the next day. On September 15, Michlik made a point to observe Pelosi's answers on the written quiz just after the command to cease work had been given and noticed that an entire section of the quiz had been left blank. Michlik apparently testified that a few moments later he observed that, even though the "approved solution" had been posted, Pelosi was writing on the quiz with an instrument other than the green pencil authorized for making corrections, probably with a piece of lead he had hidden under his fingernail. When Michlik went over to observe Pelosi's quiz paper, the sections that had earlier been left blank were filled with the correct answers. At the end of the class Michlik discussed the situation with the cadet who had originally reported seeing Pelosi cheat and the cadet said that he had also observed Pelosi writing after the approved solution had been posted.

32. James Feron, "Cadet Committee at West Point Does Away With 'The Silence,' " *New York Times* (September 12, 1973).

33. Interview with Colonel Lee D. Olvey, June 1973.

34. For an extremely detailed critique of West Point's official rationales in defending its adjudicatory systems (conduct and honor systems) and how West Point's systems compare with those of the other four United States service academies as well as with the adjudicatory systems of civilian educational institutions, see *A Prayer For Relief: The Constitutional Infirmities of the Military Academies' Conduct, Honor and Ethics Systems.* This report of a study group headed by Air Force captain Michael T. Rose carries a copyright date of 1973 but was not published by the New York University School of Law until spring 1974. We are indebted to Captain Rose for allowing us to read the report while it was in galleys. *Army Times,* October 3, 1973, 4.

35. Interview with Second Lieutenant Richard M. Saunders, June 1973. Saunders, who graduated second in the class of 1973, is the son of the head of the Department of Physics. See also *Army Times,* November 28, 1973, 4.

36. Interviews with Brigadier General Philip R. Feir, March 1973; with Colonel Sumner Willard, May 1973; with Colonel Charles H. Schilling, June 1973.

37. Interview with Captain Michael T. Rose, June 1973. Cadet contempt for the Constitution would be especially unfortunate in the view of Daniel A. Carrell, a Richmond, Virginia, attorney who taught history and political philosophy at West Point in 1968–71. "Legal loopholes are not involved in what is at issue," he argued, "and civilian concepts of due process need not be supplied in their totality. The root issue is the ascertainment of truth. Enforcement procedures at West Point may be analogized with those in prisons, where courts have required just enough procedural safeguards so as to prevent arbitrary decision making." Carrell cited a leading prison due process case [*Landman* v. *Royster*, 333 F. Supp. 621 (E. D. Va. 1971)], in which the court concluded that before a prisoner can be subjected to certain forms of punishment for violation of prison regulations, he must have received adequate written notice of the charges against him, a reasonable opportunity to prepare a defense, and a hearing before an impartial tribunal, including the right to cross-examine adverse witnesses and to present witnesses in his own behalf. Carrell also noted, "Of course, the imposition of such punishment may be much less damaging to a prisoner

than the consequences of a conviction of an honor violation are to a cadet. Moreover, *Landman* and similar cases support the view that there is no merit to the distinction that is sometimes made between 'punitive' and 'administrative' sanctions." Statement to authors, March 1974.

38. Interview with West Point cadet, May 1972.

39. Interview with Second Lieutenant Richard M. Saunders, June 1973.

40. Apparently influenced by fears that this harassment of Pelosi might work against the Academy in federal court litigation over West Point's adjudicatory system, officers moved to stop it late in 1972. The commandant of cadets, General Feir, called in each cadet class and lectured them on the impropriety of such harassment. Feir also ordered that Pelosi be transferred back to his old company, where he was known to have many supporters. Feir also altered procedures so that Pelosi's military aptitude rating would be calculated without the peer ratings from other cadets.

41. For example, when Pelosi appeared on a talk show (the Lee Leonard Show) to discuss his ordeal, a cadet called into the show to ask why Pelosi was misrepresenting, or allowing others to misrepresent, the extent and effectiveness of the silence. Pelosi acknowledged that the silence was not observed by a sizable portion of the Corps of Cadets, then added "but I didn't increase my circle of friends much either."

42. Interview with West Point officer, May 1973.

43. Interview with Brigadier General Philip R. Feir, March 1973.

44. Maxwell D. Taylor, *Swords and Plowshares* (New York, 1972) 25–26. The Baker quotation in the text is *The Cadet Honor Code and System*, 1.

45. *The New Cadet Barracks Honor Instruction Booklet* (1972), A-5-2.

46. General Ridgway's comments were made in a 1971 Founders Day speech and published in *Assembly*, XXX (Spring 1971), 21.

47. Quoted in U.S., *Congressional Record*, 92nd Congress, 1st Session (May 26, 1971), CXVII, E5091.

48. Interview with West Point officer, March 1973.

49. Interview with Colonel Sumner Willard, May 1973.

50. *The New Cadet Barracks Honor Instruction Booklet*, A-1-4 to 5, A-2-1-1, A-4-5, A-9-3, A-11-3 to 5, A-12-4.

51. *Ibid.*, A-1-1.

52. *Ibid.*, A-12-4.

53. *New York Times*, August 9, 1970; *Village Voice*, August 20, 1970.

54. Interview with West Point officer, June 1972.

55. Donham's subsequent predicament is described in stark terms in an official Academy publication:

> He filed an appeal in the U.S. District Court challenging the Department of the Army's decision. However, on 3 September 1970, the court supported the Department of the Army's decision and further directed that Cadet Donham be offered the opportunity to resign in lieu of being discharged by the

> Academy for lack of aptitude for leadership. Cadet Donham resigned, and since he had completed three years as a cadet, he was called to active duty as an enlisted man for a period of three years effective 22 September 1970. . . . After some additional legal delays, he reported on active duty and submitted an additional appeal to the courts. On 6 January 1971, the U.S. Court of Appeals reversed the U.S. District Court based on technicalities and issued instructions to stay Donham's orders to active military duty pending certain reprocessing which is now being accomplished by the Army.

See *Annual Report of the Superintendent* (West Point, 1971), 38.

56. Interview with Colonel Sumner Willard, May 1973. In the spring of 1973 General Knowlton reported, "the Supreme Court had declined to review a decision of the U.S. Court of Appeals which held that mandatory chapel should be prohibited at West Point. In accordance with this decision, all religious activities at West Point are now completely voluntary. We regret the passage of religious observance as a required part of cadet training and experience." See the superintendent's letter inside front cover of *Assembly*, XXXI (March 1973).

57. Interview with West Point officer, May 1973. In matters ranging from the approval of texts to observing the haircut regulations for officers, one of the most common rationales is the "keep your powder dry" argument. In those departments which have a reputation for liberalism, such as Social Sciences, "minor infringements" on faculty freedom are not opposed, so the argument goes, in order to preserve political capital for larger, more important curriculum fights. In those departments which have a more conservative reputation, such as Mathematics and Engineering, these issues seldom materialize, because most of the officers believe that the Military Academy should operate in the same authoritarian way as a military unit.

58. Morris Janowitz discusses similar problems in what he cites as one of the major "unresolved dilemmas of military authority. . . . What is the legitimate scope of military authority over the personal behavior of its members? . . ." See especially the "Limits of Civilianization" section of his 1971 Prologue to *The Professional Soldier*, xiii–xxxv.

59. Interview with West Point officer, May 1973.

60. Interview with West Point officer, June 1972.

61. Retired Marine Corps colonel James A. Donovan offers an uncommonly candid and accurate discussion of the inevitable tensions among professional officers in all the armed services in "Careerism" in his *Militarism, U.S.A.* (New York, 1970), 64–81. "The overiding sense of duty to follow orders," writes Colonel Donovan, "is the basis of the military professional's effective performance in the arena of defense policy planning" which occurs at "the top of the military hierarchy." He also notes that the "ideologies and ethics of the profession which motivated the officer in his youth, like the ideals of the young liberal college student, become qualified by the hard realities of family responsibility, job status, and retirement security. The middle-aged career officer has about the same self-interests as any other professional, despite his creeds of service and sacrifice."

62. Interview with four West Point cadets, May 1972. To some cadets this incident brought to mind a story in Matthew B. Ridgway's memoirs (*Soldier*, 29). Ridgway wrote of "a bitter joke that went the rounds of the Army soon after World War I:"

> At a staff meeting before a big attack some fire-eating division commander tapped at a little dot on the map with his riding crop and said:
>
> "I'd give ten thousand men to take that hill."
>
> There was a moment of silence, and then from the back of the room, where stood the battalion commanders whose men would have to go against the hill, there came an ironic voice:
>
> "Generous son-of-a-bitch, isn't he?"
>
> I've never admired such generosity, and I shall go to my grave humbly proud of the fact that on at least four occasions I have stood up at the risk of my career and denounced what I considered to be ill-considered tactical schemes which I was convinced would result in useless slaughter.

Cadets in the 1970's tend to wonder if there are many officers of general rank in the Army today with Ridgway's compassion and integrity.

63. *Ibid.*

64. January 1973 letter to authors from 1972 graduate on active duty.

65. Interview with West Point officer, January 1973.

66. Interview with West Point cadet, June 1972.

67. A sketchy history of the Honor System is provided in *The New Cadet Barracks Honor Instruction Booklet* (1972), A-2-1 to A-2-6, and in *The Cadet Honor Code and System*, 2–3. The most detailed and accurate accounts are in the dissertations by Dillard, "The Uncertain Years," Chapter 7, and by Nye "Era of Educational Reform," Chapter 3. There had been an unofficial code that the word of a cadet was his bond ever since the Thayer superintendency, but it was never formalized. There had also been isolated instances of cadets imposing punishments on each other, such as one involving cheating (1865) and another involving lying (1871). But these punishments resulted from apparently spontaneous actions by cadets, not a cohesive cadet organization. There was probably a connection between the appearance of the Vigilance Committee around 1897 and the appearance of a course entitled History of Ethics in the West Point curriculum in 1896.

68. Interview with Brigadier General Philip R. Feir, March 1973.

69. Nevertheless, this has been the approach of Heise, *The Brass Factories*, *passim*, and Galloway and Johnson, *West Point*, 100–125.

70. Interview with Colonel Edward A. Saunders, March 1973. After the cheating scandal at the Air Force Academy in 1965, West Point did modify testing procedures slightly. Previously, the same exam was given to different classes even if the classes met on different days. Since 1965 the exams have been altered for classes which have an opportunity to acquire information during the evening meal or dur-

ing the after-supper hours in the barracks. But the same exam is still given to different classes that meet on the same day.

71. The Academy's reluctance to release information on honor cases seems to be the product of mixed motives: a desire to protect accused cadets who were found innocent, an instinctive suspicion of the press, a conviction that the operation of the West Point Honor System is unique and that there is no way to adequately explain it to outsiders, fear on the part of officers at different levels in the bureaucracy that their comments will be misconstrued and their subsequent careers jeapordized, and the conviction that any report of cheating at West Point "will tarnish the image."

72. June 1973 letter to authors from a West Point cadet.

73. Interview with four West Point cadets, May 1972.

74. *New York Times*, March 5, 1964, reports the passage of the act. For many West Pointers the two most troublesome aspects of the Corps' expansion are reflected in these remarks by Colonel Gerald W. Medsger. When he was asked his opinion of the present Corps size, he replied:

> It's too big. And you can quote me. As a matter of fact, we're getting a number of indications from the present first class [1973] that they feel the same way. Obviously honor is on everyone's mind right now [because of Physics cheating scandal]. But I think the first class attribute many of the honor problems to the fact that the Corps is too large. You don't know the other people. . . . When we went into a solution room, when I was a cadet, if there was somebody there who wasn't supposed to be there, you knew it. "Hey that guy's not in our regiment." Today anybody can walk in. They don't know who he is. They don't even know if he's a classmate or not. And so it's easier for people to get away with things. I've heard a couple of cadets say, "Hey, I don't even know my honor rep. I don't really know the guy; he lives down there somewhere at the other end of the hall."
>
> I think from our standpoint, the administration's standpoint, it's harder to control and it's harder to keep tabs on. It's hard to know what they're doing, who's a good guy and who's a bad guy.

75. *Regulations: United States Corps of Cadets* (West Point, 1971).

76. Interview with Brigadier General Philip R. Feir, March 1973. Soon after he was made commandant in 1972, General Feir began a study of a way to reduce the size of the blue book.

77. *Regulations for the United States Corps of Cadets* (West Point, 1973), 1.

78. *Regulations* (1971), 125, 44–45, and *Regulations* (1973), 36, 39.

79. *The New Cadet Barracks Honor Instruction Booklet* (1972), A-4–3.

80. Cantlay to Jannarone, September 28, 1971.

81. *The New Cadet Barracks Honor Instruction Booklet* (1972), A–2–3.

82. Interview with West Point officer, June 1972.

83. Interview with cadet, May 1973.

84. When questions relating to an officer's sense of "higher law" were discussed with Lieutenant General James M. Gavin (ret.), his observations were character-

istically unorthodox. Asked if he thought the failure of at least a few West Point generals to resign when many profoundly believed major policies which were being followed in Vietnam were, and would continue to be, disastrous, General Gavin replied: "[In a] lot of ways. Lot of ways. Our values are quite odd, to say the least at the moment. For example, I think some of the heroes of our time are the young people who strenuously objected to the war in mass demonstrations in Washington and in front of St. Patrick's Cathedral. I really mean that. By what other dimensions do you judge moral courage than by the willingness of someone to stand up and be counted?" Interview with Lieutenant General Gavin, September 1973.

Chapter Seven

1. Interview with West Point officer, June 1972. Similar concerns were also expressed by C. Robert Kemble, USMA '49, who was Director of American Studies at West Point before accepting the presidency of New Mexico Military Institute in 1972. In concluding his *The Image of the Army Officer in America: Background for Current Views* (Westport, Conn., 1973), Kemble wrote:

> Our armed forces today desperately need a sense of *national* direction, and that direction must come from the people as a whole. It cannot come from within the military alone, where philosophical problems are agonized over but get lost in the practical day-by-day process of implementing political-military policy and decisions. Nor should the guidance come solely from official Washington whose short-term goals shift too conveniently with the political winds and with the personalities of appointed and elected officials. Through its government, the United States has told its soldiers for two centuries what it wants them *to do*, but it has seldom, if ever, told them what it wants them *to be*. As a result, the officer corps has largely depended on its own traditional assumptions. And if the old assumptions are wrong, they ask, what takes their place? It would seem that any philosophical redirection of the military must come from open, reasoned, and multi-sided public dialogue (202–3).

2. USMA, Department of History, *History of United States Foreign Relations, 1898–1960* (West Point, September, 1973), 1.

3. USMA, *Department of English Handbook, 1973–74* (West Point, 1973), 8.

4. Quoted in Nye, "USMA, 1900–1925," 124. Philip Rieff's discussion of "the therapeutic" as an emergent social type is helpful in understanding how far removed the West Point environment is from the experience of many Americans. Whereas cadets seem constrained by authority at every turn, "the therapeutic" has "a conclusive freedom" from society's constraints. He is free, Rieff argues, "because he can live his life among authorities so long divided that none can assert themselves strongly in their own sphere." Distrust and disrespect for authority is the new norm, a development which Rieff views as "mainly the fault of what passes for authority in our nation; the authority figures themselves are so often such inferior per-

sons that their offices can not conceal the absence of any reference beyond themselves." But even if Rieff is correct in arguing that "the opposing sides of the American scene, deviants and straights, are both suspicious of authority" and that "we are reducing politics to a mere struggle for power and more power," most West Pointers are atypical Americans in their readiness to accept the dictates of legally constituted authority figures.

See Rieff's " 'Fellow Teachers,' " *Salmagundi*, No. 20 (Summer–Fall 1972), 23–24, and a subsequent revision in *Fellow Teachers* (New York, 1973), 45–46. This issue of *Salmagundi* is, as editors Robert Boyers and Robert Orrill state, "devoted to the study of human nature in its contemporary appearance," and Philip Rieff is "a commanding presence in this volume" in accord with their belief that "Rieff's work . . . will eventually find acceptance as the single most penetrating effort of historical and socio-cultural analysis produced by an American in recent times" (3). We share the editors' view of Rieff's work.

5. Quoted in Congressional Quarterly, Inc., *Watergate: Chronology of a Crisis*, Vol. 1 (Washington, D.C., 1973), 53. General Persons is not a West Pointer but his son, Wilton Burton Persons, Jr., is a 1946 graduate and a general in the Judge Advocate General's Corps. *Register of Graduates* (1973), 563. John W. Finney discusses previous military men who have served as senior White House staff officers in "Symington Scores Haig's Dual Role," *New York Times*, May 27, 1973, 33.

6. For discussions which emphasize Haig's West Point associations, see Lou Cannon, "Haig: Nixon Staff Chief With New Style," *Washington Post*, September 30, 1973, A1, A12, and two Sunday supplement cover stories: Lloyd Shearer, "General Alexander Haig—He's Nixon's New Number One," *Parade*, October 7, 1973, 4, 5, 7, and Nick Thimmesch, "Chief of Staff," *Potomac*, in *Washington Post*, November 25, 1973, 12–15, 31, 41, 43, 45, 46. For a highly critical account of Haig's integrity and his West Point tour as a tactical officer, see Lucian K. Truscott, IV, "Mr. T and Colonel Haig," *Village Voice*, May 17, 1973.

7. Tom Braden, "Gen. Haig Deserves A Hearing," *Washington Post*, December 1, 1973, A19.

8. Thimmesch, 43 and 45. Nick Thimmesch said in a November 29, 1973, telephone interview that he tape recorded his conversations with Haig; his verbatim quotations serve as a basis for an uncommonly balanced and instructive article. On the relationship between politics, soldiering, and sports, Haig told Thimmesch:

> I can state that the military background is a very good cauldron for subsequent duty on civilian status in the bureaucracy. I don't share the concept that there is a military mind.
>
> Politics and soldiering are very, very close. It's only a soldier who can respect and admire a politician. It's a field where a man lays everything on the line to win or lose. Athletics are the same. There's a camaraderie among men who lay it all out. They're tested by the vote or they're tested in battle. When one doesn't win, the results are fatal, and in the case of the military, quite fatal. So I have a great deal of respect for politicians.

> From my perspective, I have always found that a military man can have his views respected. The military has to know its own framework in order to influence policy. There are always positions for capable military people at the highest level (12).

9. Interviews with Colonel Frederick C. Lough, head, Department of Law, May 1973; West Point officers, June and August 1973 and February 1974; and Brigadier General Elvin R. Heiberg (ret.), September 1973. Haig finished in the bottom ⅓ of his 1947 class and as late as 1969 was a relatively anonymous colonel. *Register of Graduates* (1973), 584.

10. Interview with National Security Council staff member, December 1973.

11. By early 1974 it was evident that General Haig's skills were being more realistically appraised. David S. Broder in "Operation 'Do Not Disturb,' " *Washington Post*, January 9, 1974, discussed General Haig's role in scrapping "Operation Candor," which was intended to demonstrate the White House's openness to candid discussions of criticism. In Broder's view "once Haig understood that the commander-in-chief wanted reassurance more than he wanted accurate reconnaissance, he adapted his talents to the situation" (A 24).

Rowland Evans and Robert Novak came to similar conclusions about Haig's subservience and reflexive obedience to authority in "Has a Sinister Force Corrupted Alexander Haig?" *New York*, February 7, 1974, 35–36. They noted that " a longtime military acquaintance" of Haig's told them, "Al came up in the military bureaucracy, where to get ahead you tell the boss what he wants to hear." Evans and Novak reluctantly concuded that Haig's service in the White House is clearly illuminated by "the record of the past nine months," which does not reveal a man agonizing over a creed of duty, honor, country; rather "the record . . . points powerfully to Haig's view of himself as a soldier who follows orders."

12. Most West Point cadets first see General MacArthur's phrase in context when, as plebes, they read his 1962 Thayer Award speech in "The Honor Code" section of *Bugle Notes* (1973), 116–17. In discussing the "welter of change and development" in "a new world" of the 1960's, MacArthur said, "your mission remains fixed, determined, inviolable—it is to win our wars. Everything else in your professional career is but corollary to this vital dedication. All other public purposes, all other public projects, all other public needs, great or small will find others for their accomplishment; but you are the ones who are trained to fight; yours is the profession of arms—the will to win, the sure knowledge that in war there is no substitute for victory; that if you lose the nation will be destroyed; that the very obsession of your public service must be Duty—Honor—Country."

13. Interview with Colonel John D. Foldberg, August 1973.

14. Letter to "Fellow Graduates and Friends of the Military Academy," *Assembly*, XX (Winter, 1962), inside front cover and interview with Cadet Kerry K. Pierce, February 1974.

15. Carl Stepp, "Westmoreland Runs for Governor," *Washington Post*, March 13, 1974, A2 and Joe McGinniss, "Winning Hearts and Minds in South Carolina," *Harper's*, April 1974, 65–66, 68, 70–72.

For accounts of how Westmoreland views his Army career and the nation's reluctance to voluntarily fill Army manpower needs, see his "A Soldier Looks Back," *New York Times,* June 25, 1972, Sec. E, 15, and "If Not a Volunteer Army, What Then?" *New York Times,* August 17, 1973, 31. David Halberstam's discussion of Westmoreland in *The Best and the Brightest* (New York, 1972), especially Chapters 24 and 25, draws on the author's unique access to Westmoreland's key aides in the late 1960's and early 1970's.

16. USMA, Office of Physical Education, "Every Cadet Is An Athlete!" (West Point, n.d.), 2. The Athletics section of *Bugle Notes* (1973) opens with this motto and the statement, "These words of General Douglas MacArthur have become an inherent part of the challenge that must be met by the West Point cadet; for today every cadet is required to take physical training courses and to engage in intramural or intercollegiate athletics" (253). MacArthur's historic importance to the Academy's athletic program is also stressed in *West Point: 1973–74 Catalog:* "Realizing the value of athletics to the Army, General Douglas MacArthur, who was Superintendent shortly after World War I, reorganized and strengthened the athletic system. 'The training of the athletic field, which produces in a superlative degree the attributes of fortitude, self-control, resolution, courage, mental agility and, of course, physical development, is one completely fundamental to an efficient soldiery,' General MacArthur said" (128). For a discussion of West Point football from the 1890's through the spring 1951 cheating scandal which occurred "principally among the football players and cadets who were assisting them," see Ambrose's *Duty, Honor, Country,* 303–21.

17. The belief that national powers such as Tennessee and Penn State physically beat West Point teams so soundly that they are weakened for subsequent opponents has been a commonplace at West Point in recent years. Interview with athletic director, Colonel William J. Schuder, June 1973. Comment about Army's loss to California is from *Atlanta Journal* sports editor, Furman Bisher, in "Army's No-Win Policy Abandoned for a Day," *Atlanta Journal and Constitution,* Sunday edition, October 7, 1973, D1 and D13. Listing of 1973 college football records is in the *New York Times,* December 3, 1973. Interview with Colonel John S. B. Dick, February 1974.

18. General Knowlton's statement appeared on inside front cover of *Assembly,* XXXII (December 1973). The "football factories" remark was quoted in Bob Addie's "Army-Navy Game: Crisis Point?" *Washington Post,* November 28, 1973, Sec. E, 1.

19. Quoted in Charlie Roberts' "Army'll Be Back—Cahill," *Atlanta Constitution,* October 6, 1973, D2.

20. Gordon S. White, Jr., "Crippled by an Act of Congress," *New York Times,* November 30, 1973, 43–44; see also White's related article, "Army Plans More 'Realistic' Look at Football Foes," *New York Times,* November 28, 1973, 53–55.

21. *Ibid.*

22. *Ibid.* Gordon S. White, Jr., "Army Routed by Navy, 51-0, for 10th Loss," *New York Times,* December 2, 1973, Sec. 5, 1 and 3. White noted that the crowd (91,926) was "the smallest since the Army-Navy game moved back to the big con-

crete dish [John F. Kennedy Stadium] in Philadelphia in 1946" and "many persons . . . began walking out . . . at the outset of the second half." But even these unprecedented facts were overshadowed by the enormity of Navy's victory; "The Navy coach used all 59 midshipmen suited for the game and used each of them for at least one full quarter of action."

23. Gordon S. White, Jr., "West Point Dismisses Coach Cahill," December 4, 1973, 61 and 64. An official West Point news release, dated December 13, 1973, contained no comments by Coach Cahill but rather remarks by General Knowlton: "I consider Tom [Cahill] a close friend and a fine person. He has been a great help to the Academy during some very difficult years, and has had some significant successes. In view of the won-lost record of the past season, we were going to make a coaching change, the contract expiration seemed to be the time to do it. With new coaching leadership, we feel we can be competitive again." News release supplied by USMA Information Office, February 1974.

24. Colonel Schuder is quoted in White's "Army Plans More 'Realistic' Look at Football Foes," 53.

25. Quoted in Furman Bisher's "Army's No-Win Policy Abandoned for a Day," D1.

26. Gordon S. White, Jr., "Army Hires Homer Smith, Who Leans to Wishbone," *New York Times*, January 30, 1974, 33–34. Telephone interviews with West Point officers, January 1974.

27. *Ibid.* Gordon S. White, Jr., "Army Put Soft Soap on Old Blade," *New York Times*, January 31, 1974, 39–40 and interview with Colonel Frank J. Kobes, August 1973.

28. *Ibid.* Comments about Gordon White made in telephone conversations with USMA Information Office representatives and West Point officers in October, November, and December 1973. In February, Army added Lafayette College as an eleventh game to its 1974 schedule. General Knowlton explained that the Lafayette game had been added in order to prepare Army for its game the following week against a strong Tulane team. Interview with Lieutenant General William A. Knowlton, February 1974.

29. Immediate problems which are seized upon by critics of football defeats or battlefield stalemates are financial. For instance, West Point's inter-collegiate athletic program is financed by the Army Athletic Association (AAA) which "is a self-supporting and nonprofit organization consisting of approximately 14,000 graduates of the Military Academy." The primary source of AAA revenue is receipts from football games; and, well before the 1973 season, Colonel William Schuder reported that (as a result of having "overestimated receipts for eight out of ten of the [football] games" in 1971 and a modest year in 1972 when at least "estimates were realized . . . although not a record year") it has been necessary "to increase the AAA's portion of the cadet's activity fee and to raise the AAA membership fee." Colonel Schuder noted that "the Superintendent is providing support with other funds whenever possible," but perhaps the most revealing development was—"Despite considerable efforts to secure a sponsor for our football highlights' film we have been

unsuccessful and will have to include this expense in the current budget." By the winter of 1973, months before the disastrous 0-10 season, West Point's athletic fortunes had so declined that, even with one of the nation's most celebrated football histories, the Academy could not find support from the American business community. Colonel Schuder's four-page statement of February 26, 1973, provided by USMA Department of Athletics in June 1973.

30. Academy officials were initially pleased by the publicity given to these changes after a spring and summer of "bad publicity" from the Pelosi silencing case and the physics cheating ring. James Feron's "West Point Simplifies Cadet Regulations" was featured on the front page of the *New York Times*, August 29, 1973, 1 and 18, and a UPI story appeared in the *Washington Post*, August 30, 1973, A2, under the title "West Point Overhauls Cadet Rules: Use of Common Sense Expected." However, Academy officials were annoyed by James Feron's subsequent essay, "A Strategic Withdrawal From the Old Rulebook," *New York Times*, September 2, 1973, Sec. E, 3, which demoted Lieutenant General Knowlton to "Brig. Gen." and contained other errors of fact. But what most upset them was the publication above the story of a picture of six cadets holding a plebe under a water hydrant. The picture caption used the present tense and read, "This West Point hazing technique is called 'giving the hydrant.' The photo was taken in 1913."

31. James Feron, "Cadet Committee at West Point Does Away With 'The Silence,' " *New York Times*, September 12, 1973, 1 and 12, and "West Point: Braced for Reform," *Newsweek*, September 24, 1973, 36. The *Newsweek* story defies the antimilitary bias many West Pointers assign to it with its photograph of a plebe being braced, but with the caption "Old days at the Point: End of an Era." *Newsweek* also quotes General Knowlton as denying that "West Point is going soft." Knowlton says, "We're always going to be leaner, meaner, tougher and more conservative than civilian schools."

32. "USMA Eases Life of Cadets," *Army Times*, September 12, 1973, 51, and comments from Review and Outlook section, *Wall Street Journal*, September 10, 1973.

33. Feron, "West Point Simplifies Cadet Regulations," 18.

34. Knowlton in *Assembly*, XXXII (December 1973), inside front cover.

35. *Ibid.*, 13.

36. Interview with Captain Stephen T. Lifrak, August 1973.

37. In public comments, Academy officials vehemently deny that the "self-studies" and studies by selected outsiders are pro forma. However, in the six-year period from 1968 to 1974 when we followed Academy affairs very closely, one of the most prevalent topics of discussion was the essential irrelevance (and in the view of many, properly so) of committees seeking to alter West Point's traditional mode of operation. For instance, the predominantly civilian Board of Visitors submits every year "a written report to the President of the United States" which is later released by the President under the guise of an objective civilian account of "the state of morale and discipline, curriculum, instruction, physical equipment, fiscal affairs, academic methods and other matters relating to the institution." An

officer who has worked on preparations for the annual Board visits since the mid-1960's, candidly admitted, "It's general effect is benign. Their criticisms are very muted, if they are there at all, because they let us write the thing." As for the composition of the report, the officer commented:

> We've found that the only way to do it is to write up the canned recommendations we want 'em to buy before they meet in executive session. This year we even went further and mailed them out two weeks ahead of time, and sort of apologized for it, but they did find it useful. They changed one recommendation to put a qualification there that they wouldn't support the new gymnasium addition unless the Defense Department followed through on its plan of enlarging the Corps to 4,417. But, in other words, they bought the words we put in.
>
> But, it's, it's pretty much of a charade. They are only here two and one half days and they get a series of briefings. And they totter around and have their pictures taken with the cadets. It's not that long. I've always regarded it actually as a thing to be gotten through with as little ruckus as possible. And let the Academy get back to its work. But still it's good to have somebody come and listen to the problems in confidence, I guess. Like the Supe unburdens himself usually pretty much about honor and race problems and drug problems and so on. But a lot of that stuff doesn't go into the report.

Interview with West Point officer, May 1973.

It should be emphasized that, as with much about the Academy's operation, American citizens (and in this case, elected "public servants") have contributed at least as much as the Academy to making a charade of this potentially valuable method of civilian scrutiny. Board members who participated in the 1973 assessment and who signed the report were the chairman, Major General Leif J. Sverdrup (ret.); General Albert C. Wedemeyer (ret., USMA, 1919), and Major General George H. Olmsted (ret., USMA, 1922); United States Senators Barry Goldwater and Ted Stevens; United States Congressmen William E. Minshall, John M. Murphy (USMA, 1950) and Benjamin Gilman; Dr. Whitney Halladay, president, Texas A & I; Leonard D. Henry, AVCO Corporation, New York City, and Lawrence F. Lee, Jr., chairman of the board, McMillen Corporation, Jacksonville, Florida. Two members, Senators Gale W. McGee and Joseph R. Biden, Jr., did not participate in the board's deliberations and a third member, Congressman Clarence D. Long, refused to sign the report because, as he said in a dissenting view at the end of the report, "I cannot agree with the Board's Formal Recommendation that the Defense Department 'give emphatic support to the expeditious funding and construction of a modern hospital at the Military Academy' with Fiscal 1974 appropriations." See *Report of the Board of Visitors* (1973).

38. Public relations work at the Military Academy occurs primarily in the Office of the Director of Admissions and Registrar and in the Public Affairs Office. Both have large staffs of officers, enlisted, and civilian personnel to provide public information to prospective candidates and the press. For instance, on the officer and ad-

vanced civil service levels, the Admissions and Registrar Office has a director, deputy director, reserve affairs officer, associate director for admissions, assistant director for admissions, eleven admissions officers, associate director for candidate advisory services, two admissions publications and public information officials, an associate director of data processing and a candidate testing coordinator. See "United States Military Academy Staff Directory," as of February 15, 1974. Accurate data on how much is spent on public information about the academies is very elusive. For a report on an informative General Accounting Office study, see UPI's "48 Million In Pentagon PR Unlisted," *Washington Post*, August 8, 1973, A1 and A 16.

For a discussion of public attitudes toward the American military in the 1970's and the problems faced by West Point and other military spokesmen, see Charles C. Moskos, Jr.'s *Public Opinion and the Military Establishment* (Beverly Hills, Calif.: 1971), especially, Moskos' "Introduction," ix–xvi, and "The New Estrangement: Armed Forces and American Society," 271–94; Laurence I. Radway's "Recent Trends at American Service Academies," 3–35, and Peter Karsten, " 'Professional' and 'Citizen' Officers: A Comparison of Academy and ROTC Officer Candidates," 37–61.

39. There were 260 West Pointers killed in action in Vietnam and 18 graduates missing in action or prisoners of war, 5 of whom were returned to the United States in 1973. *Register of Graduates* (1973), 854–56. In a May 22, 1974, statement to us, General Knowlton noted: "In the Vietnam War . . . the West Point graduate deaths were over ten percent of the officer deaths . . . [which] numbered 2,631." And "in the Korean War, 1,205 officers were killed and over ten percent—157—were West Point graduates."

40. Interview with Lieutenant Colonel Thomas E. Blagg, March 1973.

41. Interview with West Point cadet, May 1972.

42. Interview with West Point officer, June 1972.

43. *Ibid.* While few junior officers have read Daniel Ellsberg's work and almost none would embrace the convictions he expresses in "The Responsibility of Officials in a Criminal War," 275–309, they unknowingly share many of the convictions about the nature of the war which he develops in *Papers on the War* (New York, 1972); see especially his "The Quagmire Myth and the Stalemate Machine," 42–131.

44. Interviews with West Point officers, January and August 1973.

45. *Ibid.*

46. On August 30, 1973, General Knowlton addressed the staff and faculty at West Point: "Upon my arrival at West Point in March of 1970, I found that a great many officers were down in the mouth about the failing state of the Army and the dissolution of those qualities which we deemed so important to us and to the mission. There was a tendency to cry doom and gloom and to consider that West Point was in the approximate state of Rome when the vandals climbed the last contour line of the inner city. Since I first took recruit training in Troop B of the 3d Cavalry over 39 years ago, I have seen the Army's condition and status go up and down very much like a sine curve. And I like to portray our progress as a sine curve—partly because I believe it, and partly because the analogy is useful."

47. Interview with Colonel Manley E. Rogers, March 1973. The mean college board scores of entering plebes from 1966 to 1972 were:

	1966	*1967*	*1968*	*1969*	*1970*	*1971*	*1972*
SAT-MATH	654	649	645	635	634	622	624
SAT-VERBAL	581	575	579	563	564	554	554

A Study of the Programs of USMA (1972), 99 and *Pointer View*, May 31, 1974, 1.

48. Colonel William L. Hauser, *America's Army in Crisis: A Study in Civil-Military Relations* (Baltimore, 1973), 3–4. While Colonel Hauser's book is notable for a willingness to discuss some of the Army's problems, Hauser is also curiously reticent. In his "Preface" Colonel Hauser notes that his book "was made possible by the Army Research Associates Program" which "gives a small number of officers the opportunity to read, think, and write in the field of national security affairs." The officers selected for the program "are given a rare chance to step out of the military institution and, in the stimulating surroundings of the civilian academy, to look back with fresh insight." There is no evidence that Hauser sees any inconsistencies between these assertions and his opening remarks:

> I am an Army officer and am well aware that internal criticism *must be loyal.* The book is written in that spirit—*not to expose* the faults and troubles of the Army but to note such shortcomings as are *already public knowledge*. . . . The reference materials . . . were *taken entirely* from unclassified, public, easily available sources . . . I of course had access to official documents and the advantages of private interviews and inside knowledge, but *restricted myself*, insofar as I was able, to using such sources only as background. . . . (xii) (our italics).

49. Interview with West Point officers, February 1974.

50. Interview with Colonel Manley E. Rogers, March 23, 1973, and USMA, *An Overview of the Success of Negro Cadets at West Point: Cadet Rank, Activities, and Present Rank* (West Point, 1969). Only sixty-six blacks had graduated from West Point prior to 1969.

51. Interview with West Point cadet, May 1972.

52. Interviews with Lieutenant General William A. Knowlton, January 1973 and February 1974. During his service (1969–72) at West Point, JJE (who had worked with such programs at Yale) served as an adviser to General Knowlton on matters relating specifically to black cadets and developed the Academy's first Black Studies course, which he taught in 1971 and 1972. In the early 1970's West Point also began to sponsor "a full slate of Black History Week ceremonies, lectures, and exhibits" every winter (*Pointer View*, February 8, 1974, 1–5).

53. Interview with Brigadier General Philip R. Feir, March 23, 1973. While noting that the courts "gratuitously gave us some precise instructions as to what in view of the court would comprise sufficient due process," General Feir acknowledged that the court rendered "a correct assessment" in finding that the Academy was guilty of "failure to give them [the cadets] sufficient due process. . . . And what's more I

think it's something which we should have been able to ascertain on our own without this kind of guidance from the courts." But General Feir is most jealous of the Academy's ability to retain, free from outside interference, the power to determine the fate of individual cadets. Even in cases where a cadet "was deficient in conduct," Feir stressed the necessity of the Academy's right to assess "his potential to determine whether his potential was so outstanding—the 'potential' is a function of what he ultimately might be able to contribute to the Army—that it would override this deficiency in conduct." Feir then elaborated:

> What kind of fellow would so qualify? I'm thinking about a man who might be a Cadet Captain, a Company Commander, who has some sweet young thing down in Nyack; and, he just slips off in the dead of night down there three or four times and is caught. And those amount to significant slugs [special punishments for serious offenses]. He's reduced. Loses his job as Company Commander. Loses his stripes. And the kind of a guy who obviously can go out into the Army and make a great contribution. Well, that's the kind of potential I see which one would have to have to qualify, or override, this stigma of this failure in conduct.

54. Interview with Colonel Sumner Willard, May 11, 1973.

55. Interview with the Reverend James D. Ford, March 1973. In a September 7, 1973, story a West Point publication, *Pointer View*, announced that Chaplain Ford had been reappointed to an unprecedented third four-year term. "Being a 'three termer' is just one of three firsts Chaplain Ford has to his credit," reported *Pointer View*. "Appointed Assistant Chaplain in 1961 by former Superintendent William C. Westmoreland, Chaplain Ford was the youngest man to serve in that capacity. He is also the first Lutheran to serve as Cadet Chaplain." "He is also the only service academy chaplain to serve via Presidential appointment" (1).

56. Interview with West Point officer, May 1973. In a May 1973 interview Colonel Gerald W. Medsger cited two particularly important changes in cadet attitudes since the 1950's which suggest cadets are not as receptive to West Point "values" as they once were:

> There were a couple of significant changes in the last 10 or 15 years. . . . Back in the late 50's and early 1960's, the majority of cadets were in favor of mandatory chapel. In the late 60's and early 70's the majority of cadets were opposed. . . . Another area was in response to the question, "If I had to do it [four years at West Point] all over again, would I?" It was a dramatic *decrease* [in affirmative answers] over the same period of time.

In trying to understand better these two changes, Colonel Medsger was handicapped by the fact that "1964 through 1968" was "a sort of unenlightened period [superintendencies of James B. Lampert and Donald V. Bennett] . . . when we were not allowed to survey cadets and this is the period when these changes took place. I would love to have that data now and be able to see if it was one year that everything dropped . . . or whether it was a more gradual decrease, but it is quite clear that there was a *quantum jump* over these five years."

57. Interview with the Reverend James D. Ford, March 1973.

58. The elimination of mandatory chapel was also a matter of concern at the two other major academies. For instance, the Naval Academy's superintendent, Vice Admiral William P. Mack, emphasized to the midshipmen at Annapolis: "As officers in the naval service your personal beliefs will often be tested, and in times of stress, your men look to you for spiritual as well as professional guidance. I believe that you owe it to yourself and to your men to gain an insight into the moral, ethical and religious dimensions of leadership. Therefore, I urge you to take full advantage of your opportunities for worship and moral development." Quoted in Douglas Watson's "3 Academies Drop Mandatory Chapel," *Washington Post*, January 6, 1973, A16.

59. Interview with West Point officer, February 1974.

60. In announcing the change in superintendents, the Academy noted that Lieutenant General Knowlton "has been named Chief of Staff of the U.S. European Command headquartered in Stuttgart, Germany," and that "the command includes all U.S. Armed Forces units in Europe." Major General Berry was described as a native of Hattiesburg, Mississippi, and a former instructor in the Social Sciences Department (1953–56). Berry became "the third general officer to go directly from the 101st Airborne Division to the Superintendency. . . . The others were Generals Maxwell D. Taylor and William C. Westmoreland." USMA Public Affairs Office News Release, "New Superintendent," May 30, 1974. For a provocative profile of Berry, see Lewis H. Lapham's "Case Study of an Army Star," *Life*, September 25, 1970, 55, 56, 59–68.

61. Interviews with Lieutenant General William A. Knowlton, Colonel John S. B. Dick, Colonel Thomas E. Fitzpatrick (Deputy Commandant of Cadets), and Lieutenant Colonel Thomas P. Garigan, February 1974.

62. Statement to authors from officer on Superintendent's Special Staff, May 1974.

63. Interview with Admiral Thomas H. Moorer, June 1973.

64. Interview with Lieutenant General James M. Gavin (ret.), September 1973. Gavin has served since 1972 as Chairman of the West Point Fund Committee. "The objective" of the fund "is to obtain from private donations, gifts, and bequests, the sums needed to undertake projects benefitting the Corps of Cadets and the Military Academy for which appropriated fund support is not available" (*West Point: 1973–74 Catalog*, 164): Gavin is Chairman of the Board of the Arthur D. Little Company in Cambridge, Massachusetts.

INDEX